Advance Praise for Placing the Frontier in British North-East India

Reeju Ray's fascinating, deeply researched book is an original, theoretically sophisticated work. This book will be of much interest well beyond South Asian studies and British Empire history. It will appeal to audiences in socio-legal studies, Indigenous studies, peasant studies, and legal anthropology. The spatial and temporal constitution of peoples and places through various governance techniques is a theme drawing increasing attention from critical scholars. This book's analysis of how 'hills' and 'tribes' were constituted in the frontiers of colonial Bengal is an important and timely addition to this literature and will be of interest to readers across several disciplines.'

—Mariana Valverde, professor emeritus of
socio-legal studies at the University of Toronto

'Placing the Frontier in British North East India: Law, Custom, and Knowledge is a significant contribution to our understanding of North East India. A stimulating study with refreshing interpretation.'

—David R. Syiemlieh, historian and
former Vice Chancellor of Rajiv Gandhi University,
Arunachal Pradesh

Placing the Frontier in British North-East India

Law, Custom, and Knowledge

REEJU RAY

OXFORD
UNIVERSITY PRESS

Great Clarendon Street, Oxford, OX2 6DP,
United Kingdom

Oxford University Press is a department of the University of Oxford.
It furthers the University's objective of excellence in research, scholarship,
and education by publishing worldwide. Oxford is a registered trade mark of
Oxford University Press in the UK and in certain other countries

© Reeju Ray 2023

The moral rights of the author have been asserted

First Edition published in 2023

Impression: 1

Published in the United States of America by Oxford University Press
198 Madison Avenue, New York, NY 10016, United States of America

British Library Cataloguing in Publication Data

Data available

Library of Congress Control Number: 2022948855

ISBN 978-0-19-288708-5

DOI: 10.1093/oso/9780192887085.001.0001

Printed and bound in India by Replika Press Pvt. Ltd.

In the twilight of my last morning
I will see my friends and you,
And I will go to my grave
Regretting nothing
But an unfinished song...
—*Nāzim Hikmet Ran, 1933*

This book is dedicated to Baba

Contents

List of Figures

Acknowledgements

This has been hardest part of the book to write. Not because I am short of immense gratitude. It is simply hard to capture in words and articulate the myriad ways in which the support offered by so many people and places have ensured that this book exists. My doctoral supervisor Ishita Pande has been a steady source of inspiration, guidance, and strength. Her patience and care during difficult times and often harsh conditions of my doctoral studies made all the difference in my ability to complete my doctoral thesis. Her critical assessment of my work coupled with consistent encouragement gave me the confidence to turn the doctoral thesis into a book manuscript. Being a graduate student at Queen's University Canada would be impossible to navigate without the unwavering support of Sandra den Otter. Her warmth and generosity are only equalled by her intellectual guidance and capacity for deeply stimulating questions. Sandra's ability to be critical, realistic, and nurturing at the same time during and after graduate school contributed to the best parts of my time living in Canada. Karen Dubinsky took me out for beer during my first week in Kingston and made an intimidating place feel inviting and warm. Her seminar called Empire and Intimacies opened many new scholarly directions. Her teaching methods centred the importance of asking questions which I continue to employ in both research and teaching. It was in this seminar that I first felt confident and at home intellectually. I am thankful to my doctoral examination committee consisting of Jayeeta Sharma, Dia Da Costa, and Amitava Choudhury for their incisive comments and for pushing the ideas in my thesis. My external examiner Bhavani Raman has since been a steady source of intellectual guidance and support. The history department at Queen's University and the School of Graduate Studies where I worked as an intern, and the CFRC Queen's community radio station are places on campus where I spent the most time and learnt greatly. Friends, colleagues, and administrative staff in these places made writing the dissertation easier than it would have otherwise been. Marianna Valverde and Kanishka Goonewardena let me sit in on their graduate seminars at the University of Toronto and pushed me to think outside of the disciplinary confines of history. The theoretically rich discussions in those seminars added much to my understanding of concepts of law and space that are the core of this book.

I want to thank my partners in crime during graduate school with whom I have endured the worst and the best things about doing a PhD and without them things would have truly been bland and much harder. My dear friend and brother Scott de Groot you are an intellectual force who in addition to introducing me to the genre of horror films, encouraged me to read things outside of South Asian historiography and placed certain books and genres in my radar I would not have considered otherwise. Your influence is visible in the very title of this book. Jessica Cammaert you have been an intellectual companion and such a thoughtful roommate in the first year when I was completely lost and needed a lot of looking after. Your work ethic inspired me to get my essays done on time. Despite our terrible record of getting lost on public transport, Jess's knack for having a good time led us to the best pubs in Canada and in London. Erin and Braden thank you for all the laughs and the care with which you read my early work and provided important feedback, and for the introduction to Creemore.

My love for reading history was cultivated in the classrooms of Pine Mount School in Shillong. Dorothy Phanbuh taught history like it was a living and breathing subject. Her classes were filled with anecdotes and beautifully crafted stories that made the past so relevant to our everyday. Tranquillity Kharpuri and Eugenia Khonglah similarly ensured that high school was an enriching experience. For this and their continuing love and affection I am grateful. In college Vasudha Pande transformed my approach to reading modern Indian history. VP pushed us to interrogate our assumptions and ask questions about facts and information that we tend to take for granted. It was in her class that I felt certain about studying history after college. Prathama Bannerjee introduced words such as paradigm and epistemology among others into our undergraduate naïveté and completely changed the way we thought about knowledge. Her classes on European modernity, in particular those on the French Revolution and discussions on the ironies in the motto liberté egalité fraternité helped us build a critical vocabulary. Discussions with her outside the classroom were equally enriching. In one instance in response to my complaints about the Delhi University student elections, Prathamadi pointed out that politics is *not* a bad thing. That it is crucial to every aspect of life, in practice and thought, was an understanding brought about by those discussions and for that I am truly grateful. Meera Baijal, Prabha Rani, Kunj Gupta, and others at Lady Shri Ram College provided me with the foundation for research and teaching in history that remains unmatched.

The time spent during the masters program in history at Jawaharlal Nehru University was made up of deep learning and as much unlearning. JNU inculcated humility, empathy, and politics in my everyday practices. Filled with the most inspiring peers and teachers who demonstrated the importance of dissent, fight, and struggle it has informed my work and life in more ways than I can state. At the Centre for Historical Studies at JNU I learnt the most about modern Indian history and politics and what the two mean together. Tanikadi has remained crucial to my academic journey even after I left JNU. It was during a conversation with her in Delhi in 2019 where I felt the courage to return to this project after a hiatus which I believed was the end of my academic life. Tanikadi's constant reminders through emails and texts that my ideas, arguments, and writing are relevant truly made a difference in battling depression and returning to academic work. Her scholarship, teaching, and feminist praxis of love and care has been a source of learning, and strength I am most grateful for. Radhika Singha's classes on legal history helped create pathways for research that has culminated into this book. Her scholarship and insistence on the importance of spending long hours at archives has been indispensable to this book. Lectures, tutorials, and conversations with Mary John, Joy Pachuau, Tiplut Nongbri, Neeladri Bhattacharya, Kumkum Roy, Rajat Datta, Indivar Kamtekar, Jyoti Atwal provided the groundwork for ideas that appear in the book.

I want to thank the archivists and librarians at the National Archives of India, the British Library, Assam State Archives, the B.R. Ambedkar Central library at JNU, West Bengal State Archives in Kolkata, State Central Library, North East Hill University library in Shillong, South Asian Studies library at Cambridge University, Robarts Library at the University of Toronto, and Douglas and Stauffer libraries at Queen's University. Each person at these institutions showed care and patience in response to my anxious and sometimes hurried visits and supported me throughout the time spent researching for this book. Alone I could not have unearthed and sieved through the amount of material available to find some of the most exciting documents that form part of the primary research for this book.

In Shillong the search for resources led to me private archives and libraries, and the most precious of all sources—conversations with elders, oral historians, folklorists, and practitioners of oral traditions. The generosity with which David Syiemlieh shared with me his personal books during a time when I was quite directionless and scrambling for secondary literature is unmatched. With his guidance I found some of the most indispensable and rare books, documents, and thesis held in the NEHU library. Desmond Kharmawphlang introduced me to anthropological sources and folk literature. With his help I was able to articulate how storytelling is central to the meaning of place in the Khasi hills. The many conversations with Kong Sweetimon Rynjah gave me an expansive and rich understanding of Khasi oral history, indigenous religion, historical landscapes, and matrilineal system. With utmost generosity and thoughtfulness, and the best sense of humour Kong Sweetimon helped me navigate the ways in which the past is inhered in the present. With deeply moving anecdotes Kong Sweetimon helped me understand the sentience of landscapes I grew up around, and how matrilineal kinship forms a repository of ancestral history and storytelling. The works of Esther Syiem, Jayanta Bhattacharjee, Manorama Sharma have been helpful in shaping the early contours of my research. I am grateful to the caretakers of the Jeebon Roy Memorial Archive and in particular to Shailin Sawian for helping me navigate it. I thank Tambor Lyngdoh for the rich stories about Mawphlang's sacred groves and articulating the interstices of political economy, indigenous politics, and global conservationist movements in his narration. Rosalind thank you for the Khasi lessons and many anecdotes over endless cups of sha saw.

Harvard Law School's Institute of Global Law and Policy workshops from 2016 to 2022 have been the most helpful in turning the doctoral thesis into a book manuscript. The kindness of the intellectual community at IGLP and deeply engaged feedback in writing workshops has been a backbone for this project. I am grateful to David Kennedy, Kristen Verdeaux, Sundhya Pahuja, Rose Parfitt, Ratna Kapur, Shalini Randeria, Martti Koskenniemi, Charlie Peevers, Philippe Calvao, Oishik Sirkar, Shahd Hammouri, Priyasha Saksena, Cynthia Farid, Anna Varfolomeeva,

Fatima Osman, and Zeina Jallad all the participants I had the pleasure to meet and exchange ideas with. The friendships created at IGLP are lifelong and indispensable.

Friends—old and new—have been indispensable to my growth as a person and as an academic. Friends and comrades in Shillong have consistently grounded me by demonstrating that what appears to be a radical idea or argument in academic conferences and discourse is really part of everyday conversations, and practice in our homeland—the place I write about. Gertrude your warmth and love alongside your political activism intellectual prowess has been so inspiring. Angela your political commitment and the incredible work you do teaches me consistently about our homeland, about politics, and love. I am grateful to be able to be your friend and comrade and share this time with you. Tarun your work, vision, conversations, and anecdotes have been so very educational. Your understanding of this place reflected in your images offers historians and social scientists so much to learn from. Thank you for providing your stunning photographs for this book and making it so special. I am thankful to Rev. Kyrsoibor Pyrthuh for the deeply stimulating conversations and for sharing his expansive knowledge of Khasi history and understanding of the hills as a place. There is probably no other source of understanding history of a place greater than these nurturing relationships. I am only able to name a few but there are many more people whose empathy and politics have given shape to my work. Justin thank you for every argument, laugh, and meal you made. Having you around in Canada eased the pain of being away from home and I found family as a bonus. Gail, Cyril, Vick, Sylvester, Henry, Tara—thank you for always making returning to Shillong warm and special. Lapdiang your ability to weave history into storytelling through performance is so profoundly inspiring. Your work has challenged me to think differently about written knowledge. Janice first it was your magical storytelling that seamlessly binds fiction with history, and now it is your vision, generosity, and friendship that make me fall more deeply in love with Shillong. Your presence feels like sunshine and a giant hug and I am so happy I found you! Anurag your capacity for empathy and translating feelings into photographs is mind boggling and I am literally in awe as I type this. Ramya your kindness and resilience is so inspiring. Thank you for being on this path with me.

Pallavi, Akhila, Sangeeta, Ankita, Nayana, Tanu, Oeendrila, Charu, Anandaroop, Utathya, Prerna, Simran, Simrita, and others who made JNU more than just a place of torturous learning. Thank you for the fun times and laughter. Vanessa I have learnt greatly from your academic work and your political analysis. Thank you for helping me understand Kashmir in all its historical complexity through your work and our conversations. Serohi your gentle and kind spirit truly makes Sonipat feel like home. Thank you for the care you have shown comrade, and I cannot wait to read your brilliant thesis in the making. Saumya, Sahana, Shivangi, and Ishan thank you for the much needed laughs and insights during the final stretch of writing the manuscript. Colleagues at the Centre for Research in History at JGU especially Gitanjali, Swati, Anish, Sukumar, and everyone else who have created this stimulating space on campus and provided comments and feedback for my work. Friends and colleagues at JGU thank you for being kind and warm, and for creating an exciting workplace. I am grateful to my students for making me think. more and write better. Thank you to Anjali and Sanjula for proofreading and helping speed up a lengthy and difficult process.

Nayrouz Abu Hatoum you introduced me to the magical places of work that are cafés. Our conversations opened me up to address the multiple ways in which Palestinian history and resistance intersect with colonial history Indian borderlands. Most importantly your nurturing love during very difficult times anchored me. Thank you precious Nayrouz for telling me in the kindest way not to quit academia when I did. We still have to co-write that article and I cannot wait. Umang Antariksh thank you for your love and fairness, and opening your home to me when I was most alone. I want to thank Alison, Laura, Lindsay, Dana, Maliha, Ritika, Avi, and folks at The Goat in Kingston, Nishant, Sara Abraham, Aadi, Arzu, Jasmine, Caro, Audrey, Rocio, Nat, Gunjan, Nanky, Wren, Aruna, Simon, Nisha, Jenn, Maryam, Mariam, Hamna, Salima, Ryan, Noaman, Alios, Shaira, Nadia, Amna, folks at the Common in Toronto, and many others who helped make Canada home for a while. Urooj, Hadia, and Tuba thank you for being comrades and sisters, and for this lifelong friendship. Planning and brain storming with Arsalan and Shozab helped me sustain interest in academic work even when I had quit. I am so thankful to have had the opportunity to sketch with them the early contours of *Jamhoor* as a platform and resource for political and academic ideas.

Hūlya thank you for being my biggest ally and first friend in Toronto. You pushed my boundaries in the best ways, and opened my eyes to things I would not have otherwise seen (inside joke alert), called me out when I was wrong, held me when I was broken, and showed me such deep, consistent, and honest love. I am grateful to you for expanding what friendship has meant for me and for all that I learn from your dazzling intellect. Thank you for the love you give Bilbo who we both know is more than a pet cat. Boris, meeting you converged with the most transformative and crucial time for me and this book. Our conversations about history, fiction, fantasy, and everything in between brought intellectual curiosity, and creative and emotional resilience that I needed during the last few years. I am grateful for getting to know your mind which truly resembles a lush forest, your unwavering solidarity, and the biggest heart. Nangkyntiew, best friend does not encapsulate the relationship we have shared since our teens. You have been my sister, a teacher, and the source of so much unconditional love. Your generosity has given me the momentum during the best and worst of times such as those first few months in Delhi in 2019 among many others. Thank you for bringing Ilaria and Ashwin into my life because they bring more joy, laughter, and love into this world than I have ever known. I want to thank Suniti Baruah for understanding me in ways I possibly couldn't and holding space for me during the hardest times. Time spent with you in conversation and therapy have been indispensable in creating conditions that allowed me to write this book. My family who live in Kolkata thank you for making me always feel so loved. Whether it is archival visits or otherwise every single one of you have made me feel like I always have a home to come to. To my family in Shillong and Guwahati I am thankful for the history, and insights. Chotomama thank you for allowing me open access to the treasure trove of books in the iconic Chapala Book Stall. Deep gratitude to Jayanti Boudi and Katuda for the unconditional love and care you give, and for always having an open home for me during medical emergencies and archival visits for this book. Soham thank you for the love and laughter you brought your Dada. Misha thank you for being you and for making me such a proud Pishi. Esha I miss your kind presence and feel deep gratitude for all the time we spent together. My two grandmothers knew and understood the transformative history of this frontier and endured its impact more than I can capture. Amma and Thami it is because of you that I study history.

Biggest shout out to all my former and current pets for helping me feel so much joy in an otherwise bleak world. A special mention for the ones who were sitting with or on me at different points during the research and writing for this book—Oli, Coco, Horeen, Chandu, Biggie, Winnie, Bellatrix, and above all Bilbo who really did everything he could to bring me comfort and joy.

My parents have showed me what gentle, tough, consistent, unconditional, and grounded forms of love can be. I cannot possibly encapsulate here their role in my education, and support through long hours of writing, field work, travels, illness, dissent, and struggles with gender. Baba I wish you could hold this book in your hands but thank you for reading the earliest drafts and the many debates that ensued. Thank you for asking me what my gender is, without probably understanding the political implications and profound importance of the question. Thank you for introducing me to revolutionary poetry that shaped my earliest political opinions, much to your horror. But you continue to show me through poetry the greatness and necessity of hope. I hope you are reciting Nāzim Hikmet Ran wherever you are. Ma you are my universe and every reason I am here writing, breathing, laughing. Thank you for bearing with me and caring for me in ways no one ever can. Ma and Baba this one is all yours.

My Place

I was born in Shillong the capital of the Indian state of Meghalaya. It was a time when the newly formed borderland state inhabited by heterogenous indigenous and non-indigenous communities plunged into years of emergency laws, curfews, militancy, and armed conflict. Between the 1980s and 1990s the state capital of Shillong became a heavily militarized place. In varied ways inhabitants of the state expressed deep discomfort with and resistance to the paramilitary presence in the shape of the Border Security Force, the Central Reserve Police Force, and Assam Rifles. Stunning scenery of verdant hills, bustling markets, busy neighbourhood corners were interrupted by waves of state and inter community violence. Violence was directed sometimes at sections of migrant communities by militant and pressure groups, and at all times against tribal inhabitants of the region by the police, and paramilitary agencies. Frequent curfews meant impromptu breaks from school for uncertain durations. In the discomfort brought on by curfews, the frustration of staying away from friends, and the love of returning to school after such breaks is where I locate my initial understanding of social relationships in these hills. It was also in school that I learnt about the social distance between tribal and non-tribal identities, my 'putative identity' as a national majority, and as non-tribal or *dkhar*. While such social tensions were often invisiblized in friendships borne in classrooms and in playgrounds, prejudices based on markers of caste, class, and gender were pervasive even in these supposedly apolitical locations.

I am Sylheti. What this means to me is that I have ancestral roots in the present-day Sylhet district of Bangladesh. Both my parents were born in the north eastern province of colonial Assam. My mother was born in Shillong, and my father in a tea plantation in Darrang district. Both have only ever lived in Assam and Meghalaya. They have never even visited their respective ancestral villages in Sylhet from where their parents and grandparents had migrated in the late nineteenth and early twentieth centuries. Sylhet is 136 kms driving distance from Shillong. The distance as the crow flies is 75 kms. Yet, the term *dkhar* used to describe the 'plains people' who are outsiders to the Khasi hills carries with it sometimes an enormous distance. For instance, the word has been variously used to mark the 'outsider' or migrants—old and new. *Dkhar* is also a Khasi clan name and has various iterations denoting clans that were formed through customs whereby non-Khasi women could initiate a clan after marriage with Khasi men. Histories of mobility and exchange between inhabitants of the colonial frontier (between and across Sylhet, Khasi, Jaintia, and Garo hills that constitute present-day Meghalaya) bring to light the complexity and multivalence of borderland identities.

Boundaries between Sylhet and Khasi, Jaintia and Garo hills were made and remade during the colonial and postcolonial periods. Persistent boundary making from the early nineteenth century onwards was prone to many kinds of failure. The processes of establishing boundaries between the hills and the plains are carefully studied in this book to illuminate the conditions that produced and enhanced social differences which reverberate in the hills today. The present-day distance between different communities is not simply a result of 'outsider' discourse peddled by various anti-migrant organizations. Migrants in the nineteenth century from Sylhet and other parts of the British colonial state settled and created community silos, that echoed caste based and colonial racial prejudice against tribal inhabitants of the region. The colonial category of tribe has been repurposed for asserting caste based and other communitarian social hierarchies by migrant groups. Approaching the problem of inter-community conflict from either side (indigenous or migrant) requires a careful evaluation of differences and alliances based on class, religion, and social positions. Any homogenous view of indigenous or migrant identities and interests run the risk of being ahistorical and simplistic. Hegemonic, dominant knowledge about the frontier and its people have for centuries eluded the interstices of identities, languages, social, cultural, and politico-economy between different classificatory categories of people. The book explores this tension by detailing the role of law, geography, and other scientific disciplines in the nineteenth century.

The multiplicity of languages that constitute umbrella identities such as Achik (Garo), Hynniewtrep (Khasi), and Pnar (Jaintia) has not been described in detail in this book. This is a conscious decision in order to maintain consistency with primary archival sources, secondary literature, and ethnographic interviews. Similarly, caste which forms an important marker for the non-tribal inhabitants in the region has not been explored in this book. This is not an oversight as much as a direction taken with respect to the archival material under perusal and the nature of interviews in my fieldwork. This study acknowledges the importance of locating caste marked subjects and subjectivities in understanding the multiplicity of places and violence of spatiality in the north east of India. The need for critical and historical research on multiple and intersecting linguistic identities as well as caste-based subjectivities in the Khasi, Jaintia, and Garo hills is due to the relational nature of place making.

During the years of my doctoral studies, I learnt to critically evaluate my relationship with the place that was my object of study and my home. I found myself at an imposed physical and attempted emotional distance from it. I was enrolled in a university thousands of miles away from Meghalaya. Sitting in cold libraries and archives in Delhi, London, Toronto, and Kingston, I was often overwhelmed by sadness and anger at the persisting violence of colonial structures. These were critical moments that pushed me, through several years of debilitating anxiety and depression, to complete the doctoral dissertation and finally the book manuscript. This book is therefore not simply a product of academic research and writing. It is a result of combined love and politics that bind me to my home, and compel me to write about it. Place is a central conceptual and methodological tool in this book. It denotes historical and lived experiences combining people, landscape, law, governance, political economy, borders, knowledge, and much more. As the title suggests and themes in the book will unfold, place-making is an ongoing process, and has been essential to the writing of this book.

1

Law, Space, and Place

An Introduction

The frontier hills of the British Empire in India examined in this book are located in the present-day Indian state of Meghalaya comprising Garo, Khasi, and Jaintia districts, and Sylhet Division in Bangladesh. During the nineteenth century the words Khasi, Jaintia, and Garo came to denote both hills and tribal inhabitants in the colonial frontier of British Bengal. Colonial governance through law formulated the hills as frontier and its inhabitants as tribal. Law assumed the task of defining both people and land in relation to what was understood as an uncivilized and untamed frontier landscape. Concurrently, law enabled the drive of colonial interests into the north-eastern frontier by creating the possibility for enhanced revenue, extraction of resources, and indefinite territorial expansion. The frontier became not only a geographical location but a specific colonial politico-legal space. With a focus on colonial legal ordering through spatial and temporal processes the book identifies entanglements between frontier governance and historical subjectivities of frontier inhabitants.

The frontier in recent scholarship is variously conceptualized in terms of physical location, geographical matrix, temporal construction, and practices of governance.[1] In this book, the frontier hills history is

---

[1] Among earlier historical scholarship, Amalendu Guha's work pointed towards the importance of considering the disruption of trade and politico-economic networks between the north-east frontier region, China, and Upper Burma and the societal transformations as a result of colonial rule. Guha's work is significant because it prefigures recent scholarship that conceptualizes the 'frontier' space as produced by colonial processes. See Amalendu Guha, *Medieval and Early Colonial Assam: Society, Polity, Economy* (Kolkata: Centre for Studies in Social Sciences, 1991).
    See also Sameetah Agha and Elizabeth Kolsky, eds., *Fringes of Empire: Peoples, Places, and Spaces in Colonial India* (New York: Oxford University Press, 2009); Sanghamitra Misra, *Becoming a Borderland: The Politics of Space and Identity in Colonial Northeastern India* (New Delhi: Routledge, 2011); Indrani Chatterjee, *Forgotten Friends: Monks, Marriages, and Memories of Northeast India* (New Delhi: Oxford University Press, 2013); Neeladri Bhattacharya and

Placing the Frontier in British North-East India. Reeju Ray, Oxford University Press. © Reeju Ray 2023.
DOI: 10.1093/oso/9780192887085.003.0001

examined by interrogating the multivalence of colonial law framed by concepts of space and place. The 'where of law' as a critical analytic allows a reconsideration of key legal categories such as frontier, British and non-British territory, non-regulation areas, scheduled districts, hill tribal, settler proprietor, cultivator subject, among others. This book follows law's movement—its ebb and flow—into the north-east frontier through contractual agreements; regulations; boundary-making; jurisdictional disputes; and formulation of custom, authority, and knowledge.

The Garo, Khasi, and Jaintia hills were brought under the purview of the imperial cartographic imagination after the adjacent lands of Sylhet were included as a district of British Bengal in mid-eighteenth century. Existing social, commercial, and trade networks integrated Sylhet, and the adjoining hills within the larger Himalayan borderland region. Colonial expansion reconfigured the region's political, trade, and social ties. For instance, in 1793 the Permanent Settlement invested proprietary rights in land to a class of Zamindars who would pay a portion of the agricultural tax to the colonial state. This encouraged sedentary agricultural settlement in Sylhet's lands, displacement of non-sedentary groups, and dispossession of cultivators.[2] Further, colonial boundary-making initiatives between British and non-British territory created new and racialized hill-plain boundaries to coincide with jurisdictional divisions between Sylhet and the Garo, Khasi, and Jaintia hills. The processes, failures, and implications of these geographical and jurisdictional divisions are examined in the book.

The creation of jurisdictional units to correspond with directly administered revenue-yielding territory and ambiguously defined non-British territory produced many legal disputes. Agreements signed between local representatives or heads of communities in the hills and colonial agents assigned criminal jurisdiction to the colonial state from the early decades of the nineteenth century. Civil jurisdiction was assigned to local

Joy L. K. Pachuau, eds., *Landscape, Culture, and Belonging: Writing the History of Northeast India* (Cambridge: Cambridge University Press, 2019); Benjamin D. Hopkins, *Ruling the Savage Periphery: Frontier Governance and the Making of the Modern State* (Cambridge and London: Harvard University Press, 2020); Thomas Simpson, *The Frontier in British India: Space, Science, and Power in the Nineteenth Century* (Cambridge: Cambridge University Press, 2021). These works, among others, have been discussed further in the Introduction.

[2] See Ranajit Guha, *A Rule of Property for Bengal: An Essay on the Idea of Permanent Settlement* (Durham: Duke University Press, 1996). The book was first published in 1963.

rulers albeit with varied degrees of interference by the colonial government. Agreements and treaties signed with local authority became the legal channel through which all commercial, ideological, and military action was negotiated. Such agreements were not signed with utmost ease. David Scott, the Political Agent in the north-east frontier, was the first to initiate such treaties between local Chiefs and rulers. His travels along the frontier hills combined military expeditions, commercial contracts, and the injection of colonial law beyond the official limits of British India. His first significant policy was the creation of non-regulation areas which included the frontier hills. These areas were marked as outside colonial rule of law. There was a caveat, however, by which any colonial regulation applicable in the Bengal Presidency could be introduced in all or parts of non-regulation areas in exceptional situations. A range of situations could be considered as exceptional by relevant authorities including political resistance, commercial dissension, and diplomatic impasse.

In 1829 an armed rebellion in the Khasi hills marked the failure of British inroads through diplomacy in the frontier hills. Despite heavy military suppression of dissenting Chiefs and their armed followers, resistance in the form of guerrilla warfare continued for almost a decade. During the 1830s more treaties and contracts were signed across the Garo, Khasi, and Jaintia hills bringing land, labour, and forest resources within the ambit of colonial political economy. Long-standing jurisdictional disputes between Zamindari lands of Bengal and the frontier hills continued into the following decades regularly pushing colonial law into non-regulation areas. As a site of incessant boundary-making, the frontier allowed the expansion of commercial, jurisdictional, and civilizational reach of the colonial state. Ambiguous legality and bordering practices of the colonial state relied on categories of hill tribes, raids, barbarity, and primitivism. Together these processes created the foundation for colonial economic exploitation and a 'scientific' knowledge archive that further classified and organized communities in relation to space.

In the second half of the nineteenth century, there was an attempt to organize and reform the legal infrastructure in these frontier hills. The colonial government in Bengal commissioned two judicial and administrative reports in the 1950s which informed law and governance after the transfer of power from the East India Company to the British government in 1857. The Scheduled Districts Act of 1874 was introduced across the colony to identify and create uniform governance in areas identified as tribal.[3] In the frontier another important legislation was the Inner Line Regulation 1873 which introduced a fluid imperial boundary between British and non-British territories. Further, a new administrative province of Assam was carved out from British Bengal in 1874, which included the Garo, Khasi, and Jaintia hill districts and Sylhet.

The nineteenth century introduced new forms of political and religious authority, and new loci of power such as churches and courts that adorned parts of the hills. The lived environment was transformed with the building of roads and transport networks. The hills were decorated with military cantonments, colonial administrative buildings and residential houses, guest houses and convalescent homes for European officers and soldiers. In the Khasi hills, colonial administrators included smaller pockets such as cantonments and administrative centres within the ambit of specific laws. Some parts of the hills were incrementally or partially governed by colonial law, while others were entirely excluded even from cartographic representations as areas outside colonial rule of law. As a space of law, the hills appeared and disappeared, joining larger legal spaces and then shrinking, and subject to heterogeneous times of different legal systems and sub-systems.[4] The historical subjectivities and identities of inhabitants were profoundly impacted by colonial spatial and legal frameworks separating legal subjects along categories of tribe, caste, hills, and plains. Special legal administrative zones in the colonial frontier evolved into scheduled areas of the Indian state.

Scheduled Districts were re-christened Backward Tracts by the Government of India Act 1919. Governance in the Backward Tracts

---

[3] In a recently published article Saagar Tewari has has called into question the Scheduled Districts Act 1874 as the first iteration of the policy of scheduling in late colonial and post colonial India intended to create special governance in tribal areas of independent India. Though the Scheduled Districts Act was also applied outside of areas designated as fifth and sixth schedule areas in the north east frontier of British India, it remains important in understanding the spatiality of law in the north east frontier of British India. See Saagar Tewari, 'Framing the Fifth Schedule: Tribal Agency and the Making of the Indian Constitution', Modern Asian Studies 56, (Cambridge University Press 2022): 1556–1594. Also see, Uday Chandra, 'Liberalism and its Other: The Politics of Primitivism in Colonial and Post Colonial Indian Law', Law and Society Review 47, No, 1 (2013): 135–68

[4] Franz von Benda-Beckmann and Keebet von Benda-Beckmann, 'Places That Come and Go: A Legal Anthropological Perspective on the Temporalities of Space in Plural Legal Orders', in The Expanding Spaces of Law: A Timely Legal Geography, eds. Irus Braverman, Nicholas Blomley, David Delaney, and Alexandre Kedar (Stanford: Stanford University Press, 2014), 30–52.

assumed different scales: one for 'really backward tracts' and another for 'typically backward tracts'. The Simon Commission report in 1930 renamed 'typically backward tracts' as 'partially excluded areas' and 'really backward tracts' as 'wholly excluded areas'. This informed the Government of India Act 1935 which distinguished indirectly ruled provinces and native states from directly ruled excluded and partially excluded areas.

With the creation of the two nation-states of India and Pakistan in 1947, the Garo and Jaintia hills states joined India within the province of Assam, while Sylhet joined East Pakistan. The Khasi states signed respective agreements known as the Instrument of Accession to join the Indian union. These hills were placed under the Sixth Schedule of the Indian constitution that contains special administrative and legal provisions. Bangladesh replaced East Pakistan as the international neighbour of these frontier hills following the war of 1971. In 1972 Meghalaya (Khasi, Jaintia, and Garo hills) attained statehood by separating from Assam.

The historically tenuous and imperfect boundaries between the hills of Meghalaya and Sylhet plains continue to be sites of state violence, ethnic conflict, economic and social exchange, and human and animal mobility in the postcolonial period.[5] The distinct legal and political status of India's north-east within the Indian nation-state can be understood by uncovering the historical processes of transformation of the frontier hills. The nineteenth century is a crucial time to examine when older geographical and political conceptions were stymied but not annihilated. The book examines processes that incorporated the hills within a colonial state space in partial and provisional ways. Inhabitants remained in legal limbo oscillating between being subjected to colonial law, but not as legal British subjects. While the ambiguity of colonial legal and state apparatus in the frontier was a strategy of governance, it also produced the hills and its inhabitants as interruptions to the imperial project.[6] The frontier was thus in defiance of the very colonial spatial processes and legal representations that produced it.

---

[5] See Willem van Schendel, *The Bengal Borderland: Beyond State and Nation in South Asia* (London: Anthem Press, 2005); see also Malini Sur, *Jungle Passports: Fences, Mobility, and Citizenship at the Northeast India-Bangladesh Border* (Philadelphia: University of Pennsylvania Press, 2021).

[6] Reeju Ray, 'Interrupted Sovereignties in the North-East Frontier of British India, 1787–1870', *Modern Asian Studies* 53, no. 2 (Cambridge University Press, 2019): 606–632.

Complex negotiations between old and new spatial realities demonstrate that the frontier exemplified a variegated and uneven nature of colonial law, and locally differentiated strategies and outcomes of colonialism. Lauren Benton has demonstrated that the nature of imperial sovereignty of the different empires was always already patchy and uneven.[7] Benton's examination of imperial legal systems exposed that territorial control was not a prerequisite for imperial sovereignty and jurisdiction wandered into extra-European spaces.[8] Plurality of legal systems in Benton's formulation was a result of accommodation between pre-existing normative orders and colonial law. Yet the wide range of alternating legal temporalities (between regulation and non-regulation districts, directly and indirectly controlled and autonomous territories) and the penetrative violence of colonial law evade Benton's characterization of plural legal orders.

The violence of colonial law in political spaces such as the frontier is visible in the political role of law. Space and law acting upon each co-constituted both the north-east frontier and its inhabitants as political actors. The frontier legal space localized the political rights, social identities, and economic obligations of the various categories of inhabitants of the hills—tribal and non-tribal, Christian and non-Christian, European and Anglo-Indian. Further differentiations based on class, gender, caste, and race made it difficult to maintain consistency of legal governance. For instance, recurrent conflict between European private interests, colonial state, and local authorities exposed the severe flouting of liberal universal principles of law. The spatio-legal transformation of this region into a colonial frontier demonstrates the contingent scope of colonial liberal strategy.[9] The outcomes of colonial spatiality of law involved changes in social life, politico-economic networks, and ruler-subject relations.

To understand the nature and outcome of colonial transformation of the north-east region into a frontier, the book delves into the study of the mechanisms of colonial legal spatiality. Henri Lefebvre's complex and thick definition of space as multi-dimensional and political is used in the analysis

---

[7] Lauren Benton, *A Search for Sovereignty: Law and Geography in European Empires, 1400–1900* (New York: Cambridge University Press, 2010).

[8] Benton, *Search for Sovereignty*, 6.

[9] I argue against the notion that colonial violence, extra-judicial, and racialized legal practices were outside the scope of liberal values, or were exceptional to liberal ideology. The archive examined in this book clearly demonstrates the centrality of racialized and violent legal means in producing and reinforcing the infrastructure of law.

of the frontier as a colonial spatial project. The book thus draws attention to the Lefebvre's dialectical triad of physical practices of abstract space (frontier bordering/non-regulation), knowledge and representations of space (colonial classificatory strategies), and the lived realities (heterogeneous narratives of historical subjectivities).[10] Each of these aspects is understood through their interactive and simultaneously functioning emergence. Colonial law this book shows ran through these different elements enabling the production of the frontier hills of Garo, Khasi, and Jaintia.

To show how colonial spatiality impacted lived reality of inhabitants in these hills, the book draws attention to the process of *place-making*. The frontier hills as *place* allow a possible entry point into what precedes, interrupts, and mutually constitutes processes and conditions of colonial spatiality through law. Place is not understood in opposition to space, or as an authentic locality. Instead, places are sites of negotiation and thereby non-essentialist by definition. Doreen Massey has warned us about the commonly assumed binary between space (as abstract) and place (as situated). Instead, the frontier hills as space and place are understood in this book as coexisting sites of political negotiation and practice. Places allow, Massey states, 'to retain, while reformulating, an appreciation of the specific and the distinctive while refusing the parochial'.[11] Discussing Massey's work, Mariana Valverde points towards the ontological and methodological privileging of space over time in social theory. The accompanying marginalizing of non-linear, non-western temporalities she suggests is a crucial aspect of the history of law in colonial and postcolonial.[12] Guided by the ideas of Massey and Valverde the book explores the tensions and the overlaps between the frontier as a colonial geographic space and the hills as a place of dynamic transformation, between new and old hierarchies, between colonial and indigenous knowledge, and sovereignty and governance.

Place as political articulation is tied up with cultural identity. While place-making can be understood as resistance to colonial spatiality, it has

---

[10] Henri Lefebvre, *The Production of Space*, trans. Donald Nicholson-Smith (Oxford: Blackwell Publishing, 1991).

[11] Doreen Massey, 'Geographies of Responsibility', *Geografiska Annaler Series B, Human Geography* 86, no. 1 (2004): 5–18. See also Doreen Massey, *Space, Place, Gender* (Cambridge: Polity Press, 1994).

[12] Mariana Valverde, '"Time Thickens, Takes on Flesh": Spatiotemporal Dynamics in Law', in *The Expanding Spaces of Law: A Timely Legal Geography*, eds. Irus Braverman, Nicholas Blomley, David Delaney, and Alexandre Kedar (Stanford: Stanford University Press, 2014), 53–76.

also manifested in uncritical fetishizing of alternative geographies that reinforce rigid spatio-temporal categories such as tribe, frontier, and nation.[13] For instance, present-day discourses on indigeneity and custom in the Khasi hills are embedded in conceptions of the past shaped by colonial and national discourses on tribal identity, customary law, and frontier governance. It is important to challenge historically the notions of a place embedded in essentialist and exclusive characteristics of belonging. The attempt here is not to present a neat and resolved argument showcasing place as an alternative geography but instead as embedded in spatial processes. The book searches within the messy interstices of colonial spatio-legal representation and local self-representation to find the possible imaginative resources with which communities counteract and challenge dominant, hierarchical, and normalized spatiality.

The incorporation of place in this analysis enables archival and disciplinary possibilities beyond written and documented historical sources on colonial north-east India. In addition to colonial government documents and correspondence, different disciplinary formulations of land and people by geographers, botanists, geologists, and anthropologists are juxtaposed with oral traditions and oral histories, legends and folktales that allow a critical reading of interactions between different systems of knowledge. These sources allow us to witness not only the murky and interrelated classifications of colonial and indigenous knowledge forms, but also cite the ways past inheres in the present lives of inhabitants of these hills.

Frontier Histories of Colonial India

The book locates itself within the fields of colonial legal history, law and society, and indigenous studies. This section will demonstrate how this book's historical research engages with these fields of study by highlighting key concepts, arguments, and theoretical approaches. Only a small slice of relevant literature is discussed here, while there is a rich and extensive scholarship that has informed this book.

---

[13] In Chapter 2, I have examined the spatio-temporality of legal categories to show how they formed interruptions to colonial spatiality and law. These ideas have also been developed in detail in Ray, 'Interrupted Sovereignties', 606–632.

Figure 1.1 J. G. Bartholomew, Eastern Bengal and Assam with Bhutan. Imperial Gazetteer of India. Vol. 11. New edition, published under the authority of His Majesty's Secretary of State for India in Council. Oxford: Clarendon, 1907–1909. National Archives of India.

Recent scholarship on colonial frontiers of British India has wrested the histories of communities in the north-east from the totalizing narratives of empire and nation. Some have demonstrated the dynamic political-economic systems and thriving social formations that had, in the past, produced a geographic seamlessness between places now separated by international borders. Others have highlighted an understanding of the interrelations of global, national, and regional histories.

Ben Hopkins in his book states that frontier is an 'ideational space', within which state power manifests through peculiar administrative practices. This he terms as frontier governmentality. Through comparative case studies of global imperial frontiers in colonial India, Africa, North and South America, Hopkins shows that frontiers are conceptual spaces 'made and maintained through constant, repeated, and publicly

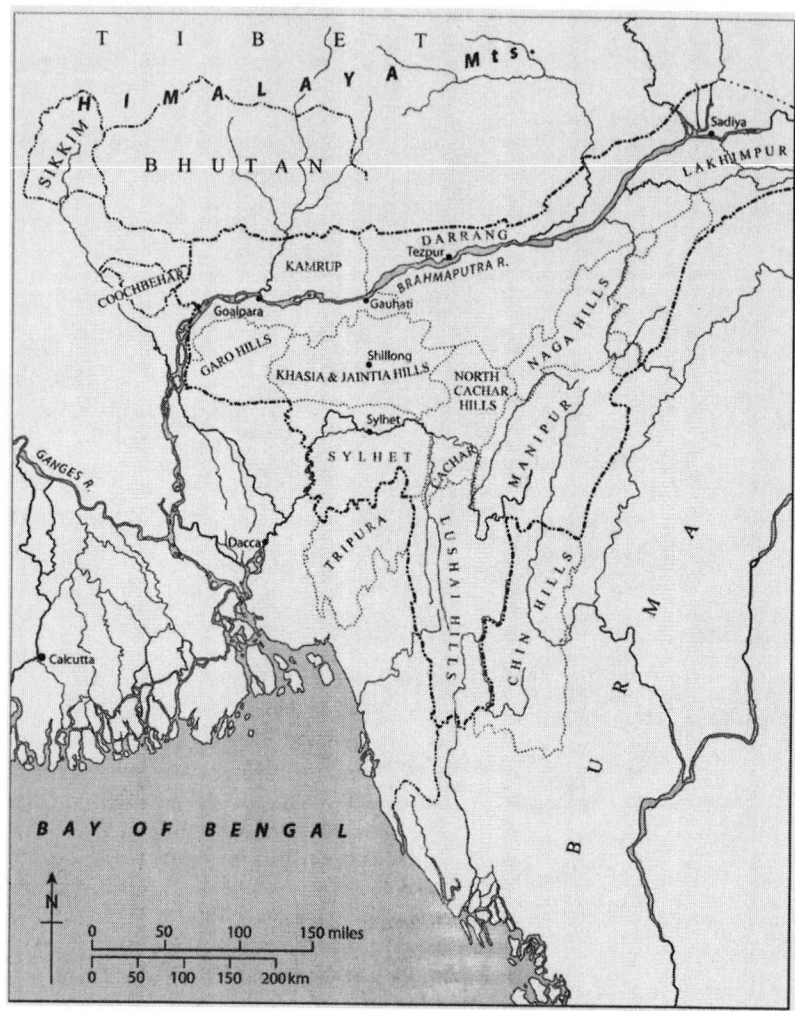

Figure 1.2 The North East Frontier in 1931. Map by Ramya Swayamprakash derived from David Zou and Satish Kumar 'Mapping a Colonial Borderland: Objectifying the Geo-Body of India's Northeast'. *The Journal of Asian Studies* 70, no. 1 (2011). Adapted from C S. Mullen Census of India 1931. Vol III: Assam.

visible acts of ... sovereignty.[14] Hopkins argues that due to the economic dependence of frontier spaces or 'fiscal pits', specific forms of legal codes, administration through indirect rule, and plural sovereignty became ubiquitous features of frontier governmentality.

While there was limited, irregular, or nominal formal taxation on land in the north-eastern frontier hills, the economic value of the region is reflective in the large-scale capital investments made by the East India Company, and many more joint-stock companies and traders. Bodhisattva Kar's study on capital and speculation in the north-east frontier demonstrates the large numbers of contracts signed between frontier inhabitants and commercial agents. He states, 'in 1869, 38 joint stock companies were engaged in tea industry in the north eastern frontier. Their nominal capital amounted to nearly four millions and a half sterling pounds and called-up capital three millions. Very soon, scores of other companies—specializing in timber and saw mills, rubber and gittapercha, ivory and minor forest products, oil and mining, and railways and transport—followed the suit of tea.'[15] Capital flowed into the frontier beyond the imperial jurisdictional limits, with the involvement and support of colonial government.

Kar's argument provides a significant departure in history writing on colonial north-east by bringing focus to the emergence of capitalist political economy in a region that was historically classified as primitive and thereby as outside the time of capital. This argument also has implications for indigenous studies in South Asia that have overwhelmingly focused on representation and identity of tribes and adivasis. Importantly, some of these studies have shown the historically shifting and plurality of Adivasi identities.[16] Yet the archival and theoretical possibilities of such

---

[14] Hopkins, *Ruling the Savage Periphery*, 15.

[15] Bodhisattva Kar, 'Nomadic Capital and Speculative Tribes: A Culture of Contracts in the Northeastern Frontier of British India', *The Indian Economic and Social History Review* 53, no. 1 (2016): 41–67.

[16] The most recent (among a rich array of) literature on tribes and adivasi communities in India is Sangeeta Dasgupta's extensively researched and incisive study on Oraons and Tana Bhagats in present-day Jharkhand. In Dasgupta's introduction, she provides a comprehensive account of the historiographical debates and contributions on the histories of adivasis. She shows how the notion of tribe shifted in meaning and usage during the colonial period, and its political implications in the postcolonial period. Dasgupta's work combines the colonial archive and the memory archive by centring the multiple voices of Oraons. See Sangeeta Dasgupta, *Reordering Adivasi Worlds: Representation, Resistance, Memory* (India: Oxford University Press, 2022).

histories remain bound within binary notions of universality of primitive on the one hand and localized and often parochial socio-political contexts on the other. In this book tribe is understood as a colonial category of law inscribed upon the social and political lives of frontier communities. Questions of belonging, legality, rights, and politics are historically shaped through the heuristics of tribe and more recently indigeneity in north-east India. This book does not delve into the historiographical debates on the multiple deployments of tribe and indigeneity. Instead, the book shows the conditions for the production of categories such as tribe as a corollary to the separation of hills and plains.

Prior to Kar's work, an important historiographical intervention that enables rich 'archival possibilities' has been the detangling of historical research from national boundaries. Drawing attention to the relationship between geographical history of the frontier and the social realities in recent decades, David Ludden poses a rhetorical question: 'where is Assam?' He argues that the history of the region cannot be contained within the gridlines of national geography. Social histories, he states, can be identified in multiple and mobile spaces. This means that certain histories remain invisible in the type of knowledge that nationalizes histories of communities, culture, identities, and even weather.[17] In another essay that exemplifies his argument, Ludden shows that colonial territorialization in Bengal established the first modern boundary, put in place to separate the Khasi hills from the Sylhet plains. The boundary was modern in the sense that it not only physically separated the hills and plains, but also played on social differentiation between inhabitants. This boundary was made, he writes, to limit the claims of Khasi rulers to lands in the

---

See also Bengt. G. Karlsson and T. B. Subba, eds., *Indigeneity in India* (London: Kegan Paul, 2006); Vinita Damodaran, 'Colonial Constructions of the "Tribe" in India: The Case of Chotanagpur', *Indian Historical Review* 33, no. 1 (2006): 44–75; Daniel J. Rycroft and Sangeeta Dasgupta, eds., *The Politics of Belonging in India: Becoming Adivasi* (London and New York: Routledge, 2011); Nandini Sundar, *Subalterns and Sovereigns: An Anthropological History of Bastar, 1854–1996* (New Delhi and New York: Oxford University Press, 1997).

[17] David Ludden, 'Where Is Assam? Using Geographical History to Locate Current Social Realities', *CENISEAS Papers*, no. 1 (Guwahati: Centre for Northeast India, South and Southeast Asia Studies, Omeo Kumar Das Institute for Social Change and Development, 2003). https://nyuscholars.nyu.edu/en/publications/where-is-assam-using-geographical-history-to-locate-current-socia

plains appropriated under the Permanent Settlement.[18] Arguing against Ludden's postulation that social and ethnic differences were considered by Company officials while drawing boundaries, Gunnel Cederlof states that boundaries were neither rigid nor fixed in the early nineteenth century.[19] Commercial concerns trumped state making and racialized governance of divide and rule in the early decades of the nineteenth century the Company's according to Cederlof.

It is true that boundary-making initiatives between Sylhet and the Khasi hills were incomplete and partial due to ecology, climate, and specific requirements of governance. However, it is evident in colonial record on boundary disputes in the frontier hills that the colonial administrators from the late eighteenth century heavily relied on racial characterizations such as the hill tribal to enable law's travels into non-British territory. Such characterizations attributed spatial and temporal meanings to identities of frontier inhabitants with implications for colonial governance and commercial interests. This book shows that racial classifications between hills and plains, tribal and non-tribal, underwrote strategic use of ambiguous legal policy, and shifting jurisdictional boundaries in the north-eastern region.

The imprecision of boundaries was characteristic of pre-colonial Mughal and Ahom kingdoms in this region. These larger kingdoms alongside smaller ones such as the Khasi and Jaintia polities witnessed overlapping political sovereignty and changing fealty and reciprocity between subjects and authorities. Sanghamitra Mishra shows how shared sovereignty between the Zamindar in Goalpara in northern Bengal, the monarch of Bhutan, the Dalai Lama of Tibet, Ahom dynasty in Assam, and other smaller nodes of power were reformulated with colonial expansion into the Himalayan borderlands (see Figure 1.1 and 1.2). Changes in marketing practices, trading connections, and land settlement patterns

---

[18] David Ludden, 'Investing in Nature around Sylhet: An Excursion into Geographical History', *Economic and Political Weekly* 38, no. 48 (November 2003): 5080–5088; Misra, *Becoming a Borderland*, 22.

[19] Gunnel Cederlöf, 'Fixed Boundaries, Fluid Landscapes: British Expansion into Northern East Bengal in the 1820s', *The Indian Economic and Social History Review* 46, no. 4 (2009): 513–540.

transformed this interconnected space and challenged multiple and overlapping authority, she argues.[20] Mishra contends that colonial officials failed to understand the nature of overlapping sovereignties, and ambiguous boundaries between different rulers in the region. Yet, the judicial archive on the Garo, Khasi, and Jaintia hills shows that ambiguity and jurisdictional confusion in fact helped to further entrench colonial power in the frontier hills.

Contrary to Sharma's interlocutors who were unable to comprehend the multiplicity of sovereign authority, colonial administrators in the frontier hills employed plural sovereignty and ambiguous, and often overlapping jurisdiction as a strategy of governance. David Scott who held the highest political office in the north-east frontier as Political Agent and his successors like Francis Jenkins were crucial in creating the particulars of this form of governance. This meant allowing existing tropes of customary authority and norms, albeit with significant adaptations for colonial sovereignty. Plural sovereignty was encoded as law through the practice of indirect rule. However, indirect rule was not a stage in the development of colonial control and governance as historians have previously argued. Indirect rule was a strategy of plural legal and sovereign governance where in customary rulers remained markers of continuity of pre-colonial autonomy. Yet, as in the case of Khasi states examined in this book, Chiefs and local rulers were stripped of political power, decentring their authority. Not unlike the case of colonial Egypt, as Samera Esmeir skilfully demonstrates, a temporal split between the modern and premodern induced the process of decentring the commanding role of the sovereign. Modern colonial law could thereby rightfully claim its role in paving the trajectory towards freedom and civilization.[21] In the same way, colonial law integrated rather than excluded the frontier hills within the universal parameters of liberal governmentality. This book further

---

[20] For a similar study by Indrani Chatterjee examining transformations in geographical conceptions and politico-economic networks, see Chatterjee, *Forgotten Friends.*

[21] Law's temporalization, as Esmeir has skilfully shown, involved the *inclusion* of colonial subjects within a universal framework as juridical humans. This departs from the pervasive notion of the exclusion of colonial subjects from the universal principles of enlightenment and the concomitant expectation that only through full integration within those principles could the colonized be rescued from the waiting room of history. The violence inhered within processes of inclusion, shown by Esmeir, helps in understanding the violence of law and discourse of rights. See Samera Esmeir, *Juridical Humanity: A Colonial History* (Stanford: Stanford University Press, 2012).

shows how plural sovereignty and entanglements of law, custom, and commerce decentred the political role of Chiefs in Khasi polities.

Plural legal ordering of the north-east frontier accompanied large-scale transformation of the landscape for purposes of enhanced revenue through large-scale plantations and mining.[22] Politico-economic transformations and changes in demographic composition of colonial Assam led to the intensification of caste violence, and racialized subject categories such as tribal and coolie became increasingly visible in colonial legal proceedings. The plantation has been understood as a site of exceptional legal violence. In her study of Assam's plantations as exceptional spaces of law Elizabeth Kolsky points towards a 'legal void' defined by everyday racialized violence.[23] Legal spaces like plantations Kolsky argues demonstrate the gap between goals set by principles of liberal universal justice and extra-legal practices in colonial contexts. It is important to point out here that frontier spaces, including plantations, were not aberrations in liberal governance. Frontier spaces were included within the ambit of colonial law through strategic discourse of their exceptionality and difference. The violence that accompanied extra territorial jurisdiction and exceptional legislation were mechanisms central to colonial rule and liberal governance. This important point helps move away from the general tendency of viewing frontier regions as units in themselves as either spaces of exception or before law.

In a comparative study of the north-east and north-west frontiers of British India Thomas Simpson challenges the view of frontier spaces as isolable, fixed, and uniform.[24] He shows that border-making enclosed these spaces as regions and produced shifting and contested boundaries. The Naga hills' amorphous borders, Simpson shows, were celebrated and little effort was made to lay down rigid boundaries.[25] Just as in the Garo and Khasi hills, the vague boundaries between British territory and non-British territory in the Naga hills allowed easy access for military

---

[22] For a comprehensive study of Assam's changing landscape marked by tea plantations, see Jayeeta Sharma, *Empire's Garden: Assam and the Making of India* (Durham and London: Duke University Press, 2011).

[23] Elizabeth Kolsky, *Colonial Justice in British India: White Violence and the Rule of Law* (Cambridge: Cambridge University Press, 2010).

[24] See Simpson, *Frontier in British India*. See also Thomas Simpson, 'Bordering and Frontier-Making in Nineteenth-Century British India', *The Historical Journal* 58, no. 2 (2015): 513–542.

[25] Simpson, *Frontier in British India* and Simpson, 'Bordering and Frontier-Making', 513–542.

expeditions sometimes guised as geographical surveys and sometimes explicitly for punitive purposes. Simpson argues that colonial officials were aware of the failures of imperial liberalism, and shortcomings of imperial knowledge systems.

Agents of empire, Simpson states invoking Helen Tilley, often rejected European civilizational discourse challenging 'truth claims that accepted European examples and standards as the norm'.[26] The colonial state power he argues was thus itself fragmentary adding further complexity to the 'fractal' frontier landscape.[27] Inconsistency and diversity of 'men in the spot' Simpson highlights as key features of frontier governance. Albeit this is an important observation, like Andrew May's study of recalcitrant and rebellious Welsh missionaries in the Khasi hills, the focus remains on the contradictions inherent in the colonial project and lived experience of imperial agents. Even if individual officers or missionaries resisted, critiqued, and challenged the imperial apparatus their voices and actions impacted localized experiences within the contours of a colonial exploitative framework. Large-scale transformative policies, in areas of law, administration, political economy, and knowledge were informed by colonial governing ideology that was uniformly violent.

The universal parameters of law and jurisdiction formulated by colonial intellectuals were important in shaping legal pluralism, in places as far from the imperial centre as the frontier hills examined here. For instance, Henry Maine's ideas about customary laws and indirect rule had a profound influence on the attitude of the colonial administration towards semi-independent and princely states.[28] Karuna Mantena notes that Henry Maine's fears of the inevitability of the 'radical undoing

---

[26] Helen Tilley quoted in Simpson, *Frontier in British India*, 7. See Helen Tilley, *Africa as a Living Laboratory: Empire, Development, and the Problem of Scientific Knowledge, 1870–1950* (Chicago and London: University of Chicago Press, 2011), 314–315.

[27] Simpson, *Frontier in British India*, 12.
Mandy Sadan has developed the idea of the fractal frontier, suggesting multiple layers of fragmentation of spaces and communities of colonial borderlands in Mandy Sadan, *Being and Becoming Kachin: Histories beyond the State in the Borderworlds of Burma* (Oxford: Oxford University Press, 2013).

[28] Henry Sumner Maine (1822–1888)—a jurist, legal theorist, and colonial administrator between 1863 and 1869—was highly influential in the implementation of changes in colonial legal and administrative policies in British India in the second half of the nineteenth century. For an analysis of Maine's formulation of indirect rule in the colony, see Karuna Mantena, *Alibis of Empire: Henry Maine and the Ends of Liberal Imperialism* (Princeton and Oxford: Princeton University Press, 2010).

of customary basis of village community under imperial rule' resulting in atomized private property, led to his formulation of an alternative strategy, a solution in the form of indirect rule.[29] The colony-wide appreciation of indirect rule as an appropriate form of governance manifested in the frontier hills with reconstituted relationships between colonial administrators, customary authority, and subjects. Encouraged by a desire to stymie private trade monopoly, the colonial state reformulated the terms of economic activity through new agreements signed with customary authority. Although transfer in the administrative reins from Company to Crown came with a declaration of an official policy to separate governance along with colonial and customary aspects, and an official sanction of legal pluralism through indirect rule. Instead on the ground there was a hardening of state structures and assertion of colonial sovereignty. In the frontier hills in the late nineteenth-century colonial policy reflect not so much a distancing from local institutions, instead a more thorough involvement in civil disputes including inheritance and succession of ruling clans, and ruler subject relations circumscribed by custom.

The interstices of commerce, custom, and plural sovereignty examined in this book reflect the way imperial ideology mutated and manifested through local colonial agents, albeit retaining its universally violent and transformative character. Law appeared in these hills not simply as a tool used by the state but as fundamental to the shaping of political space itself. Imprecision of borders, and thereby of law and governance was a useful strategy.[30] Critical legal scholars and legal geographers have contributed to our understanding of the constitutive relationship between law, geography, and hierarchical relations of power. Racialized spatio-legal reasoning employed by colonial administrators enables a reorientation of our understanding of law as objective and complete. Colonial law through jurisdictional and revenue boundary-making operations created divisions between the Garo, Khasi, and Jaintia hills and Sylhet plains by invoking the spectre of hill tribal. Categories such as tribal and indigenous continue to be laden with the combined logic of civilizational

---

[29] Mantena, *Alibis*, 121.
[30] See Irus Braverman, Nicholas Blomley, David Delaney, and Alexandre Kedar, eds., *The Expanding Spaces of Law: A Timely Legal Geography* (Stanford: Stanford University Press, 2014).

discrimination and spatial hierarchization.[31] This book shows the myriad ways in which law appears in the frontier hills, and the engagement and resistance of inhabitants interacting with colonial law.

Chapters

The book begins with an examination of colonial law-making and boundary-making initiatives from the late eighteenth century onwards. Chapters 2–4 focus on the interaction between colonial spatiality and law. A shifting and complex interchange between colonial administrators at various levels of the government, local elites' contested interpretation of customs, and challenges posed by inhabitants to such interpretations are examined. Chapter 2 takes us along the travels of David Scott, the architect of law in the north-east frontier of the British Empire. Before being promoted to the role of Political Agent of the North-East Frontier, David Scott as Magistrate of Rangpur in the province of Assam engineered a legal framework that excluded inhabitants of the frontier from Bengal Regulations. The formulation of tribal in the north-east as a spatial and legal category enabled the exclusion of parts or entire hill ranges in the frontier from the framework of the Bengal Regulations. In non-regulation provinces laws in operation elsewhere in the colony were suspended in favour of special laws or no laws. Further, any law existing in regulation areas could be imposed in the non-regulation areas if deemed necessary.

Negotiations and conflicts with local rulers, and changes in political topography are examined in Chapter 3. This chapter follows the setting up of colonial legal infrastructure in the hills, and attendant processes of spatial transformation. The policy of non-regulation initiated by David Scott followed by decrees, and the signing of agreements with Khasi states, while parts of the Garo and Jaintiah hills were brought within imprecise form of direct colonial administration. Absence of a uniform legal policy was characteristic of colonial governance in the frontier hills. The

---

[31] Prathama Banerjee, *Politics of Time: 'Primitives' and History-Writing in a Colonial Society* (New Delhi and Oxford: Oxford University Press, 2006).

chapter demonstrates conflicting and overlapping roles, responsibilities, and jurisdictions of different courts and judicial forums in the frontier hill districts. Ambiguities in the jurisdictional powers of the Political Agent allowed him unlimited powers. With the increasing powers of the Political Agent and other local colonial officials such as district administrators, and magistrates, the role of the Khasi Syiem also shifted. The latter is examined in the following chapter.

Chapter 4 focuses on the entwined historical emergence of law and custom in the frontier hills visible in the changing role of rulers of Khasi states known as Syiem. Colonial state's ability to impose law and jurisdiction anywhere in hills and over anyone produced significant departures in the meaning of customary authority. This was further complicated by the presence of private traders some of whom had immense power and influence in governance and administration. In the second half of the nineteenth-century legal reforms, and structural changes in administrative and judicial system in the hills were legalized through new agreements signed with Syiems. Laws governing property and succession were subjected to debate and analysis by legal and political theorists through the nineteenth century.[32] In the Khasi hills, debates on aspects of law led to the reconfiguration of custom, to suit the politico-economic concerns of the colonial state across the theatre of Empire. This chapter provides insight into the working of legal pluralism not as a system of accommodation and agency of the colonized, but as a strategy of hierarchical governance.

The book then turns to a contrapuntal reading of scientific and non-scientific narratives from the nineteenth century and addresses the way colonial scientific knowledge shaped the hills as a legal space. Chapter 5 examines colonial knowledge and sciences that characterized frontier inhabitants in relation to geographical landscape. Imperial scientific disciplines starting with geography, botany, and geology in the first half of the nineteenth century, and ethnography, ethnology, and anthropology in the second half impacted the understanding of space and place in

---

[32] Sandra den Otter, 'A Legislating Empire: Victorian Political Theorists, Codes of Law, and Empire', in *Victorian Visions of a Global Order: Empire and International Relations in Nineteenth-Century Political Thought*, ed. Duncan Bell (Cambridge: Cambridge University Press, 2007), 89–112.

the frontier hills. The characteristic invariance and prejudicial under-standing noticeable in colonial knowledge on tribes was not simply an inability of colonial administrators, travelling scientists, and missionaries to comprehend societies in the Garo, Khasi, Jaintia hills. Instead, such generalizations, slippages, and ambiguity in colonial liberal formulations were ideologically and politically motivated.

The last two chapters present a discussion on literary and non-literary sources, highlighting heterogeneous conceptions of history, self, and belonging in the hills. Chapter 6 examines print literature and cultural articulations of identity in the Khasi hills initiated by English-educated Khasi men. Christian missionaries not only introduced new religious ideologies and cosmological conceptions but also engaged in the production of standardized Khasi language and grammar. The emergence of a Khasi public sphere in the late nineteenth century re-flected socio-religious assertion of indigenous Khasi faith informed by and produced through interactions between multiple religious and social organizations such as the Brahmo Samaj and Unitarian Church. The Khasi Young Men's Association, later named Seng Khasi Movement, was formed in 1899 as an anticolonial social movement to protect indigenous religion. Khasi and English publications in jour-nals, and newspapers from this time reflect articulations of hill-based identity.

Chapter 7, the final chapter of the book, highlights embodied and situated experiences of frontier hill inhabitants by exploring their re-lationship to landscape, environment, and the changing spatiality of new jurisdictional boundaries, lines of communication, enhanced economic mobility, and social architecture. This chapter will show how notions of place cut across and weave through spatial practices tra-jectories and interrelations. Place-making is essentially time-bound—whether linear, cyclical, or iterative. The heterogeneity of place and its narratives provide access to non-linear histories. In contemporary so-cieties of the erstwhile frontier multiple and coexisting understand-ings of spaces and places can be found. In the Khasi hills there are spaces wherein temporality is not understood only in linear terms. For instance, social spaces defined by matrilineal kinship (*iing* and *kpoh*), religious spaces (sacred forests), and political spaces like *darbars* are sites of conflict, hierarchy, and power built on social relations that inform each other.[33] Statutory and constitutional laws are inscribed into such spaces that are framed in terms of custom. A host of laws on land, forest, environment, and customary rights provides such spaces with legitimacy, and thereby informs social norms and power relations in the hills. Law in turn claims validity through these spaces.

To explain the above point the book shows the profound spatial and legal changes of the nineteenth century that manifested in the relationship between people and their surroundings. These changes remain part of the living memory of inhabitants of the hills and form an integral part of the present. A living memory archive can be accessed in coexisting linear and non-linear conceptions of the past contained in landscapes marked with memory stones, and oral sources. These sources provide a departure from western teleological, positivist, and literary historical narratives.[34] Non-literary forms of knowledge such as oral traditions and histories, legends and folktales have engaged with written histories for over two centuries, and in the present such interactions inflect a relationship between older concerns and new politico-social interests. Contemporary discourses on indigeneity and custom in the Khasi hills are embedded in conceptions of the past shaped by colonial and national discourses on tribal identity, customary law, and frontier governance. Many such narratives rely on homogenous conceptions of ethnic identity and collocated claims to rights, culture, and space. Law appears in this book as central to the creation of the frontier space, and place-based identity. The book thus intervenes in historiographical debates that reflect intersecting concerns of frontier historians, law and society scholars, and indigenous and minority histories of South Asia.

[33] For a theorization of law's multiple spaces in a different context, see Benda-Beckmann, 'Places that Come and Go', 30–52.
[34] Historians such as Ajay Skaria, among others, have pointed towards the radical archival possibilities in memory and oral narratives.

2

Frontiers of Law

In 1787 Robert Lindsay, private merchant and resident collector of revenues for the British East India Company in Sylhet, wrote a report informing the Government of Bengal of communities bordering British Bengal on its northern and eastern frontiers. He described the geographical limits of the area in which inhabitants of Khasi polities lived. He included within these limits 'mountainous country' stretching to the northwest extremity of Sylhet and the eastern boundaries of Cachar (including within this demarcation the Garo and Jaintia Hills). Lindsay added, the mountains are 'inaccessible to a foreign enemy and every part of them are beyond the company's provinces.'[1] Lindsay wrote this report in response to growing concerns among higher officials about events described as raids into British territory. Raids became a central concern across frontier areas leading to the formulation of a series of actions and policies to settle jurisdictions along the borders between the hills and plains. This chapter lays out the colonial mapping of jurisdictional and topographical divisions in the north-east frontier of the British empire in India. By examining the role of law and jurisdiction in separating British and non-British territory, hills and plains, tribe and caste, the chapter demonstrates concomitant processes of law-making and frontier-making.

The primitive status ascribed to 'hill tribals' was bound up with their marginality, their non-revenue yielding power, and their 'inaccessibility'.[2] In fact so-called hill polities extended into the Sylhet plains, thus preventing any convenient topographical division between British and non-British territories. Centuries of accumulated knowledge emanating from inter-imperial networks produced an idea of the legal primitivism

---

[1] Board of Revenue Papers, 29 December 1787, No. 10, Assam State Archives (ASA).
[2] Board of Revenue Papers 1782, File No. 8, Serial No. 3, ASA; Board of Revenue Papers 1783, File No. 12, Serial No. 2, ASA; Board of Revenue Papers, 9 November 1787, No.13, ASA.

Placing the Frontier in British North-East India. Reeju Ray, Oxford University Press. © Reeju Ray 2023.
DOI: 10.1093/oso/9780192887085.003.0002

of hill polities in the north-east frontier of British India.[3] The north eastern frontier was a strategically important region for the East India Company because for defensive purposes in addition to revenue generation through trade and agriculture. China and Burma were powerful neighbours, in addition to several gradations of kingdoms and polities spread across the Himalayan borderlands. With the grant of Diwani by the Mughal Court in Delhi in 1775, Bengal came under the administrative and judicial control of the East India Company. In the late eighteenth century the East India Company was hesitant to expand its administration into mountainous terrain beyond the revenue-yielding agricultural plains, markets, and established trading outposts in the foothills such as at Pandua in Khasi territory.[4] From the mid-eighteenth century to the early decades of the nineteenth century, the Company's ambitions in the region evolved from accessing markets in Burma and China to ensuring the security of Bengal from Burmese encroachment by establishing itself as a dominant political power.[5] By the early nineteenth century shifting geopolitical concerns, particularly the positions of the kingdoms of Assam (Ahom), Manipur, Cachar, and Jaintia, propelled colonial judicial administration into the frontier hills of the Garo, Khasi, and Jaintia territories.

The East India Company's reach into the Garo, Khasi, and Jaintia Hills began with punitive expeditions and geographical and revenue surveys, which in overlapping ways, were harbingers of colonial law.[6] These efforts

[3] Hills have historically, and perhaps globally, been associated with socio-political forms that mark a distinct 'non-civility' in relation to plains, cities, and towns. See Lauren Benton, *A Search for Sovereignty: Law and Geography in European Empires, 1400–1900* (New York: Cambridge University Press, 2010), 222–236.
Hills have also been understood as interrupters of civilizing forces, and as places of refuge for those who seek to evade taxation and assimilation into imperial political economies. James C. Scott, *The Art of Not Being Governed: An Anarchist History of Upland Southeast Asia* (New Haven and New York: Yale University Press, 2009).

[4] The EIC was one of many trading interests in Sylhet in the eighteenth century. The foothills were marked by dynamic market centres like Pandua, where trade was carried out between Khasis, Bengalis, Armenians, English, and Afghan traders. See Gunnel Cederlöf, 'Fixed Boundaries, Fluid Landscapes: British Expansion into Northern East Bengal in the 1820s', *The Indian Economic and Social History Review* 46, no. 4 (2009): 518.

[5] Gunnel Cederlöf, *Founding an Empire on India's North-Eastern Frontiers, 1790–1840: Climate, Commerce, Polity* (New Delhi: Oxford University Press, 2014), 4.

[6] In their article 'The Travels of Law: Indian Ocean Itineraries', Renisa Mawani and Iza Hussin ask, 'what is law and how does it travel?' I take a cue from this question to enquire into law's itinerancy in the north-east frontier of the British empire in India. See Renisa Mawani and Iza Hussin, 'The Travels of Law: Indian Ocean Itineraries', *Law and History Review* 32, no. 4 (2014): 733–747.

produced a large corpus of geographical information that gives the illusion of a seamless frontier space.[7] This frontier, however, was not a uniform administrative unit by any means, nor was there any uniformity of juridical order. Gaps in territorial control and fragmented sovereignty across imperial spaces produced what has been termed as 'anomalous legal zones' wherein normative principles of law were suspended or altogether absent.[8] However, such 'anomalies' were characteristic of colonial rule of law in British India not only in legally differentiated spaces but also more pervasively as representations of difference.[9] Differentiation and domestication became concomitant colonial strategies that created the frontier through law.

Colonial law according to Hussain negotiated two Enlightenment concepts: primitivism (marking an absence of law) and oriental despotism (suggesting excessive rule).[10] The frontier hills were marked by an absence of law while the discourse of primitives was further legitimated through a dual backwardness: temporal and spatial.[11] Prathama Bannerjee has shown that civilizational hierarchies were measured by both time and space as units on a scale of progress and informed processes of representation of the primitive.[12] Conditions of legality and the

---

[7] The archive of cartographic information, cadastral surveys, and commissioned and non-commissioned travellers' accounts enabled an imagining of the frontier as spatially bounded. Matthew Edney has shown that the incorporation of multiple cartographic representations, and multiple sources of geographic information to produce single maps constructed a 'communal view' that subsumed and superseded individual views. He described the resulting gaze as a concerted observation. These singular observations are all understood in relation to other observations along the geographer's route, or other relative observations producing a larger conceptual framework or an absolute space. See Matthew H. Edney, *Mapping an Empire: The Geographical Construction of British India, 1765–1843* (Chicago: University of Chicago Press, 1997), 64.

[8] Lauren Benton uses Gerald L. Neuman's concept of anomalous legal zones to describe the patches within imperial spaces where normative laws can be suspended. See Gerald L. Neuman, 'Anomalous Zones', *Stanford Law Review* 48, no. 5 (May, 1996): 1197–1234.

[9] Radhika Singha has pointed out that the colonial state attempted to create an encompassing typology of tribal and incorporated groups like the Thugs, Pindaris, Bhils, and others. Such classifications enabled distinguishing between productive revenue yielding subjects and non-revenue yielding subjects. More significantly, such classifications enabled legal coercive measures against certain groups, culminating in the Criminal Tribes Act of 1871. See Radhika Singha, *A Despotism of Law: Crime and Justice in Early Colonial India* (Delhi and New York: Oxford University Press, 1998). See also Nasser Hussain, 'Towards a Jurisprudence of Emergency: Colonialism and the Rule of Law', *Law and Critique* 10 (1999): 93–115.

[10] Hussain, 'Jurisprudence'.

[11] Ajay Skaria, 'Shades of Wildness: Tribe, Caste, and Gender in Western India', *The Journal of Asian Studies* 56, no. 3 (August 1997): 724.

[12] Prathama Banerjee, *Politics of Time: 'Primitives' and History-Writing in a Colonial Society* (New Delhi and Oxford: Oxford University Press, 2006). Banerjee invokes Hegel's concept of

emerging legal order in the frontier hills of Bengal constructed space as anomalous where normative laws did not apply. Identifying frontier inhabitants as primitive was an important part of creating anomalous legal zones.[13]

This chapter examines decrees, regulations, treaties, that often doubled up as military expeditions and produced the hills as legally differentiated spaces. Prominent among them is the Bengal Regulation XII of 1833 that legalized the existence of exceptional administrative and legal zones in which the laws or regulations of the Bengal Presidency would not apply.[14] For decades prior to this regulation, local administrators in the frontier districts grappled with ways to define and establish jurisdiction, separating British-acquired territories from those outside of them. Frustrated by an inability to mark the precise boundary of British territory, administrators used special juridical powers to punish transgressing non-British subjects. Ambiguity and uncertainty about jurisdiction and boundaries thus made way for colonial law's travel into the frontier hills.[15]

The material and ideological conditions of production of legal spaces in the northeast frontier of the British Empire in India in the first half of the nineteenth century have been examined below. The first section focuses on the various contingent and strategic processes through which colonial law moved into these regions, where it was invoked and for what purposes, and what it sought to achieve or prevent. The second section examines official and non-official geographical narratives that demonstrate the entanglements of law and geography. The final section

---

spatialized temporality to define the founding moment of modernity that facilitated the understanding of 'an-other land as an-other time'.

[13] Renisa Mawani, 'Law as Temporality: Colonial Politics and Indian Settlers', *UC Irvine Law Review* 4, no. 1 (2014): 65–95. See also Sudipta Sen, 'Unfinished Conquest: Residual Sovereignty and the Legal Foundations of the British Empire in India', *Law, Culture, and the Humanities* 9, no. 2 (2013): 232–239.

[14] Bengal Regulation XII 1833, quoted in Uday Chandra, 'Liberalism and Its Other: The Politics of Primitivism in Colonial and Postcolonial Indian Law', *Law and Society Review* 47, no. 1 (2013): 135–168.

[15] Renisa Mawani and Iza Hussin show that colonial law's indeterminacy was crucial to its travels across time and space, in Mawani and Hussin, 'The Travels', 6.

concludes by arguing that if colonial law sought to tame the challenges of the frontier space, it was contradictory and prone to failure.[16]

Law's Travel

The notion that hill inhabitants of frontier polities were responsible for raids into British territories justified punitive expeditions. Raids by Garo 'mountaineers' on the frontier of Rangpur district formed the basis of several British policies to protect as well as expand revenue in trade and agriculture in the frontier districts. Persistent raids resulted in the formulation of a policy of administration to guide jurisdiction in the hills, namely Regulation X (1822). The architect of Regulation X was David Scott, magistrate of Rangpur, a frontier district of Bengal adjoining the Garo Hills. His strategic ability to combine violence with diplomacy in the non-British territories helped in his rise as the first Political Agent of the North East.[17]

David Scott questioned the suitability of the Bengal Regulations in the frontier hills and insisted on establishing a special code of regulations. These rules, according to Scott, would provide security to Europeans as well as help civilize the tribal communities. Colonial control over Garo territory was graded in terms of jurisdictional power.[18] Distinctions between Garos rested on whether or not they were revenue yielding, and also on the basis of their location in villages, clans, or the higher hills.[19] However, such distinctions were fictive since clans, villages, and topography overlapped.[20]

---

[16] For an analysis of the processes of taming of space as a strategy of repressing not only the spatial but multiple temporalities, see Doreen Massey, *For Space* (Delhi: SAGE Publications, 2005), 69–70.

[17] Reports of David Scott dated 15 August 1818 and 10 November 1820 the former showing the result of his enquiries in the Garo villages and the pergunnahs of Curryburree and Caloomalopara and the latter giving information of a murder committed on a Garo and his four young children by the two inhabitants of the villages of Dodanpara in pergunnah Meekpara, Boards Collections 1825–1826, 21848–21862, Vol. 819, Judicial No. 16 IOR.

[18] Ibid.

[19] Ibid.

[20] Jayanta Bhusan Bhattacharjee, *The Garos and the English, 1765–1874* (Shillong and New Delhi: Radiant Publishers, 1988), 65. See also Alexander Mackenzie, *History of the Relations of the Government with the Hill Tribes of the North-East Frontier of Bengal* (1884; Reprint, Cambridge: Cambridge University Press, 2012).

The regulation did not establish a judicial policy for the 'non-regulated' tracts. Instead, it was built on the premise that regulations in operation in Bengal could not be applied in these spaces, and therefore it allowed room for the creation of special laws when required. The regulation lacked clarity in terms of the colonial government's judicial policy, but created a centralized executive with magisterial, judicial, and revenue powers.[21] Without any specific legal and judicial policies in the hills, and an ability on the part of the colonial administrators to apply any law as deemed necessary, the reach of colonial power expanded greatly in the frontier.

Following the passage of Regulation X, David Scott gained prominence in the colonial administration and travelled across the frontier hills to either subdue or enter into contractual relations with local authorities identified as sovereigns. During the same period, the threat of Burmese advance into British territory provoked large geographical expeditions and surveys, and commissioned reports by the Company government.[22] For example, between 1827 and 1829, Lieutenant Thomas Fischer conducted multiple surveys on the frontiers of Sylhet and Mymensing districts bordering the frontier hills.[23] His report repeatedly referenced in subsequent surveys and expeditions, and noted which boundaries had been disputed in the previous decades. Such reports, discussed in detail later in this chapter, provide insight into the violence of imperial expansion in the frontier area as simultaneously epistemological and embodied.

Agreements signed during the early decades of the nineteenth century across the Garo, Khasi, and Jaintiah Hills embodied the travel of law.[24] Conditions leading up to these agreements, and their intended

---

[21] Richard Clarke, comp., *The Regulations of the Government of Fort William in Bengal, in Force at the End of 1853: To Which Are Added, the Acts of the Government of India in Force in that Presidency*, vol. 2 (London: J. H. Cox, 1854), 659–663.

[22] For instance: R Wilcox, 'Memoir of a Survey of Asam and the Neighbouring Countries, Executed in 1825-6-7-8', *Asiatic Researches* 17 (Calcutta: Bengal Military Printing Press, 1832): 314–469; William Robinson, *A Descriptive Account of Asam: With a Sketch of the Local Geography and a Concise History of the Tea-Plant of Asam, to Which Is Added a Short Account of the Neighbouring Tribes, Exhibiting Their History, Manners, and Customs* (London: Thomas Ostell and Co., 1841); H. Walters, 'A Journey across Pandua Hills, Near Silhet, in Bengal', *Asiatic Researches* 17 (Calcutta: Bengal Military Printing Press, 1832). See also Thomas Fischer's surveys among others.

[23] Board of Revenue Papers 48, File No. 8-100, ASA.

[24] C. U. Aitchison, *A Collection of Treaties, Engagements and Sanads Relating to India and Neighbouring Countries*, vol. 12 (Calcutta: Government of India Central Publication Branch, 1931).

and unintended outcomes varied. The Jaintia Raja's territory was split into two administrative units divided among a melange of jurisdictions. After a military expedition in 1774 Raja Ram Singh was forced to retreat into the hills while the Company took control of the Jaintia lands in Sylhet.[25] In the years preceding the Anglo-Burmese war (1824–1826), the Jaintia Raja among other local rulers signed agreements of alliance with the Company. The allegiance of the Raja in the event of war with Burma was the focal point, but the treaty set in motion the official containment of the Jaintia polity to the hills (see Figure 2.1).[26] The treaty signed between David Scott and Ram Singh was a precursor to formal annexation on pretexts of British moral concerns about the 'barbaric' practices by Jaintia subjects.[27] Agreements signed with chiefs often contained a clause that identified various practices as immoral and unethical. For instance, agreements with Garo chiefs at the frontier of Mymensing included a clause that forbade storing or displaying human skulls in houses.[28]

The question of jurisdiction in the annexed Jaintia territory developed into a series of debates about the relationship between jurisdictional units, administrative ease, and topographical fluidity.[29] With the passing of Act VI in 1835, Company jurisdiction was extended into the hills of Jaintia. This act empowered Captain Lister, the commandant of the Sylhet Light Infantry and newly appointed political agent to act in the capacity of magistrate combining military, policing, executive, and

[25] David Reid Syiemlieh, *British Administration in Meghalaya: Policy and Pattern* (New Delhi: Heritage Publishers, 1989), 17. See also Cederlöf, *Founding*, 60–61.

[26] Aitchison, *A Collection of Treaties*, 118–119.

[27] For examples of alleged kidnapping of British subjects from the Sylhet plains, for the purpose of human sacrifice, recorded in official correspondence and in officially produced historical accounts, see R. B. Pemberton, *Report on the Eastern Frontier of India* (1835; Reprint, New Delhi: Mittal Publishers 2000), 210–221 and Mackenzie, *History of the Relations*, 217–244.

[28] Bodhisattva Kar has demonstrated that the anxieties of colonial officials regarding practices of headhunting were linked to efforts to establish sovereignty and dominance. See Bodhisattva Kar, 'Heads in the Naga Hills', in *New Cultural Histories of India: Materiality and Practices*, eds. Partha Chatterjee, Tapati Guha-Thakurta, and Bodhisattva Kar (New Delhi: Oxford University Press, 2014), 335–370.

[29] For instance, after a part of the Jaintia lands known as the Seven Reaches or Shat Bank was annexed to Cachar, the commissioner of Sylhet wrote to the Sudder Board of Revenue insisting that the Shat Bank 'naturally' belonged to Sylhet. The correspondence indicates that there was a general opinion that once Shat Bank was amalgamated into Sylhet and all the laws and regulations of settlement imposed upon it the same could be extended to the rest of the Jaintia territory. The Government of Bengal sanctioned the former under Act XXI of 1836. From Secretary to the Government of India to the Revenue Department, Government of Bengal, BG Papers 1837, no.353, ASA.

No. IV.

Treaty concluded between David Scott, Esq., Agent to the Governor-General, on the part of the Honorable East India Company and Rajah Ram Sing, ruler of Jy-Jynteepore of Jynteah.

ARTICLE 1.

Rajah Ram Sing acknowledges allegiance to the Honorable Company, and places his country of Jynteah under their protection. Mutual friendship and amity shall always be maintained between the Honorable Company and the Rajah.

ARTICLE 2.

The internal government of the country shall be conducted by the Rajah, and the jurisdiction of the British Courts of Justice shall not extend there. The Rajah will always attend to the welfare of his subjects, and observe the ancient customs of government, but should any unforseen abuse arise in the adminis-tration of affairs, he agrees to rectify the same agreeably to the advice of the Gov-ernor-General in Council.

ARTICLE 3.

The Honorable Company engages to protect the territory of Jynteah from external enemies, and to arbitrate any differences that may arise between the Rajah and other States. The Rajah agrees to abide by such arbitration, and to hold no political correspondence or communication with foreign powers, except with the consent of the British Government.

ARTICLE 4.

In the event of the Honorable Company being engaged in war to the east-ward of the Berhampooter, the Rajah engages to assist with all his forces, and to afford every other facility in his power in furtherance of such military opera-tions.

ARTICLE 5.

The Rajah agrees, in concert with the British local Authorities, to adopt all measures that may be necessary for the maintenance, in the district of Sylhet, of the arrangements in force in the Judicial, Opium and Salt Departments.

Executed this 10th of March 1824, corresponding with the 28th of Fagoon 1230 B.S., at Rajahgunge.

D. SCOTT,
Agent to the Governor-General.

SEAL AND SIGNATURE OF RAJAH
RAM SING OF JYNTEAH.

Figure 2.1 Treaty of Allegiance executed by Raja Ram Singh of Jaintia, dated 10 March 1824, C CU Aitchison, A Collection of Treaties, Engagements and Sanads Relating to India and Neighbouring Countries Vol. XII, Calcutta: Government of India Central Publication Branch 1931.

judicial functions.[30] Additionally, *Dolois* or headmen in the Jaintia Hills were recast, just like Laskars in the Garo Hills, as juridical agents of the Company.

Company relations with the sovereign Khasi polities shifted following the outbreak of rebellions in the hills against the Company in 1829.[31] Several sovereign *Syiems* (heads of polities) allied to disavow former agreements and expel the encroaching colonial government.[32] Company officials Lieutenant Bedingfield and Captain Burlton who had been part of geographical surveys and explorations in the hills were killed while supervising the construction of a road connecting Sylhet with Assam through Nongkhlaw polity.[33] David Scott, also present in Nongkhlaw at the time, narrowly escaped the insurgents led by Tirot Singh Syiem of Nongkhlaw (see Figure 2.2).[34] The incident described as 'the Nongkhlaw Massacre' in colonial reports and published accounts was followed by military offensives to subjugate the Khasi polities and renewed agreements with *Syiems*.

Following the 'Nongkhlaw Massacre' violent subjugation in these hills ranged from visible acts such as burning rebellious villages to more insidious forms including revised agreements coercively signed with Chiefs. The revised agreements enhanced the colonial monopoly

---

[30] Foreign Political, 7 February 1835, no.101, National Archives of India (NAI).

[31] Cederlöf shows that the nature of relations between the Khasi chiefs and the company was primarily dictated by the rich limestone trade until the 1820s. Several agreements were drawn up with the company to control the market and secure leases on the quarries in the hills. Many disputes arising from these trading agreements were also registered by the Bengal judicial department, but the minutes of the judicial department show that the company was not interested in settling disputes between Khasi syiems as much as it was in maintaining a stronghold over the market. See Cederlöf, *Founding,* 164–168.

[32] In an agreement signed between the *Syiem* of Nongkhlaw and David Scott in 1824, the *Syiem* agreed to comply with Scott's request for unrestricted passage of troops between Assam and Sylhet. He also agreed to furnish the materials required for the construction of the road on payment, and to keep the road in repair after its completion. He agreed to 'serve with his followers', 'to rule his subjects according to the rules of his country', and to carry out public business 'according to ancient customs, without the interference of the British Government'. See Aitchison, *A Collection of Treaties,* 122–123.

[33] References to the two men are found in geographical accounts of surveys and explorations in the 1820s discussed in the next chapter.

[34] Colonial reports, gazetteers, and official histories recorded this incident. These include, among others, reports by R. B. Pemberton, *Report on the Eastern Frontier of India* (1835); A. J. M. Mills, *Report on the Khasi and Jaintia Hills, 1853* (Assam: Secretariat Printing Office, 1901); W. J. Allen, *Report on the Administration of the Cossyah and Jynteah Hill Territory* (Calcutta: Bengal Hurkaru Press, 1858) as well as books published by colonial officials. See Edward A. Gait, *A History of Assam* (Calcutta: Thacker, Spink & Co., 1906).

No. VIII.

ARTICLES of AGREEMENT entered into by MR. DAVID SCOTT, AGENT to the GOV-
ERNOR-GENERAL, on behalf of the HONORABLE COMPANY, AND TEERUT SING
ASHEMLEE, called the WHITE RAJAH, CHIEF of NUNGKLOW,—1826.

ARTICLE 1.

Rajah Teerut Sing, the Ruler of Nungklow and its dependencies, with the
advice and consent of his relations, dependent Lushkurs and Sirdars in Council
assembled, voluntarily agrees to become subject to the Honorable Company, and
places his country under their protection.

ARTICLE 2.

The said Rajah agrees to give a free passage for troops through his country
to go and to come between Assam and Sylhet.

ARTICLE 3.

The Rajah agrees to furnish materials for the construction of a road through
his territories, receiving payment for the same, and after its completion to adopt
such measures as may be necessary to keep it in repair.

ARTICLE 4.

The Agent to the Governor-General agrees, on the part of the Honorable Company, to protect the Rajah's country from foreign enemies, and if any other Chief
injures him, to enquire into the facts, and if it appear that he has been unjustly
attacked, to afford him due support. The Rajah on his part agrees to abide by
such decision, and not to hold any intercourse or correspondence on political
matters with any foreign Chief without the consent of the British Government.

ARTICLE 5.

The Rajah agrees that, in the event of the Honorable Company carrying on
hostilities with any other power, he will serve with all his followers as far to the
eastward as Kulliabar in Assam, his men being entitled to receive subsistence
money from the British Government when employed on the Plains.

ARTICLE 6.

The Rajah promises to rule his subjects according to laws of his country, keep-
ing them pleased and contented, and carrying on the public business according
to ancient custom, without the interference of the British Government; but if
any person should commit violence in the Honorable Company's Territory, and
take refuge in the Rajah's country, he agrees to seize and deliver them up.

*Dated at Gowhatty this 30th November 1826, corresponding with the 16th Aghun
1233.*

D. SCOTT,

Agent to the Governor-General.

Similar Agreement entered into by the Chief of Khyrim.

Figure 2.2   Agreement of allegiance executed by Raja Tirot Singh
of Nongkhlaw, dated 30 November 1826, A Collection of Treaties,
Engagements and Sanads Relating to India and Neighbouring Countries
Vol. XII, Calcutta: Government of India Central Publication Branch 1931.

over resources in the hills, including limestone crucial for trade and for building roads and infrastructure.[35] The terms of subjection and humiliation are captured in an agreement between the Company and the Syiem of Mowsunram Poonjee (Mawsynram) (see Figure 2.3):

> My village having been burnt down on the part of the British Government, and now being a waste, I hereby acknowledge my submission to the government, and furnish this agreement, with the object of again settling on the spot, to the effect that I and my people will rebuild and reoccupy the village as subjects of the Government, and will obey such orders as you may, from time to time, issue on us.[36]

Although the Company reinstated surrendered *Syiems* to their positions through the signing of agreements, severe restrictions were placed on their authority.[37] The restored *Syiems* were liable for treason if they showed any form of opposition to the Company government and heavy fines were imposed as an additional punitive measure.[38] In 1833 Tirot Singh was confined in Dacca jail following a failed negotiation for reinstatement to his position as Chief of Nongkhlaw.

Which law enabled the incarceration of Tirot Singh who was identified as a sovereign by the colonial state? Would he have been allowed to retain his position if he had signed an agreement acceptable to the British? Was he imprisoned for instigating rebellion and causing the deaths of British subjects including Europeans? Or was he punished for not agreeing to the terms of subjection? There are no available or clear answers to these questions. A second treaty was signed with Tirot Singh's nine-year-old heir Rujjum Singh on 29 March 1834. Nongkhlaw was classified as a dependent territory and brought under the jurisdiction of the colonial political agent.[39]

---

[35] Aitchison, *A Collection of Treaties*, 127–132.
[36] Ibid., 133.
[37] According to a letter from David Scott to General Swinton, the territories that had rebelled alongside Nongkhlaw were to be 'held under Sunads granted by the Government ... the Chiefs would be amenable for treason for resistance to our authority and ... liable for removal in the case of continued oppression', and a new successor would be elected 'subject to the approval of the Governor General'. Foreign Political, 9 April 1830, no.49–50, NAI.
[38] Foreign Political, 27 May 1834, no.78, NAI.
[39] Aitchison, *A Collection of Treaties*, 137–138.

No. XVIII.

TRANSLATION of an AGREEMENT given by AHDOR SING, RAJAH of MOWSUNRAM
POONJEE, in the year 1831.

AHDOR SING, *Rajah*.

To

THE AGENT TO THE GOVERNOR-GENERAL,

North-East Frontier.

The written Agreement of Ahdor Sing, Rajah, resident of Mowsunram Poonjee,
given to the following effect :—

My village having been burnt down on the part of the British Government,
and being now a waste, I hereby acknowledge my submission to the Government,
and furnish this Agreement, with the object of again settling on the spot, to the
effect that I and my people will re-build and re-occupy the village as subjects
of the Government, and will obey such orders as you may, from time to time,
issue to us.

That I will take measures for apprehending the enemies of the Government
if I should hear of their being in my village or its vicinity, and I will also convey
immediate information of the same to Captain Townshend, and if I have no particular news to communicate, I will merely wait on him every month.

That if I violate these Engagements, I will, without any demur, abide by
whatever orders you may think proper to pass.

Dated this 17th of December 1831, corresponding with the 3rd of Pous 1238 B.S.
Witnessed by :

DEWAN SING DUBASHIA, *resident of Cherra Poonjee.*

OOMEE COSSIAH, *resident of Cherra Poonjee.*

—————

Figure 2.3   Agreement of Allegiance executed by Adhor Singh, Chief
of Mawsynram, dated 17 December 1831, A Collection of Treaties,
Engagements and Sanads Relating to India and Neighbouring Countries
Vol. XII, Calcutta: Government of India Central Publication Branch 1931.

The renewed agreements and violent suppression of resistance led to
the passing of Act VI in 1835, which sanctioned the jurisdiction of the
political agent in the Khasi Hills under the superintendence of *Sudder
Dewani Adalat* or Supreme Court of Revenue in Bengal and *Nizamut*

Adalat or the Criminal Court of Appeal.[40] The extension of judicial over-view of colonial courts ensured a certain amount of conformity with re-gulations spread across the colony. The colonial station of Cherrapoonjee, which was a cantonment and an enclave for European settlers and his own office, was the only place in the hills over which the political agent of-ficially exercised sole jurisdiction. The terms of the treaty signed in 1829 gave the *Syiem* of Sorah, where Cherrapoonjee was located, jurisdiction in the rest of the polity in cases involving Khasi subjects. It is imperative to note that the *Syiem* of Sorah supported the Company in tracking down rebels and resistant chiefs.

Syiems continued to hold juridical authority over their chieftaincies according to the agreements. However, jurisdictional powers of the *Syiem* were truncated. In cases involving Bengali (read Sylheti) and Khasi in-habitants the *Syiem* would share authority with the political agent in de-ciding cases.[41] The *Syiem* of Sorah by treaty, and the *Syiems* of Khyrim, Langrin, Nongstoin, and Nongspun with whom no treaty had been signed held sole criminal and civil jurisdiction over their respective polities. In twenty-two Khasi polities apart from the five mentioned above, the pol-itical agent stationed at Cherrapoonjee acting in the capacity of magis-trate was authorized to try criminal cases considered 'heinous' in nature involving British and non-British subjects.[42] A hierarchy of *Syiems* and chiefdoms emerged with some chiefs who retained more independent status than others. Significantly, the Nongkhlaw Massacre resulted in the chiefs being legally bound to render services to the Company in order for them to retain their political position.

The policy of non-regulation initiated by David Scott, followed by decrees and agreements brought the frontier hills within the colonial legal-judicial framework. Customary authority assumed new meaning as male heads of polities were identified as sovereigns.[43] Judicial authority of Khasi Syiems was graded in terms of the level of influence the polit-ical agent could impose on different polities. Overall, the political agent

---

[40] Orders of 29 September 1835 that included 'Jaintiah territory' as part of the Khasi hills were modified by ACT XXI of 1836, which sanctioned the annexation of the Jaintiah territory to Sylhet, but Mills states that only the 'plain country on this side was brought under this order'. See Mills, *Report*, 9.

[41] Aitchison, *A Collection of Treaties*, 126–127.

[42] Syiemlieh, *British Administration*, 98.

[43] Kar, 'Heads in the Naga Hills', 335–370.

was sanctioned to impose colonial jurisdiction anywhere in the hills and over anyone. Non-British subjects of these polities were drawn into the ambit of colonial legal apparatus and debarred from any legal rights at the same time. Visible in court cases concerning boundary disputes judicial reform in the Khasi Jaintia Hills from the mid-nineteenth century, far from establishing clear jurisdictional boundaries, lack of clarity around boundaries between British and non-British territory, semi-independence, dependence, and autonomy allowed strategic employment of colonial power with unregulated violence. The following section will examine processes through which the movement of law mapped the Khasi hills.

Mapping the Hills

Henry Walters, a judge in the sessions court of British Bengal's eastern district of Sylhet, travelled across the frontier hills in 1828 and wrote an account of his travels that provide an insight into the combined legal and geographical knowledge being produced through colonial discourse.[44] The Calcutta Military Press subsequently published Walters's 'Journey across the Pandua Hills near Sylhet' in the 1832 edition of *Asiatic Researches*. At the very outset of his account, Walters informed the reader of an important colonial policy that had taken shape in the preceding decades. He asserted that the hill people had to be kept 'in check' and contained in the hills, that their presence in the plains was a menace, and that all the Khasis living in the Sylhet plains were subjects of the Company. This warning and the spatial typology Walters invoked between inhabitants of the plains as British subjects and the non-British subjects of the hills, echoed Robert Lindsay, David Scott, Francis Jenkins, and other colonial administrators' formulations of tribal spaces and the use of colonial law in such spaces. A close reading of Walters's travel account provides insight into the dual colonial processes of domestication and differentiation in the anomalous and ambiguous legal landscape.

Although Walters wrote his travel account in 1828, it only acquired importance in the eyes of colonial authorities after the 'Nongkhlaw

---

[44] Walters, 'Journey'.

Massacre' the following year. In addition to the military expeditions and the suppression of armed resistance discussed in the previous section, colonial encounters in the Khasi hills in 1829 placed an importance on literary and scientific publications on this region. Judge Walters's account can be classified as both a travel account and a geographical narrative. Mathew Edney pointed out that Walters was not a surveyor, geographer, or explorer, but a judge. Yet his narrative of the journey across the hills combines technical geographical observations with personal reflections on travel.[45] While the geographical measurements, descriptions of geology, and ethnographic accounts of the inhabitants of the hills boast scientific methods, his reflections also domesticate the frontier landscape by presenting to the European reader sentimental comparisons with England. This account demonstrates the corporeal movement of colonial law, and law's entanglement with colonial knowledge production.

Walters's account of his travels in the Khasi hills, like many contemporary publications, used a style of personal travel narrative, an increasingly popular genre at the time. Edney states that geographical and travel narratives often overlapped and the differences between the two lie in the use of self-references. While travel accounts generally contained authorial self-references, geographical accounts did not. Significant overlaps between personal and more scientific writing are found not only in Walters's account but also in many others, such as William Robinson's *A Descriptive Account of Asam* published in 1841 and Thomas Fischer's revenue survey of Sylhet discussed in this next section.[46] Henry Walters's account also shared many similarities with official publications such as R. Wilcox's *Memoir of a Survey of Asam and the Neighbouring Countries, Executed in 1825-6-7-8* published in 1833.[47] In Wilcox's words, this work was a 'detailed account of the progress of our geographical discoveries on the N. E. Frontier'.[48]

It is evident in these publications that colonial spatiality involved the incorporation of multiple cartographic representations and multiple sources of geographic information to produce single maps constructing a 'communal view' that subsumed and superseded individual

---

[45] Edney, *Mapping an Empire.*
[46] Robinson, *Descriptive Account of Asam.*
[47] Wilcox, 'Memoir', 314–469.
[48] Ibid.

views.[49] Commissioned for the purpose of collating multiple observations and geographical studies for a single spatial understanding of the north-east frontier, Wilcox provided details of a series of geographical surveys of Assam and regions to the northeast of Bengal. These details were derived from multiple observations by different surveyors at different times from the mid-eighteenth century onwards integrated multiple views into a singular vision and informed and directed the political advance in the region. The various sources Wilcox drew on included narratives of journeys published in scattered newspapers or periodicals, and also new information including, but not limited to, statistical enquiries. Two things become very clear in Wilcox's observations of the journals he used as sources. First, military expeditions went hand-in-hand with geographical survey operations, showing the corporeal and epistemological violence that enabled the movement of colonial law into these regions. Second, visual representations gave life to the frontier landscapes either in contrast to (absence of law), or analogous with (as the primitive stage on the civilizational scale) Europe.[50]

Returning to Henry Walters whose account, the distinctions made between inhabitants of the hills who had to be checked and contained and people from the plains who had to be protected represented non-revenue yielding non-British subjects and revenue-yielding British subjects respectively. Pandua, identified as a frontier village, provided a physical marker of this separation. It is important to note that ideas developed in the late eighteenth century, visible in Robert Lindsay's report on the Khasis, made their way into colonial discourse in the nineteenth century. For example, Walters wrote, 'from hence [Pandua] the Cassias obtain their rice, cloth, salt, and in fact all the necessaries of life, in exchange for honey, way, oranges, cinnamon, betelnut, &c.[sic], the produce of their hills'.[51] He did not make note of the fact that the Khasi polities of Nongstoin, Cheyla, and Rambrai, among others, extended into the plains. Walters's emphasis on the hill-plain distinction and corresponding

---

[49] Edney, *Mapping an Empire*, 64.
[50] David Arnold's concept of 'tropicality' suggests that Indian tropics were as much encountered as created. A significant element of this creation was the use of tropes, comparisons, and associations with temperate Europe or other tropics. In doing so, the colonial Indian tropics were conceived of as the bad tropics. See David Arnold, *The Tropics and the Traveling Gaze: India, Landscape, and Science, 1800–1856* (Seattle: University of Washington Press, 2006), 110–146.
[51] Walters, 'Journey', 500.

separation between British and non-British subjects was not simply a product of his reliance on early colonial records. As a judge on the Sudder court of Sylhet, Walters was well acquainted with the political landscape of the vicinity, as well as the many judicial disputes over boundaries. The absence of such information in his account points to corresponding topographical and mark jurisdictional distinctions. Civilizational hierarchies informed the legal and geographical reordering. The comparisons between Khasis and Garos who were neither homogenous nor identified as separate ethnic categories coincided with jurisdictional divisions of the frontier hills.[52] While legal differentiation of landscapes and people was an imperial strategy, to overcome the danger and uncertainties of the unknown frontier it was domesticated through knowledge production. Domestication as a literary tool is found in Walters' account.

Walters interspersed his narrative with romantic comparisons of the scenic beauty of the region with British landscapes. A number of sketches, in particular of stone monuments or memorial stones, help the reader connect the frontier hills with Britain's pre-historic past by, for instance, comparing memorial stones to Stonehenge and other pre-historic megalithic structures in Cornwall and Wales. His awe and pleasure at encountering artefacts in these distant hills that reminded him of primitive British monuments enabled Walters to situate tribal culture and social formations as temporally backward. Nostalgia helped to tame frontier inhabitants into primitives; a characterization that enabled the advance of colonial law. Walters wrote,

Doubtless these ancient monuments were appropriated to the same purpose ....If this was the case, how singular it is that customs of nations, in the same stage of society indeed, but situated at such immeasurable distance from each other, should be found so exactly to coincide! If any doubt exists as to the purpose for which the monuments in Britain were erected, is it not dissipated by observation, as to the actual use of similar monuments in this country at the present day?[53]

[52] Comparisons between different tribes and their physical attributes became even more significant in the latter half of the century with the flourishing of the disciplines of anthropology and ethnography.

[53] Walters, 'Journey', 505.

Such descriptions readily transform dangerous landscapes into consumable, relatable domestic spaces, thus advancing colonial initiatives to carve out administrative pockets in the hills. He was elated when on the way to Nongkhlaw he found, 'with one steep descent and little streams here and there, the valleys stiff and white with *hoarfrost!* The first I have seen since leaving England fifteen years ago'.[54] In support of a proposed sanatorium to be built at Sorah polity, Walters compared the site with the hills in Bathford.

> The elevation is about five thousand feet above the level of the sea. The air is cool, light, and refreshing; and although the sun is hot, it is not noxious. The hill is free from jungle, covered with fine pasture and flowers, but rocky—and the ravines filled with trees and shrubs—I can almost fancy myself on the top of Bannerdown![55]

Geographic narratives like the ones discussed here included visual representations and cartographic images. Maps were not only meant to create a unified vision of the Empire but also used as a visual aid for European travellers and explorers, and as official references for colonial administrators.[56] Most colonial maps of the Khasi-Jaintia demonstrated the importance of communication networks and transportation routes passing through the hills.[57] The interruption to imperial sovereignty presented by the frontier hills was overcome in cartographic representations. These maps highlighted the lines of communication between British territories of Sylhet and Assam through the hills, and across important nodes of power interspersed throughout these extra-imperial spaces.

Apart from an emphasis on roads, guest houses, and a few important stops along the designated routes, the maps did not contain any other information. The distance between Sylhet and colonial stations in the hills

---

[54] Ibid., 506.

[55] Ibid., 505.

[56] For an analysis of cartographic productions that created the sense of a unified empire, see Edney, *Mapping an Empire.*

[57] The maps used in this chapter are only those selected few that the National Archives of India authorities permit to be copied and used. The policy of the Indian Government to restrict cartographic information of its frontier region restricts the ability of researches in many disciplines to thoroughly examine parts of the subcontinent that have become international boundaries and remain unstable, contended spaces where state oppression is heightened in many ways in the cause of establishing nation sovereignty.

was marked on some maps, while others noted the heights of different points. For example, the two-part map, titled 'Roads in the Khassia Hills District', showed the communication routes between Assam and Sylhet through the Khasi hills, obliterating landscape features and place names across the non-British territories of the hills (see Figures 2.4a and 2.4b). Roads on these maps seem to cut across large empty spaces. This map was published in 1883 when the colonial state had made significant political inroads into the Khasi Hills. Colonial geography accompanied by colonial law actively superseded and rendered invisible the local geographical imagination. Yet, such a process was incomplete, and neither entirely functional nor absolute.

The contingent realities of political relations and the imprecision of boundaries persistently eroded the discursive frontier that maps and narratives created. The objectivity of geographical knowledge and the power of scientific methods of enquiry were subverted by the active landscape explorers and surveyors encountered.[58] Tensions between a discursive construction of colonial space and the inter-subjective conceptualization of place by local inhabitants, between the hills as a laboratory of science and as a landscape imbued with memory, myth, and history, between new and old meanings, persisted throughout the colonial and postcolonial period. Such tensions, contentions, and entanglements undercut the dominance of colonial knowledge and fractured colonial law.

Imprecise Boundaries

An emerging association between topography and political and cultural forms, always already imperfect, is visible in the reproduction of survey information from judicial discourse on boundary disputes. Geographical surveys that doubled as revenue surveys were instrumental in extending colonial jurisdiction on the frontier. The surveys discussed in the following pages were tools used to formulate new notions of sovereignty and jurisdiction.

---

[58] For a detailed discussion of science as culture, see Kavita Philip, 'English Mud: Towards a Critical Cultural Studies of Colonial Science', *Cultural Studies* 12, no. 3 (1998): 300–331.

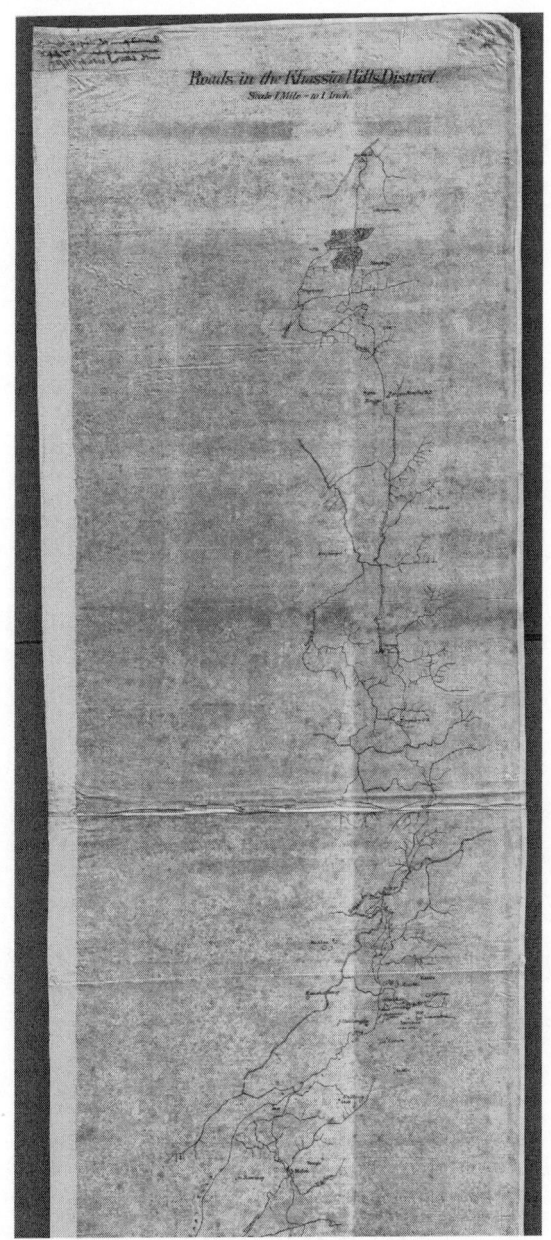

Figure 2.4a A two-part reproduction of a map, titled, 'Roads in the Khassia Hills District', 1883, signed Major R. E., Executive Engineer, Khasi Jaintiah Hills Division.

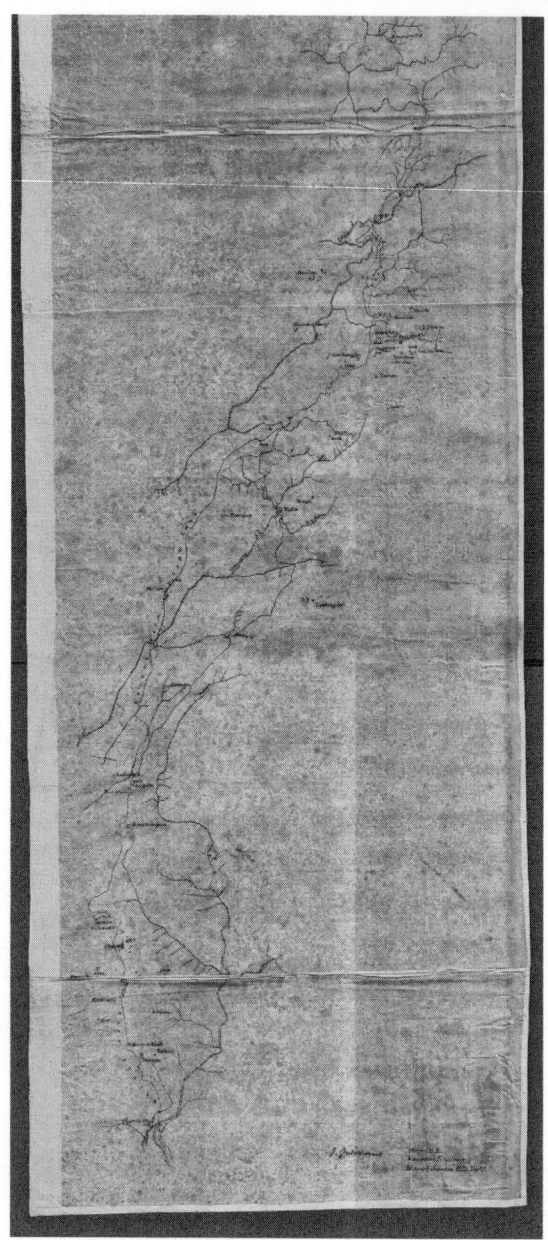

Figure 2.4b The second part of reproduction of a map, titled, 'Roads in the Khassia Hills District', 1883, signed Major R. E., Executive Engineer, Khasi Jaintiah Hills Division. National Archives of India.

Early on in the nineteenth century, the Company began to identify landscape features like mountains, hills, and rivers as natural boundaries in a bid to demarcate British and non-British territory. Land was classified largely in terms of taxed and non-taxed. The means of transforming non-agricultural or non-taxed agricultural land into a revenue-yielding resource was found through legislation. For instance, according to Regulation II of 1828–29 non-assessed lands, including those held as grants by religious orders or beneficiaries of the erstwhile state, could be appropriated for 'public revenue'.[59] It is significant to note that even after Sylhet became a separate administrative and revenue unit, and collector Robert Lindsay converted Pandua into a frontier outpost signalling the extent of Company jurisdiction on the plains, the river Surma continued to be understood as a natural boundary. Such imprecision in colonial jurisdiction characterized both the effort to mark boundaries and the disputes around them.

Natural boundaries like rivers were used to define frontiers in pre-colonial Bengal between the Mughal Empire and other dynastic powers and smaller autonomous polities. This practice was replicated by colonial survey operations in the nineteenth century.[60] However, colonial officials did not simply fail to comprehend that political and territorial distinctions in the pre-colonial period were imprecise. Rather the effort to supersede fluid boundaries between different sovereign powers by marking jurisdictional limits gave colonial law both vitality and legitimacy. Efforts to mark precise boundaries were prone to failure and so enabled colonial administrators to strategically employ extra-territorial jurisdiction and severe violence within the ambit of the law.

Boundaries between the Khasi, Jaintia, Garo Hills, Bengal, and Assam, remained contentious throughout the nineteenth century. The process of demarcating boundaries was a long one, and disputes over boundaries persisted despite numerous surveys. Early surveys like James Rennell's were deemed erroneous by later surveyors on account of the changing nature of landscape due to climate and ecology.[61] Landscapes encountered by early geographers were active with political, social, and economic

---

[59] See Chatterjee, *Forgotten Friends*, 81–126.

[60] For a substantiation of this premise with respect to the Tibet, Goalpara, and Cachar regions, see Misra, *Becoming a Borderland*, 19–41.

[61] Cederlöf, 'Fixed Boundaries', 515.

movements. Yet they appeared in topographical and revenue surveys as canvases upon which only new boundaries had an active role.[62] For instance, in Fischer's rough map the two most prominent features are the Surma River as a natural boundary and Thomas Fischer's proposed boundary between the Company's agricultural revenue yielding land in the plains and the hill territory.

In 1835 Francis Jenkins wrote, '[it] seems expedient that the question of boundary should be decisively arranged early for the present want of a determined frontier keeps the borders in a very unsettled state and may lead to breaches of the peace.'[63] These breaches continued into the following decades because the boundaries marked by the British in their early surveys were inapplicable to on-the-ground realities. Disputes between the new proprietors who settled in the Sylhet and subjects of Khasi *Syiems* who had been using the Sylhet lowlands for agriculture, grazing, and other purposes, discussed later in the chapter, demonstrate the contentious nature of territorial and topographical divisions. Lieutenant Thomas Fischer's survey of 1827–28 became the focal point of many discussions and disputes, political and judicial, through the mid-nineteenth century. The survey was ordered in 1823, but the first report was only presented to the collector of Sylhet in December 1827, delayed by the Anglo-Burmese war on the northeast frontier. The purpose of this survey according to Fischer was to ascertain in detail the quantity of land in each estate of Sylhet and thereby assess land revenue. But Fischer provided sufficient geographic detail to facilitate other imperial purposes including military excursions across non-British territories.[64]

Fischer's survey was supplemented by a more specific report on the boundary between the Khasi Jaintiah Hills and Sylhet addressed to the magistrate at Dacca. In his words, it consisted of 'a map of the country contiguous to the Cossya independent hill estate together with a statement of proceedings and the information collected for the definition of the boundary and the settlement of the disputes between the landholders of this district and the Hill Chiefs.'[65] The map shown is an early

[62] See Figures 2.5a and 2.5b.

[63] Foreign Political, 11 February 1835, no. 90, NAI.

[64] Board of Revenue Papers 48, File No. 8–100, ASA.

[65] I was only able to get an earlier draft of the map (which is not scaled) and not the one that was published along with the report because it shows present-day international borders and is against NAI policy.

draft to which corrections were made in the margins. The river Surma is represented as a natural boundary while a red line along the river, in places extending north of the river and in others extending south, shows the boundary line Fischer suggested. The map indicated the proposed boundary between Sylhet and Jaintia Hills incorporating strategic lands along the Surma within direct Company control. The names of villages on the southern side of the river were marked whereas the hill territory did not show any place names. The map depicted topographical divisions superimposed with imagined distinctions between British territory and non-British territory. In Fischer's rough map the two most prominent features are the natural boundary—the Surma river and the proposed boundary by Fischer between Company's agricultural revenue territory or plains territory and the hills territory. With respect to Jaintiah territory the Company transgressed all the boundaries that had previously been acknowledged i.e. until 1835. However, certain boundaries were relevant for creating political territories and jurisdictional classifications.

Between 1827 and 1829, Fischer surveyed the frontier west of Pandua: 'Bansicoora on the boundary of Mymensing and near which the Cossya estates join the Garrows.'[66] His report noted which boundaries were disputed in previous decades and those acknowledged by local authorities. Fisher reproduced local understandings of places by marking boundaries such as hillocks, rivers, streams, and lakes, along with the names of villages, but measurements of distance and other technical jargon of topographical surveys are absent. For instance, Fischer wrote,

From Yiski Barri (at which my former report terminated) the boundary runs North east, along the Pian R. [river] to the mouth of the Dabree R. up which it is continued to the fork of the latter with the Dullai, it then bends south west along Oloo Chera from which it diverges by the course of Kaloo Cherra to Phukan Khal an insignificant stream running into the last named Cherra from whence it runs on the east side of a small Jheel to the head of the Kourei Khal along the course of which it continues to the Sonnae nulla and passes to Rangamittill teela, a hillock on the right bank of the river ....From Yiski barri to the fork of the dulaie and Dobree our frontier is bounded by the Rajahs of Jynteah and

Kyram ....From the fork of Dulaie the boundary runs between Pundwa and the estate of the Cherra rajah on whose part an agent attended, who in conjunction with the land holders pointed out the line above described.[67]

The report aimed to mark a boundary between British territories and the Khasi Hills by employing local pre-existing categories and by examining boundary disputes. In the case of a dispute on lands bordering the Maharam polity, Fischer referred to a case brought to the Sudder court of Sylhet in 1806 by Talukdars who claimed the 'low hills covered with jungle'. The court 'decided against them [Talukdars], awarding all the continuous chain of hills branching from the mountains to the Cosseahs and leaving the plain country including the detached hillocks to the Talukdars.'[68] Cases such as this established precedents for judicial enquiries into future boundary disputes. Contradictory notions of what constituted plains territory and where the hills produced recurring disputes.

Additionally, Fischer's report contained vague and unclear characterizations of the landscape. He wrote with reference to another dispute that,

the foot of the mountain is acknowledged to be boundary both by the Chiefs of Muchungpoonjee and the inhabitants of the plains and this rule is generally admitted along the remainder of the Frontier line by the Chief of Nusteng [Nongstoin] on the side of the Cossyas and the land holders of Purgunnahs Laour and Bansicoora on ours. In this instance the observation of this rule for the determination of the boundary is attended with little difficulty as there are no minor ranges branching from the main chain of mountains but the later rise abruptly leaving in general a marked indication of their commencement.[69]

It was hard to characterize where the hills ended because hillocks and undulating lands did not merge into the Sylhet plains in any precise manner (see Figure 2.5). In the situation described above, a portion of

---

[67] Ibid.
[68] Ibid.
[69] Ibid.

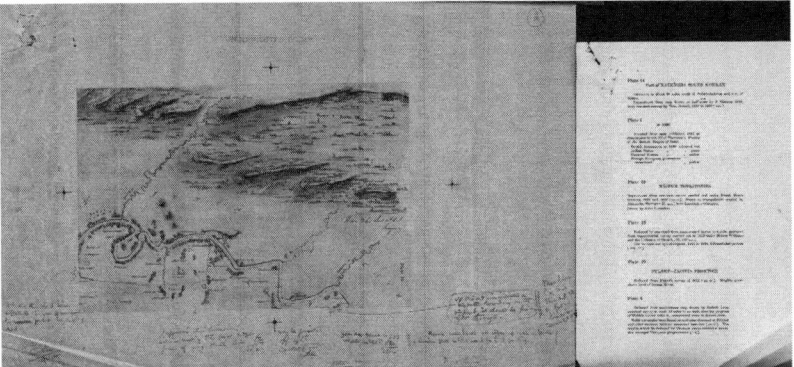

Figure 2.5 Thomas Fischer, Sketch of proposed boundary between Sylhet plains and Jaintia territory, 1827–1828. Assam State Archives.

undefined land between the actual mountain range and its mirror ranges was considered a confirmed frontier ending at the foot of the main chain of mountains. In reality, as the quotation demonstrates, 'natural boundaries' were not used as boundaries by both the *Syiem* of Nongstoin and Zamindars in Sylhet. It was only through political negotiations with the *Syiem* of Nongstoin that the boundary was confirmed.[70] Settlers and proprietors in the Sylhet plains were employed to police the boundaries demarcated by this survey. Zamindars were compensated for their efforts to maintain a distinction between British and non-British territory. With reference to a grant made to the Zamindars of Sylhet to the land north of the Surma River, Fischer wrote that the grant was made 'on condition of defending the frontier and *confining* Cossyas to their mountains.'[71] In addition, physical markers such as masonry pillars were constructed along the boundary line. Fischer's notes reveal the motive, intent, and methods used to mark and maintain boundaries. Jurisdictional and geographical reordering were entangled processes enabled by the categorization of inhabitants of Khasi polities as hill tribal.

As early as 1789, orders were issued by the Bengal Government to define the boundary between British and non-British territory. The

---

[70] Ibid.
[71] Fischer's account does not provide a date or the details of this grant, but he wrote that the grant was given.

revenue collector informed political authorities in the hills that raids into Company territory could not be permitted. However, Fisher noted that no actual measures were taken to define the precise limits of Company lands, 'but it was intended to include all the lowlands within the Company's frontier leaving to the Cossyas the undisputed possession of the mountains.'[72] Not only did Fisher acknowledge the impracticality of demarcating precise boundaries but also pointed out that the colonial administrators' intention to fix boundaries did not match actual efforts to do so.

He stated that it was difficult to ascertain strictly where the mountains ended and the lowlands began, 'the former being often intersected by low ranges of hills branching from the latter as well as by isolated range of hillocks the connexion of which with the main chain in a wooded impervious country cannot satisfactorily be ascertained.'[73] These difficulties, he concluded, resulted in new boundary lines drawn with a 'spirit of moderation' resulting in a lot of plain countries north of the Surma River to be left under the authority of the *Syiems*. Such imprecision in jurisdictional and territorial boundaries was effectively used as a colonial strategy to tame the challenges faced by imperial sovereignty on colonial frontiers discussed in detail in the next chapter.

Bengal Regulation XII of 1833 formalized the imprecision of jurisdictional boundaries through the creation of legal zones where colonial law could not be applied except when deemed necessary by colonial administrators. Such a classification created ambiguity around the legal status of the Garo, Khasi, and Jaintia hills. Were the inhabitants of these hills colonial legal subjects? Confronted with landscapes, and people who could not be confined within rigid classificatory schemas—geographical, ethnic, or legal colonial administrators in the frontier relied on innovative and strategic use of colonial power. These included combined spatio-temporal and legal processes. The reordering of the hills into a frontier space required identifying landscapes, inhabitants, and societies in terms of legal primitivism. This meant that the frontier was at once a differentiated space that needed to be tamed through law, and identified

[72] Board of Revenue Papers 48, File No. 8–100, ASA.
[73] Ibid.

as analogous to a primitive stage of European civilization and thereby domesticated.

This chapter has introduced the initial discursive and material imagining of the frontier hills by colonial administrators between the late eighteenth and mid-nineteenth centuries. By locating the travels of law, contrapuntal reading of colonial travel narratives written by legal experts, examining geographical and revenue surveys by military officers this chapter has re-examined the nature of law-making and frontier-making. The following chapter elaborates on the arguments made in this chapter by closely examining jurisdictional boundary disputes between Bengal, Garo, Khasi, Jaintia hills, and Assam. It will show exactly how the imprecision of jurisdictional boundaries extended colonial law into non-British territories.

3

Games of Jurisdictions

The 'game of jurisdiction', as Mariana Valverde points out, determined not only who governed but also how governance was shaped.[1] Concerns over boundaries separating British and non-British territories and frontier jurisdiction were enhanced after agreements with local rulers and representatives of communities in the Garo, Khasi, and Jaintia hills in the 1820s and 1830s. In delineating jurisdiction, law-making went hand-in-hand with boundary-making. Establishment of jurisdiction entailed the dual processes of locating authority and of placing limits upon that authority. Hybrid notions of sovereignty, including a Hobbesian one centred on a singular sovereign authority, travelled with colonial agents into the frontier, where such ideas were reflected in the treaties and agreements made concerning those regions.[2] The inherent epistemological and ontological diversity underpinning Western notions of sovereignty meant that imperial sovereignty in the frontier was always already ambiguous, imprecise, and strategic. Imprecision and ambiguity formed, in part, strategic elements to imperial governance; but they equally represented imperial responses to encounters with the incommensurable and varied forms of authority and ruler-subject relations in the frontier hills. This chapter explores the duality of colonial governance in the frontier.

Since their inception, imperial states, as Lauren Benton has argued, occupied a patchwork, uneven formation in which strongholds were intersected by autonomous or semi-autonomous zones. Sovereignty was measured by the degree of legal authority that an imperial state possessed. Legal authority remained plural across both time and geographical space. Imperial legal sovereignty was thus always fragmented, lumpy,

---

[1] Mariana Valverde, *Chronotopes of Law: Jurisdiction, Scale and Governance* (Oxford and New York: Routledge, 2015), 82–87.

[2] Ian Hunter, 'Global Justice and Regional Metaphysics: On the Critical History of the Law of Nature and Nations', in *Law and Politics in British Colonial Thought: Transpositions of Empire*, eds. Shaunnagh Dorsett and Ian Hunter (New York: Palgrave Macmillan, 2010), 11–29.

Placing the Frontier in British North-East India. Reeju Ray, Oxford University Press. © Reeju Ray 2023. DOI: 10.1093/oso/9780192887085.003.0003

and uneven.[3] Building on Benton's thesis, Eric Lewis Beverley has argued that the frontier between the Bombay presidency and the princely state of Hyderabad represented 'a tangled configuration of fragmented sovereignties' that could not be completely controlled by state policies. Beverley's concept of 'fragmented sovereignties' resonates with Benton's idea of a patchwork of coexisting and plural legal orders. Beverley departs from Benton's schema, however, by arguing that a fragmentary jural landscape did not constitute an early stage in the formation of imperial states only to be later superseded by a consolidated imperial state, but rather that this legal fragmentation was characteristic of imperial frontier zones even in the heyday of empire. Judicial complexity, changing meanings, and differentiated legal rules enforced in the frontier zone: all worked to make the frontier a site both of creativity and of power.[4] This chapter will show that the fluidity and liminality of the frontier in fact allowed for the accommodation and proliferation of oppressive and racialized colonial categories of governance.[5] Fluidity, imprecision, and ambiguity over jurisdictional boundaries were all conducive to severe forms of violence.[6]

The previous chapter demonstrated how British sovereignty was inscribed in the epistemological and corporeal violence of the imperial state's legal regime. Lack of clarity over judicial policies along with the imprecision of legal rules allowed the EIC government to take any law that was applicable in the Bengal Presidency and impose it in the Garo, Khasi, and Jaintia. Efforts to establish clear jurisdictional boundaries were facilitated by the creation of geographical knowledge about the frontier. This chapter will examine the processes of boundary-making in the nineteenth century regarding the Garo, Khasi, and Jaintia hills, as well as Assam and Sylhet. But rather than analysing relationships of authority as seen through trade, diplomatic arrangements, and asymmetric wars (of which there were many), this chapter instead highlights the tensions

[3] Lauren Benton, *A Search for Sovereignty: Law and Geography in European Empires, 1400–1900* (New York: Cambridge University Press, 2010), 1–39.

[4] See Eric Lewis Beverley, 'Frontier as Resource: Law, Crime, and Sovereignty on the Margins of Empire', *Comparative Studies in Society and History* 55, no. 2 (2013): 241–272.

[5] Here, I refer both to historical and contemporary instances of political and social mobilization that rely on colonial spatio-temporal constructions of primitive, tribal, backward, etc.

[6] Elizabeth Kolsky, 'The Colonial Rule of Law and the Legal Regime of Exception: Frontier "Fanaticism" and State Violence in British India', *The American Historical Review* 120, no. 4 (2015): 1218–1246; Thomas Simpson, 'Bordering and Frontier-Making in Nineteenth-Century British India', *The Historical Journal* 58, no. 2 (2015): 513–542.

within emerging ruler-subject relations, within colonial spatial and civilizational categories, and within colonial sovereignty. By looking at the constant flux of jurisdictional boundaries—visible in the recurrent disputes, raids, and incommensurable practices of authority in the Khasi hills that the colonial authorities defined as blackmail and nomadism— we can see how the contested nature of sovereignty functioned as a strategy of imperial governance. This chapter further examines what happens to colonial sovereignty in its varied jurisdictional encounters.

In 1835, the role of the Political Agent to the north-east frontier was significantly expanded.[7] The 1835 Act empowered Captain Lister, the commandant of the Sylhet Light Infantry and Political Agent, to act as magistrate with jurisdiction over cases involving British subjects, as well as those that were considered to be 'heinous crimes'.[8] Lister's son-in-law, a British trader named Henry Inglis, was appointed as his assistant. The Act also rearranged the north-eastern frontier into new jurisdictional districts, a process that gave different officers charge over the following territories: Sylhet was placed under the commissioner of Dhaka, Assam, and the north-eastern part of Rangpore came under Captain Francis Jenkins' authority, and Upper and Lower Cachar fell to Thomas Fischer as judge and collector.[9] The Khasi and Jaintia hills themselves were combined into one district, although the nature of jurisdictional powers differed between the two. The Act of 1835 further allowed for the formal annexation of the entire Jaintia territory. The Jaintia polity had been split into two administrative units and divided among several jurisdictions. As early as 1774, the EIC took control of the Jaintia lands in Sylhet.[10] The Jaintia Rajah created his new seat of power in Nartiang in the hills.[11]

[7] IOR/F/4/1555/63494, Legislative no. 5, 24 August 1835.

[8] Foreign Political, 7 February 1835, no. 101, NAI; IOR/F/4/1555/63494: 11 February 1835.

[9] IOR/F/4/1555/63494: December 1834–August 1835.

[10] David R. Syiemlieh, *British Administration in Meghalaya: Policy and Pattern* (New Delhi: Heritage Publishers, 1989).

[11] Board of Revenue Papers, April 1789, No. 8, ASA; IOR/F/4/1583, Political Proceedings 64360, 15 June 1835, pp. 41–45. The Jaintiah polity was similar in structure to the Khasi polities and had grown in size and influence before the EIC had made headway in the frontier. The EIC's concerns over the control of the river Surma, where Jaintiah Rajah Chatra Singh levied tolls on the boats of European merchants, was the cause of conflict between the two powers. A military contingent was sent to the Sylhet frontier in 1774 and, after a short-lived confrontation, the Jaintiah Rajah left his capital Jaintiapore in Sylhet and fled to the hills. The particular concerns of the EIC in relation to the Jaintiah Kingdom can be found in Edward A. Gait, *A History of Assam* (Calcutta: Thacker, Spink and Co., 1906), 319; see also Syiemlieh, *British Administration*, 17.

In the years preceding the Anglo-Burmese war, David Scott renewed agreements with the Jaintia Rajah.[12] The treaty signed between Scott and the Jaintia Rajah Ram Singh was a precursor to the formal annexation of the territory on the grounds of British moral concerns over alleged human sacrifices made by the inhabitants of a Jaintia district, which was referred to in 1821 as Gobali.[13] Agreements signed with the Jaintia chiefs often contained a clause that identified certain practices as immoral and unethical, and hence also illegal.[14] In a letter to the commissioner of Dacca in 1835, the former Rajah of Jaintia wrote,

> In the human sacrifice of 1832 at Goba in which I am suspected I was not then Rajah nor had I any control over people of Jynteah ... I had no knowledge of the matter the circumstances of the sacrifice ... My ancestors were, as well as I have had been, ever Governments faithful friends and during the Burmese war with everything in our power we assisted.[15]

The Government of Bengal came to the conclusion that because there was 'no legal heir according to custom ... perhaps no other course set to adopt than the annexation of Jynteah [sic] to our territory and we have only to express our hope that the necessary measures have been taken ascertaining as correctly as possible the resources of the country'.[16] Act VI of 1835 extended Company jurisdiction into the hills of Jaintia. The *Dolois*

[12] C. U. Aitchison, *A Collection of Treaties*, 118–119.

[13] Foreign Political, 25 September 1835, no. 44, NAI; IOR/F/4/1583, Political Proceedings 64360, 15 June 1835. Examples of the alleged kidnapping of British subjects from the Sylhet plains for the purpose of human sacrifice can be found not only in official correspondence but also in published historical accounts.
See Alexander Mackenzie, *History of the Relations of the Government with the Hill Tribes of the North-East Frontier of Bengal* (1884; Reprint, Cambridge: Cambridge University Press, 2012), 217–244.

[14] Similarly, in formal agreements signed between the Company and the Garo chiefs at the frontier of Mymensing, a clause was often included that forbade the storing or displaying of human skulls in their houses. Bodhisattva Kar has shown that headhunting tribes of the frontier became the targets of colonial efforts to find singular authority or headmen to represent the figure of the sovereign. The allegorical power of heads linked sovereignty and primitivity. See Bodhisattva Kar, 'Heads in the Naga Hills', in *New Cultural Histories of India: Materiality and Practices*, eds. Partha Chatterjee, Tapati Guha-Thakurta, and Bodhisattva Kar (New Delhi: Oxford University Press, 2014), 335–370.

[15] IOR/F/4/1583, Political Proceedings 64360, 15 June 1835, pp. 41–5.

[16] Ibid., p. 11.

or headmen in the Jaintia hills were employed as juridical agents of the Company.[17]

In the annexed Jaintia territory, law's spatial and temporal specificity manifested itself in a series of debates over the relationship between jurisdictional units, administrative ease, and topographical fluidity. For instance, the part of the Jaintia lands known either as the Seven Reaches or Shat Bank was annexed to Cachar. The Commissioner of Sylhet wrote to the *Sudder* Board of Revenue insisting that the Shat Bank 'naturally' belonged to Sylhet. There was a general opinion that once Shat Bank was amalgamated into Sylhet, and all the laws and regulations of settlement were imposed upon it, then the same process could be extended to the rest of the Jaintia territory. The Government of Bengal sanctioned the former under Act XXI of 1836.[18] A report submitted to the Commissioner of Dacca in 1837 highlighted the importance of jurisdictional divisions alongside the division of district administration even when the matter concerned a 'small patch of land'.[19] Small patches of land in and around the borders of newly made districts caused the frontier administrator much trouble by causing repeated conflicts between jurisdictional divisions.

Direct Administration, Taxation, and Protests in the Jaintia Hills

Although there were no recorded rebellions in the Khasi-Jaintia hills in 1857, the responses of the colonial state to the colony-wide rebellions impacted the frontier region. Judicial and fiscal delegations were sent to the Khasi-Jaintia Hills under A. J. M. Mills and W. J. Allen in 1853 and 1858 respectively. These two reports played a significant role in informing colonial policy towards the hills during the second half of the nineteenth century, and will be discussed in greater detail in the following chapter.

---

[17] IOR/F/4/819, Boards Collections 1825–1826, 21848–21862, vol. 819, Judicial no. 16 and IOR/F/4/1583, Political Proceedings, February 1835.

[18] From Secretary to the Government of India to the Revenue Department, Government of Bengal, BG Papers 1837, no. 353, ASA.

[19] 'Report on the Revenue, villages, population in Jaintiah after British Conquest', prepared by the Revenue Department Government of Bengal, 4 October 1837; Bengal Government Files (BG) 334, ASA.

W. J. Allen had recommended that administration over the hills be placed under a colonial officer. This officer, in Allen's recommendations, would slowly assume the powers of the *Dolois* and Sirdars, thereby gradually making the local headmen redundant. He also suggested establishing a court similar to that of the Santhal Parganas in Bengal.[20] Allen further recommended the imposition of a house tax. In March 1859, the Agent to the Governor-General was instructed to make arrangements for carrying this measure into effect. Despite their opinion that the collection of the house tax would be the 'least distastefully collected', the confidence of the colonial officers would in the end be proven wrong.[21]

In 1860, in a letter sent to Francis Jenkins, B. Shadwell reported that although tax collection had been successful in some parts of the Jaintia hills, in others, in contrast, '[the] inhabitants of that place en-masse opposed his making a new census of their village and refused to pay any rents. The rest of the villages in Jynteah Hills then followed their example'.[22] According to Shadwell's report, the protest, in the first instance, amounted to the refusal to pay newly imposed taxes. Petitions from villagers demanded that they only be held liable to pay their rents to the government, and even in those circumstances, they would only pay them through their Rajah. Because of the villagers' petitions, however, the colonial administrators found reason to implicate the Rajah, suggesting that he had instigated the rebellions; this accusation was only retracted once the Rajah provided the administrators with information about the protestors and rebels. The *Dolois*, similarly, were summoned to provide information concerning the 'feelings of discontent brewing among the people'.[23]

The officiating commissioner of Assam, acting in accordance with the suggestions made in Shadwell's letter, agreed that the collection of revenue should be stopped until the administrators received orders from higher authorities indicating how to respond to the villagers' non-payment of revenue as a form of protest. Soon after this correspondence, the Political

---

[20] W. J. Allen, *Report on the Administration of the Cossyah and Jynteah Hill Territory* (Calcutta: Bengal Hurkaru Press, 1858), 69.

[21] Home Public A, 19 May 1860, no. 676, NAI.

[22] Letter from B. Shadwell to Francis Jenkins, dated 25 February 1860, Cherrapoonjee, in Assam Commissioner's Papers (AC), 399, ASA.

[23] Letter from B. Shadwell to Francis Jenkins, dated 25 February 1860, Cherrapoonjee, in Assam Commissioner's Papers (AC), 399, ASA.

Agent sent another letter which stated that he had received intelligence of a planned uprising in the Khasi and Jaintia hills.[24] A report submitted by the DC provided details of the uprising. It is clear from the DC's report that the armed nature of the uprising was highly exaggerated. Some of the *Dolois*, when interviewed by DC Shadwell, denied that they had played a role in instigating the people to rebel. Shadwell was quick to implicate the *Dolois*, however, because they had 'taken no steps to realise the revenue of their respective villages'.[25] This was considered sufficient grounds to confine them and put them under the watch of a military guard. Faced with acts of intimidation and violence, some of the *Dolois* were led to agree to the collection of taxes for the colonial government; others, conversely, including the *Dolois* of Nartiang and Nongpoonjee, remained ambiguous in their responses. A military detachment was then sent to Nongpoonjee based on intelligence alleging that the villagers were building blockades with the explicit aim of preventing colonial tax collectors from entering the village. The military detachment stopped by villages along the way forcing them to comply with the new tax requirements, and then defeated the armed rebels in Nongpoonjee. DC Shadwell wrote, 'I deemed it necessary to coerce them to submission if they still meditated resisting us, before I proceeded to Nongpoonjee, so that I might not leave my enemies in the rear'.[26]

Resistance to the forcible collection of revenue was made manifest in several ways, including the refusal to pay rents, villagers' petitions, the desertion of villages, and actual armed rebellion, to name a few. In Nartiang, the new *Dolois* led a rebellion comprised of a large number of people who later found strategic refuge in the forests once the colonial military had arrived on the scene. The military detachment and colonial officers remained prone to successive attacks by the rebels who were hiding in the forested hills and able to make sudden and unexpected attacks whenever the colonial forces ascended the hills—the same tactics that had been used in the rebellions led by Tirot Singh in 1829. The villages that resisted paying taxes were led by the village headmen, just as those that did

---

[24] Ibid.
[25] Ibid.
[26] Letter from B. Shadwell to Francis Jenkins, dated 25 February 1860, Cherrapoonjee, in Assam Commissioner's Papers (hereafter as AC) 399, ASA.

comply and pay the new taxes were also led by their respective *Dolois*.[27] U. Kiang Nongbah was remembered in both written and oral histories as the leader of the rebellion.[28] The leadership of Kiang Nongbah is significant since he was neither a *Syiem*, nor a *Dolois*. As significant as his role is in the history of the Jaintia hills, and in the history of this rebellion in particular, the rebellions of 1860–63 were neither homogenous nor were they centralized.

The DC's report stated that the villages which had remained submissive did so on the advice of their *Dolois*. Shadwell, in recompense, rewarded these *Dolois* with the right to hold their elected positions for life, instead of for the duration of their stipulated tenure. Further, Shadwell's report made recommendations to increase the strength of the detachment in the hills to at least 500 men, and, even after the suppression of all armed resistance, 300 soldiers were to be present at all times.[29] Meanwhile, the former Rajah of Jaintia, in a memorandum, insisted that he had had no reason to incite the rebellions, and, moreover, that he was aware that he lacked the means and the power to resist the colonial state.[30] Even so, the colonial authorities in Bengal were convinced that even if the people had only used the Rajah's name to invoke him as their symbolic leader, the only way for them to intimidate the people thoroughly, thereby aiming to prevent further resistance, was for them to remove the Rajah from the hills and bring him to Dhaka. So too for the Rajah's brother-in-law and his niece's husband, who were also suspected to have been instigators in the rebellion.[31]

The protests that broke out in 1863 were in response to the newly declared property tax. The pre-emptive measures taken by the colonial state of employing military guards and of calling for more troop numbers in order to intimidate and coerce reluctant villagers into paying the taxes failed to yield the state's desired results. The colonial state thus resorted to

---

[27] Home Department, Public A, 16 July 1862, no. 56, NAI; Home Department, Public A, 16 July 1862, no. 157, NAI; Home Department, Public B, 16 July 1862, no. 57, NAI.

[28] Helen Giri, *The Khasis under British Rule: 1824–1947* (New Delhi: Regency Publications, 1998), 92.

[29] Giri, *Khasis*, 92.

[30] Rajah Indro Sing's Memorandum, translated by Captain Rowlatt, Principal Assistant to the Commissioner, Khasi Jaintiah Hills, in AC 399, ASA.

[31] From A. R. Young, Secretary to the Government of Bengal to the Agent to the Governor General in the North East Frontier, 11 June 1860, no. 247, in AC 399, ASA.

its old and favoured method: it closed the markets in the Jaintia hills that were located along the border with the Khasi polities of Khyrim, Assam, and Sylhet.[32] These were key market centres, located at different points around the perimeter of the hills. An old ally of the British, the *Syiem* of Khyrim responded to these tactics by extending his support to the British in their efforts to capture the rebels. The colonial officers were then able to communicate to the government that the Jaintia Rebellion had ended in late 1863.[33]

As a result of these protests, the British reorganized the Jaintia hills according to a new administrative layout, along with new terms to describe it. According to the recommendations made by the government of Bengal, the reason for these changes was that 'this uncivilized race' could not be ruled in the same way as most of the other parts of the empire.[34] The *Dolois* were stripped of their official status. Their authority over the courts, police, and tax collection was handed over to a magistrate with charge over a sub-division of the Jaintia hills, and who reported directly to the District Deputy Commissioner. Spatial, administrative, and judicial reordering complemented each other.

Violence of Boundaries

Spatio-legal categories such as 'hill tribal', 'settler proprietor', 'cultivator', and 'non-British subject' appear in colonial judicial files and reports, and their appearance serves to map the violent processes of colonial law-making and the administrative and judicial reshuffling of boundaries. Instances of corporeal and epistemological violence reveal the interrupted nature of colonial authority and of new ruler-subject relations. This section will examine violent processes of boundary-making and the limits of colonial territorialization along the frontier, focusing on the boundaries between the Khasi hills and Sylhet, between the Garo and Khasi hills, between the Jaintia hills and Sylhet, and between the Khasi hills and Assam.

---

[32] Home Public A, 10 September 1862, no. 51, NAI.
[33] Syiemlieh, *British Administration*, 93–94.
[34] Home Public A, 25 September 1862, no. 59, NAI.

The history of colonial territorialization relied on a combination of geographical-military excursion, which was then articulated and consolidated through the drawing of conceptual boundaries to demarcate space, expressed in terms of 'law' or 'lawlessness'. The piecemeal settlement whereby communities from the plains moved into the Khasi hills, and the specific socio-political formations that developed over centuries of territorialization as a result, were, according to David Ludden, a response to and informed by greater territorialization in the plains under the Mughal empire. The communities that now live in the hills had once occupied the low lands of Sylhet, from as far as the Gangetic basin reaching into Bihar, and within this territory they practised shifting rice cultivation, according to David Ludden and Khasi historian Hamlet Bareh. Ludden writes, 'after 1600 and again after 1800, the accelerated expansion of sedentary agriculture drove shifting cultivators out of the plains. It also increased violence between contending interests on the land; confined tribal societies to the hills, and produced new political forms in the mountains'.[35] The boundaries laid down by the colonial state in the early decades of the nineteenth century sharpened the perceived differences between the inhabitants of the hills and those of the plains.

Gunnel Cederlof's ecological study convincingly demonstrates the tension between the fluidity of natural landscapes and the boundedness in regions where fixed colonial boundaries were being drawn. Cederlof departs from Ludden's characterization of processes of nineteenth-century boundary-making, and instead insists on the central role played by commerce in the organization of social and political relationships. However, colonial responses to 'raids' during the late eighteenth century, examined in the previous chapter, along with the urgency to define jurisdiction all throughout the nineteenth century, were colonial strategies of governance that were predicated upon civilizational and spatio-legal categories such as 'hill tribal'.

Processes of differentiation fed into the internal logic of colonial law and jurisdiction. Yet the inhabitants of Khasi polities in both the foothills and the plains, as well as communities that were both Khasi and Sylheti (read Bengali), deeply disturbed the neat spatial and civilizational

---

[35] David Ludden, 'Investing in Nature Around Sylhet: An Excursion into Geographical History', *Economic and Political Weekly* 38, no. 48 (November 2003): 5080–5081.

categorizations of the colonial state. Although the landscape in Sylhet and its frontier resisted the type of permanent characterization as one thing or another, as shown by Cederlof's detailed study, nevertheless, the colonial state's geographical and legal representations of that landscape were made in purportedly objective or scientific terms that intersected with racialized or civilizational terms.

Efforts to create and maintain jurisdictional boundaries continued well into the second half of the nineteenth century. After 1858, sustained efforts were made to deny any form of sovereignty to the Khasi *Syiems*. The ensuing debates over the settling of boundaries reflected the intrinsic tensions that underpinned imperial sovereignty in these frontier hills. In January 1870, Government of Bengal issued orders for the suspension of a topographical survey of the Khasi, Jaintia, and Garo Hills. The Surveyor-General of India, however, requested that this restriction be lifted. In his personal correspondence with the lieutenant governor of Bengal, he stated that the local survey officer had been given the instruction to carry on the survey operations alongside 'a good military reconnaissance of the Garrow hills, penetrating into the interior, only as far as he may do so with safety'.[36]

The avowed purpose of this survey, according to the Surveyor-General, was to ensure that blank spaces on existing maps be filled out. Clearly, the topographical survey was at the same time intended as a military operation to prevent or subjugate any resistance. The Surveyor-General insisted that the survey should continue, despite the Government of Bengal's stated lack of funds. He added that the survey of the Garo hills, along with those in the Naga Hills and Manipur regions, as per orders of the Government of India, would not be completed if it were suspended, even temporarily, due to a lack of funds. This letter formed part of a chain of correspondence between several tiers of colonial officials and officers who oversaw the topographical survey.

Alexander Mackenzie, a British civil servant who took part in several colonial survey operations and retired as the Lieutenant General of British India, concurred with the Surveyor-General. In a letter to the Government of India, Mackenzie stated that the economic concerns that

---

[36] Letter from Surveyor General of India to the Secretary to the Government of India, Home Department, Geographical Branch Part B, 27 January 1870, nos. 9/15, NAI.

were driving the orders for suspension of the survey were the very same reasons for why that survey ought to be completed. The survey, he believed, would prevent long-term fiscal loss to the government.[37] Just as with Fischer's surveys of 1827–29, the military-cartographic operations of the second half of the nineteenth century facilitated the identification of arable land in order to increase the amount of land under cultivation and to categorize it as revenue-yielding.

Additional arguments for the continuation of the survey operation were advanced in the exchange of letters. Some of the reasons offered for the continuation of the survey were more political than economic. In a letter from the Deputy Superintendent of the Topographical Survey, the deputy stated that the rebellions in the Jaintia hills against the state in 1861–62 could have been averted if the officers had known the geography better.[38] He further stated, 'It is impossible to underrate the knowledge of a country especially where jungle clad, intricate and mountainous, when a force has importunately to march into it [sic]'.[39] Such statements demonstrate how cartographic representations identified inhabitants as one with the landscape. They—the landscape and its inhabitants—were unpredictable and unknown, in need of mapping and of political control. The government rescinded the suspension, at least in part, and survey operations were resumed in the Khasi and Garo hills.[40] The interruptions to the violence of map-making and boundary-making are evident in statements such as those made by Surveyor General H. L. Thullier in a letter to Alexander Mackenzie. He complained about several obstacles to the survey, including labour costs, but, most significantly, he added that the 'maps of Khasi, Naga and Garrow Hills will be to a certain extent blank and unsatisfactory, and much remains to be done'.[41]

---

[37] Letter from Alexander Mackenzie, Secretary to the Government of Bengal to the Secretary to the Government of India, Home Department, Geographical Branch Part B, 31 January 1870, nos. 9/15, NAI.

[38] Home Department, Geographical Branch Part B, 5 January 1870, nos. 9/15, NAI. This letter stated several other reasons that were considered less grave, but equally important. These included the breaking-up of a team of trained surveyor officials, the financial loss to the government in the form of the measuring instruments that had been bought expressly for this purpose, and so on.

[39] Home Department, Geographical Branch Part B, 5 January 1870, nos. 9/15, NAI.

[40] Board of Revenue Papers 48, file nos. 8/100, ASA.

[41] Letter from H. L. Thullier, Surveyor General of India, to the Secretary to the Government of Bengal, 5 January 1870, nos. 9/15, Geographical Branch Part B, Home Department, NAI.

The large amount of correspondence during the nineteenth century on boundary-making and resolving persistent disputes between British and non-British territories reflects something of the interrupted nature of colonial sovereignty in the frontier regions of the Khasi, Jaintia, and Garo hills.[42] But as will be discussed presently, there was a specific concern over the boundary between the Garo and Khasi hills in particular that reveals even more of the tensions that simmered beneath the surface when colonial powers sought to establish their sovereignty in the frontier.

Dividing the Khasi Hills and the Garo Hill District: Ethnic Separation or Jurisdiction?

The need to demarcate a jurisdictional boundary between the Garo and Khasi hills only became pressing in the second half of the nineteenth century. Laws enacted in this period attempted to define relations between different authorities. Act XXII of 1869, also called the Garo Hills Act, came into force from 1870. It replaced Regulation X of 1822, and sanctioned the extension of *any* law, or any portion of law, that had been passed by the British Government into the Garo Hills. The Garo Hills Act could also be extended to the Khasi, Jaintia, and Naga hills by notification in the Calcutta Gazette.[43] This meant that the colonial government secured the right to impose the Garo Hills Act or parts of it to the frontier hills as and when it was deemed necessary. Yet, jurisdictional boundaries between the hill districts had to be ascertained. This was because despite the increasingly centralized claims of authority made by the lieutenant governor, actual jurisdictional boundaries remained in flux.

In a letter to the Commissioner of Cooch Behar, Alexander Mackenzie, the officiating secretary to the Government of Bengal in the Judicial Department, provides some insights into the survey operations in frontier hills in the second half of the century. Mackenzie stated that the 'primary object of the expedition' was to *separate* the Khasi and Garo hills. He insisted that this separation would not be achieved 'until the

---

[42] See Reeju Ray, 'Interrupted Sovereignties in the North-East Frontier of British India, 1787–1870', *Modern Asian Studies* 53, no. 2 (Cambridge University Press, 2019): 606–632.

[43] Mackenzie, *History of the Relations*, 262–263.

independent Garo circle in the centre of the hills [was] brought into subjection.'[44] Separating the two regions entailed the categorization of the inhabitants of British territory (that is, most of the Garo hills) and those of the Khasi polities as ethnically different from each other. The Khasis and Garos were understood to be distinct based on their different languages. However, in villages on the cusp of the Khasi and Garo hills, dialects could not be distinguished as either Khasi or Garo. Additionally, the authority of Khasi *Syiems* in the adjoining polities, Rambrai and Nongstoin in particular, was not so strictly demarcated, and the villages bordering villages Garo and Khasi regions often owed allegiance to both *Syiems*. The flexibility and plurality of ruler-subject relations further complicated colonial boundary-making based jurisdiction and revenue.[45]

The boundary line that was created to separate the Garo and Khasi hills, which topographically formed part of a single mountain chain, was designed purely for administrative convenience. The indeterminate views amongst those people who were defined as Garo concerning whom they considered to be their ruler confused the colonial officials. The colonial district administration's correspondence suggests that officials had wanted to define sovereignty as precise, indivisible, and territorially demarcated. Yet in the border villages, inhabitants owed their allegiance and paid tribute to the *Syiems* of Nongstoin and Rambrai polities respectively. The practice of recognizing both *Syiems* as holders of politico-spiritual authority, or, in the terms of the colonial state, as sovereign heads with jurisdictional authority, was deemed cumbersome in the view of colonial officials. They therefore insisted upon demarcating a territorial boundary that would limit each of the respective *Syiems*' jurisdiction.

The process of establishing a boundary that marked the jurisdictional limits of the *Syiems* of Rambrai and Nongstoin depended upon the support and the participation of both of them. Their authority was essential to conduct the village durbars or councils that had been summoned by the colonial government. In these councils, information on new boundaries was announced alongside the new revenue arrangements that accompanied them. The presence of the *Syiems*, it was hoped, would preclude the possibility of any major resistance to these changes. Further,

[44] Board of Revenue Papers 48, file nos. 8/100, ASA.
[45] Ibid.

the *Syiems*' presence also helped legitimize the authority of colonial district official, whose role was to represent Company jurisdiction in those pockets of the Khasi hills under the direct governance of the colonial state. The authority of the DC of the Khasi hills, though it was officially restricted to colonial stations, was nevertheless extended to matters of the succession of *Syiems*, as well as to all other kinds of civil dispute. The colonial state was not the first to introduce multiple nodes and figures of authority, and this made the work of colonial officials in these polities much easier.

Dual jurisdiction (between the *Syiem* and the colonial district administration) was established in those border villages whose inhabitants owed allegiance and paid taxes to the Khasi *Syiems*, but who fell within the newly defined Garo hills boundary. In such villages, the DC would collect dues 'paying them over to the Khasi chiefs, less 25%'.[46] Many new villages that were outside direct colonial control should be annexed and 'put at once on par with villages already dependent'.[47] The colonial government ensured that in the violent subjugation of these villages, no Khasis were employed 'for offensive purposes or in any other capacity than as coolies'.[48] The government recognized the dangers in employing Khasis to coerce or to suppress the Garos through violent means.

Even so, the ethnic differentiation was not entirely reliable. The overlaps between independent and dependent villages in the Garo hills, as well as Garos and Khasis in villages in the prescribed border, precluded and interrupted colonial spatio-temporal classifications. In other words, in the bordering villages independent and dependent, or Khasi and Garo were not distinct categories, and the framework guiding colonial military offensives notwithstanding its violence was inherently flawed. The military offensives against independent villages were meant to place them on par with colonially dependent villages, and thereby to create homogeneity among Garo-British subjects.

In 1873, the commissioner of Assam wrote a pressing letter to the DC of the Khasi hills urging, once again, the necessity to complete the settlement of the boundary between Garo hills and the Khasi-Jaintia hills.

[46] Ibid.
[47] Ibid.
[48] Ibid.

Preparations were undertaken for the demarcation of the boundary, and included the placement of military units from the native infantry at the newly delineated border separating the Khasi from the Garo hills. Colonial violence manifested itself not only in military offensives as has been discussed, but also in collective forms of punishment, such as the closure of market centres or the acts of violence unleashed by European entrepreneurs that were protected by law. The complexity of jurisdiction and the movement of law across the hills enabled such violence.[49]

The commissioner of Assam wrote to the DC a second time, and insisted on pursuing the objective of 'disconnecting the Garrows from the Khasis'.[50] The difficulties in determining whether a village was really Garo or Khasi, according to local officials, undermined colonial sovereignty, not only in the Khasi and Garo hills, but also in the adjoining settled territories.[51] Officials' inability to identify certain villages as one or the other was exacerbated by the fact that some British subjects like 'the Assamese [did] not distinguish between Garrows and Khasis in speaking of the people of the low hills south of Nusteng [Noingstoin] but always cast them as Garrows'.[52] Neither of the *Syiems* of Nongstoin and Rambrai, moreover, were able to provide a precise list of each village that paid allegiance to them. Colonial officials interpreted this imprecision to mean that doubt had been cast over the legitimacy of the claims made by each of the *Syiems* for jurisdiction over villages. The DC of the Khasi hills restated a claim made by an official a decade earlier in 1863. The memorandum stated the following,

I suspect the real explanation of the matter is that these States [Nongstoin and Rambrai] have whenever they felt themselves strong enough, levied blackmail upon them [the Garos] ... no doubt the authority of the Khasia Raja is little more than nominal, but it is highly desirable that those communities should be assigned to him who acknowledge his rule and speak the Khasia language. The great importance of having a well-defined boundary, the people living on one side of which will be subject to your [British] jurisdiction, and those on the

[49] Ibid.
[50] Assam Commissioner's Papers, 1871–1873, file no. 635, ASA.
[51] Ibid.
[52] Ibid.

other to the Rajas of Nongsteng and Ramrye (for I believe both claim to the north east) must be borne in mind.[53]

The irregularity of levying of tribute by *Syiems* was translated here as *blackmail*.[54] There was a significance of calling the irregularity of tribute payment blackmail instead of customary. The existing system between the *Syiems* and the inhabitants of these villages lacked the coherence of time-bound taxation. Thus, colonial officials denied that the said relationship represented one between a ruler and his subjects. The absence of regular or timely taxation was considered a gross violation of the rights of a ruler according to colonial officials. Officials further understood that the villagers' recognition of the political and spiritual rights of more than one *Syiem* could be taken as an indication that the *Syiems'* enjoyed only nominal authority. The use of terminology such as blackmail aided officials in their subjugation of local authorities, and in their goals of colonial border-making. Terms such as 'blackmail' formed part of a governance strategy for those landscapes and communities that eluded the normal frameworks of colonial classificatory knowledge.

Several of the villages in question were inhabited by groups identified as Lyngams. These were people who were described as having been 'produced by the intermarriage of the Khasis and Garos', and their existence also complicated the attempts at making boundaries along the lines desired by local officials.[55] Forty-nine villages were identified as being inhabited by Lyngams, living under the jurisdiction of Nongstoin. The 1873 memorandum contained a short description of the Lyngams' social and cultural attributes, which were seen to combine elements of both Garo and Khasi communities.[56] The Lyngams challenged British efforts to confine and make sedentary subjects out of the hills' inhabitants, particularly

---

[53] Deputy Commissioner Colonel Haughten quoted in, 'Memorandum on Khasia and Garo Boundary carried out by Colonel Bivar, Deputy Commissioner, Garo Hills, and Captain Woodthrope, R. E., Survey officer, in March 1873', Assam Commissioner's Papers, 1871–1873, file no. 635, ASA.

[54] For a discussion of how the British saw existing practices, such as *posa* tribute relationship between hill and plains inhabitants in the Brahmaputra valley, and translated them into terms like blackmail—a process that inflected colonial border making—see Simpson, 'Bordering and Frontier-Making', 513–542.

[55] Assam Commissioner's Papers, 1871–1873, file no. 635, ASA.

[56] Lyngams were included in anthropologist P. R. T. Gordon's monograph entitled *The Khasis*, thereby establishing that they were not Garos, but Khasis. See Philip R. T. Gurdon, *The Khasis* (1907; Reprint, New Delhi: Cosmo Publications, 1987), 17.

within the annexed parts of the Garo hills. These groups were described as, 'very nomadic in their habits and rarely [lived] long on the same village site'.[57] For colonial officials, the nomadism of some of the inhabitants in the Garos was part of the same linguistic register in which irregular taxation practices by the *Syiems* had been described as blackmail. The memorandum stated that the irregular and arbitrary collection of levies by the *Syiems* was acceptable to the Garos because 'by doing so they [inhabitants of the villages] enjoy comparative immunity and escape all control, and avoid the more direct and searching [British] Government which they would be liable to under the Deputy Commissioner, Garo Hills'.[58]

To resolve the problem of these Lyngam villages, and the challenges these posed for colonial ethnic separation, the villages were stripped from the jurisdiction of the Khasi chiefs. Eighteen villages recognized the authority of no local chief or *Syiem* at all. These villages were brought under the direct control of the British government. Through a rearrangement of jurisdictional boundaries, Nongstoin polity was stripped of land and subjects, while the *Syiem* was awarded a few villages as compensation.[59]

Demarcating the boundaries 'separating the Khasias from the Garos as far as possible' was strategic. There were occasions when 'intricate boundaries ... through heavy jungles and the densest swamps' were given a preference over natural boundaries.[60] For instance, suggestions to use the Radiac River that ran from the northern portion of the Garo hills down to the plains as a boundary were found to be impractical. With this natural boundary, several villages—described as 'purely Garo'—that paid taxes to the government and had no connection with the Khasi *Syiems* would fall under the boundary jurisdiction of the *Syiem* of Rambrai. There were also 'purely Khasi villages' that fell on the Garo (British) side of that boundary. The reliance on a natural boundary to settle boundaries of revenue and jurisdiction meant that the *Syiem's* relationship with several villages under his jurisdiction was severed—Khasi, Garo, and Lyngam.

The establishment of this boundary also clearly explained the changes being applied to the very notion of authority in the frontier hills.

---

57 Assam Commissioner's Papers, 1871–1873, file no. 635, ASA.
58 Ibid.
59 Ibid.
60 Ibid.

A resolution passed by the Political department of the Government of Bengal concluded that the *Syiems* had 'no territorial rights' over their own immediate subjects. The Government, in turn, would retain all rights of timber, minerals, elephants, fisheries, etc.[61]

This resolution emphasized that the *Syiems* had to be reminded not to collect taxes west of the new boundary. To affirm the new boundary and make it visible, officials discussed several options, including placing 'cairns of stone', masonry pillars, or iron posts along the agreed dividing line.[62] The demarcation of the boundary by various measures, including military operations, remained unsatisfactory, and the cooperation of the Khasi *Syiems* was found to be the most effective way to establish colonial legitimacy.[63]

Many villages showed deference to the *Syiems* and cooperated in boundary-demarcation operations because of the presence of one or the other *Syiem*. Village depositions during boundary commission operations demonstrate that without the *Syiem*, the colonial officers were unable to extract information or gain the cooperation of a village's inhabitants. The boundary settlement was secured by compensating the *Syiems* for their rights over villages that fell on the west of the boundary line (i.e. the Garo hills).[64] The government decided that the Syiems were to be 'liberally treated' for their cooperation, while the chiefs in turn were reminded that objections would not be entertained. The chiefs performed an essential role during depositions of villagers and announcement of new jurisdictional boundaries and new rulers. Their presence gave legitimacy to colonial administrators as new rulers.

The archive of material used as a point-of-reference for this survey operation included older surveys, geographical narratives, and depositions of the *Syiems* and inhabitants of villages at the boundaries, as well as petitions and other locally collected information. However, the memorandum by local administrators on the boundary between Garo and Khasi hills dismissed the depositions collected in 1839 from the chief of Nongstoin and his family members as 'highly unsatisfactory'.[65] The 1839

---

[61] Resolution passed by the Political Department of the Government of Bengal, 24 October 1873, Assam Commissioner's Papers, 1871–1873, file no. 635, ASA.

[62] Assam Commissioner's Papers, 1871–1873, file no. 635, ASA.

[63] Ibid.

[64] Ibid.

[65] Ibid.

depositions did not help colonial cartographic mapping along ethnic lines. There was continued acknowledgement that the authority of the *Syiem* of Nongstoin extended into some villages that had paid taxes to the colonial government from the early nineteenth century onwards.[66]

Contending Colonial Jurisdictions

In the second half of the century, Shillong replaced Cherrapoonjee as the headquarters for the north-east frontier agency. The Khasi and Jaintia hills had been combined into a single political district. The administrative and jurisdictional separation of the Garo and Khasi hills had now been successfully achieved. The Scheduled Districts Act was passed in 1874, which identified tribal areas throughout British India, as well as the application of special laws within them. This spatial re-ordering helped British officials separate and determine what lay within the hill district, and what remained under Sylhet jurisdiction. In the following discussion concerning disputes that arose in the border region of the Sylhet and Jaintia hills, it becomes clear that the stakes had shifted.

In March 1874, the Government of Bengal, in a letter to the commissioner of Dacca, pointed out that two European planters named in the correspondence as Halford Brownlow and Hart had illegally encroached into Jaintia hill territory. Unsurprisingly, colonial authorities stationed in the Sylhet and in the Khasi-Jaintia hills were uncertain as to which side of the jurisdictional boundary this disputed land fell. The government thus ordered a halt to any grants or leases of land in and around the border that had been made without the approval of the DC of the Khasi-Jaintia hills. The government also demanded an official report on the types of lease that had been granted by the Collector of Sylhet.[67] This situation developed into a conflict between the Collector of Sylhet and the DC of the Khasi-Jaintia hills. Disagreements between them stemmed from the unresolved nature of jurisdictional boundaries.

---

[66] Ibid. Also, Report from Captain H. J. Peet, DC of the Garo Hills, to the Commissioner of the Cooch Behar Division, 31 March 1871, Assam Commissioner's Papers, 1871–1873, file no. 635, ASA.

[67] Dacca Commissioner's File, file no. 110, serial nos. 1–20, 11 March 1874, ASA.

A report prepared by the sub-district collector of Sylhet, Sambhu Narayan Singh, and by J. B. Shadwell, the extra-assistant commissioner of the hills district, explained the nature and cause of the dispute. A comparison between two maps, one in Bengali from 1840 (later corroborated by the surveyor of India to be the correct map) and an English map, showed that the disputed lands belonged to the Khasi-Jaintia Hills jurisdiction. The enquiry revealed that Mr Brownlow had occupied lands without a land deed or *patta* from the Sylhet administration. The *patta* he provided pertained to lands that belonged to the hill district.

Referring to the case of Brownlow, a cultivator named Roop Ram was interviewed, and he claimed that there were eighteen settlement holders who sold portions of the disputed lands to Brownlow. He was unable to account for lands that were not owned by any of these eighteen landholders. He also stated that these eighteen settlements had paid rents to the Sylhet treasury, but were transferred to the Shillong district treasury a year earlier. Other cultivators, like Loai Chowkidar, Jain Mahomed, Nobin Lasker, Gholam Iwa, and Batai Kazi, who all tilled or owned lands in the region, confirmed in their interviews that the lands in question belonged to the hills. Dhanai Nuah Sikdar, employed as the *jamadar* of the contested lands, was the only interviewee who claimed that he had no information about the boundaries of these districts. And one of the cultivators, who was believed to have sold land to Hart, claimed that he had not in fact sold any land to the planter.

On the surface, this dispute reflected the ambiguous relationship between the competing jurisdictions of the colonial authorities in the hills on the one hand, and the collector of Sylhet on the other. It seems to have arisen from miscommunication and from disagreements caused by faulty maps. The involvement of the office of Surveyor-General of India in this local dispute attested to the inability of local authorities to determine the lines of contested boundaries. In a letter from the Surveyor-General of India, the boundary was described in the following words,

the foot of the hills or the surveyed line of the cultivated villages in the plains alone form part of the Jynteah district attached to Sylhet according to the Survey of 1838.... The hilly portion of the north of the villages specified in your letter ... ought to be held as appertaining to the hill jurisdiction. The intermediate area defined by the straight lines to the peaks was fixed merely to show the extent of the survey and how the hill peaks were laid down. It is in no way connected with the total area of the district as given on the published general map ... the straight line shows the triangulation area, as it is called, have given rise to the misunderstanding. But I have never had any other opinion that what I now give you—the plains belong to Sylhet, the hills to the political agency.[68]

The Surveyor-General pointed out that a particular map that incorrectly depicted areas that were under the Sylhet district, and had been published without his approval, had led to the confusion. He forwarded a correct version of the map and also referred to a book titled *Atlas of India* which, according to him, also contained the correct demarcations of the boundary.

During this enquiry, another dispute was discussed in which the European planter referred to as Hart had occupied hillocks forming part of the larger chain of Jaintia hills, but that had been excluded from the Survey of Lieutenant Thuillier. A land settlement holder or *zamindar*, referred to as Durreny Choudry [sic], was interviewed, along with several others, who all acknowledged that they had sold lands that were part of the hill district, and that they also paid rents for these lands to the Sylhet Collector.[69] In his deposition, Hart alleged that a deep watercourse or ravine separated the main chain of the hills from the specific hillocks that he had occupied. He therefore considered the hillocks to be part of the plains, rather than of the hills. The local authorities found no trace of such a stream or natural boundary.[70]

The two cases exacerbated existing conflicts between the colonial authorities in Sylhet and those in the hills district. The report from the Commissioner of Revenue in Dhaka to the Government of Bengal stated that colonial authorities in the hills believe the collector of Sylhet was surreptitiously extending his jurisdiction to Jaintia hills.[71] The collector

---

[68] Letter from H. L. Thullier, Surveyor General of India, to H. C. Sutherland, Commissioner of Sylhet, Dacca Commissioner's File, file no. 110, serial nos. 1–20, 11 April 1874, ASA.

[69] 'Choudhury' was a title associated with the Bengali land-holding class.

[70] Dacca Commissioner's File, file no. 110, serial nos. 1–20, ASA.

[71] Report from the Commissioner of Revenue, Dacca Division to Secretary to the Government of Bengal, Dacca Commissioner's File, file no. 110, serial nos. 1–20, 12 May 1874, ASA.

of Sylhet was found responsible for issuing leases to the two planters Brownlow and Hart, and for transferring to them the right of using the resources from the disputed lands.[72] Yet, the report concluded that the dispute was the result of a faulty map; and thus, the Collector was exonerated.[73] As a result, two changes were introduced. First, an order was passed to replace defective maps with the correct ones. Second, all the land records and *pattas* referring to lands that were admitted being within Khasi-Jaintia territorial jurisdiction were, henceforth, to be transferred from the Sylhet Collector's office to the office of the DC of the Khasi-Jaintia hills.[74] Even though the enquiry identified the actions of the two European planters as 'illegal encroachment', neither of them was held responsible for occupying those lands by deceit and lies, as per the testimonials of the cultivators.

The encroachment into the hills by European planters, sanctioned by the Collector of Sylhet, was seen as a serious transgression, but one that could ultimately be explained as arising from a problem of incomplete or faulty knowledge. This highlighted the persistent problem of where, in fact, did the hills end? Extant correspondence and reports suggest that the claims and counterclaims between colonial officials at the local, regional, and state levels, eventually tried to arrive at a jurisdictional hill-plain divide. This was interrupted time and time again by the very nature of the foothills' undulating landscape, where the hills merged into the plains. The creation of a new cartographic imagination through surveys and maps to define colonial jurisdiction and its limits proved to be incomplete and unsatisfactory. Colonial sovereignty was interrupted by the very logics and frames used by colonial administrators, and the knowledge that was produced through maps and surveys.

In this chapter I have argued that jurisdictional disputes throughout the nineteenth century reveal a complex intersection of colonial law

---

[72] Elizabeth Kolsky has shown that the presence of non-official Europeans who were neither Company subjects nor colonized was a central component driving efforts to codify law in nineteenth-century colonial India. Further, the universal rhetoric of codification was undercut by the need to assert the 'differences' of the indigenous populations in order to restrict their legal rights, and this was the inherent contradiction of the colonial civilizing mission. See Elizabeth Kolsky, *Colonial Justice in British India: White Violence and the Rule of Law* (Cambridge: Cambridge University Press, 2010).

[73] Report from the Commissioner of Revenue, Dacca Division to Secretary to the Government of Bengal, Dacca Commissioner's File, file no. 110, serial nos. 1–20, 12 May 1874, ASA.

[74] Ibid.

and sovereignty as strategies of governance.[75] The imprecision of physical boundaries between hills and plains allowed for the fluidity of jurisdiction, a fluidity that simultaneously relied on civilizational and ethnic classifications to describe inhabitants of the region. Local communities played a significant role in informing, challenging, and engaging with the colonial officials who persistently failed to arrive at jurisdictional certainty and administrative stability in the frontier. The significance for the local authority such as the Khasi *Syiems* in stating and negotiating the terms of jurisdictional boundary-making is also a moment of transformation in ruler-subject relations. Through law's arteries, the role of colonial officials now included mediating and finally dictating the relationship between subjects and local rulers. The violence of border-making was at the core of imperial sovereignty as a governance strategy.

[75] Board of Revenue Papers 48, File Nos. 8–100, ASA.

4

Colonial Governance and Customary Authority

In 1822, David Scott, the Political Agent of the Governor in the North East who was stationed in the Khasi hills, expressed that there were numerous local customs 'which it will be better to permit them [frontier inhabitants] to follow than to attempt at present to introduce a uniform mode of procedure throughout the whole extent of the frontier'.[1] Treaties confirming the right to male customary authority were signed with the designated heads of Khasi polities that were classified as 'dependent' or 'semi-independent', depending on their strategic location and their respective histories of resistance to Company authority.[2] There were polities that did not sign treaties, though such autonomous polities are rarely mentioned in government records. The polities in the Khasi hills—dependent, semi-independent, or independent—were defined as non-British territory. Within non-British hill polities, however, colonial stations were carved out that were directly administered by the East India Company. Jurisdiction was shared between the *Syiems* and Political Agent of the East India Company.[3]

Central to the administration of the non-British territories was local authority. Consider the *Zamindars* who were revenue collecting agents under the Mughal empire, and they were granted landed proprietary

---

[1] Letter from David Scott, Agent to the Governor General in the North east to W. B. Bayly, Chief Secretary to the Bengal Government, Revenue Department Consultations, 24 July 1822, no. 13, India Office Records.

[2] For instance, the Khasi state of Nongkhlaw, which led many other states into a decade long rebellion that started in 1829, was completely subjugated after the Syiem. Tirot Singh and his allies were captured. The state of Khyrim, on the other hand, which had helped the Company forces during these rebellions, was ascribed a semi-independent status.

[3] By the Act of 1835, the Political Agent in the Khasi Hills was placed in charge of civil and criminal cases under the superintendence of the supreme revenue court or *sudder dewani* and criminal court or *nizamut adalats*; but the orders of 29 September 1835 that included Jaintia territory as part of the Khasi hills were modified by Act XXI of 1836, which sanctioned the annexation of the same to Sylhet.

Placing the Frontier in British North-East India. Reeju Ray, Oxford University Press. © Reeju Ray 2023.
DOI: 10.1093/oso/9780192887085.003.0004

rights by the EIC under the Permanent Settlement Act of 1793. These revenue agents turned into landlords served as intermediaries and paid a fixed revenue to the colonial government. This new 'rule of property' in Bengal overwrote tenants' many existing customary rights. The boundary disputes examined in the previous chapters, as well as the government correspondence on establishing jurisdictional boundaries between the frontier hills and the Bengal plains, were to a large extent precipitated by colonial efforts to preserve the newly-created capitalist, agricultural *zamindari* estates.[4]

Unlike *zamindars* or the rulers of princely states, headmen, or chiefs in the Garo, Khasi, and Jaintiah hills were coded as non-proprietary, customary authority. For instance *Syiems* were understood to be different from landlords of large estates. The nature of authority of variously termed heads of polities such as *Syiems*, Wahadadars in the Khasi hills, Dollois and Sirdars in the Jaintiah hills, Laskars in the Garo hills varied. This chapter will show that the authority of the political agent and other colonial officials was reinforced with the strengthening of colonial notions of custom and customary authority.

In 1835 the Political Agent who was stationed in the Khasi hills was given magisterial duties in addition to his military and administrative functions. However, the precise nature of the Political Agent's authority and jurisdiction was not clearly stated.[5] He could henceforth refer criminal cases to the high courts in Bengal or Assam, depending on the gravity of the offence.[6] Criminal and civil cases were subject to different jurisdictions—customary and colonial respectively. The plural legal order enabled the Company to have penal authority over its non-subjects. While most Khasi *Syiems* were allowed to retain juridical authority within the territorial scope of their chieftaincies, the Political Agent acquired the power to intervene in major civil disputes.[7]

---

[4] Andrew Sartori, 'A Liberal Discourse of Custom in Colonial Bengal', *Past & Present* 212, no. 1 (2011): 163–197.

[5] The vagueness regarding the role of the Political Agent within Khasi polities gave excessive discretionary powers to the colonial state. The ambiguity and non-uniformity of colonial legal order was not an exception but a pervasive feature of imperial rule of law. See Ann Laura Stoler, 'On Degrees of Imperial Sovereignty', *Public Culture* 18, no. 1 (2006): 125–126.

[6] Mills, *Report*, 9.

[7] The word *Syiem* is spelled interchangeably with *Siem* in colonial records. I have chosen to use the current spelling of *Syiem*, unless it is used within quotations. I have adopted a similar approach with other terms (e.g., *Dolois* for *Dollois*, *Khasi* for *Cossya* or *Khasia*, *Jaintia* for *Jaintiah*,

Local authority was integrated into the colonial state through their evolving relationships with colonial agents including district commissioners, magistrates, judges, lawyers, missionaries, and, most importantly, private traders. Jurisdictional disputes offer an understanding of the myriad forms these relationships took. The lack of a shared legal identity for everyone who inhabited the hills created asymmetries between the Europeans, hill inhabitants of differently graded polities, and inhabitants of directly ruled areas. The presence of a large number of Europeans—private traders, entrepreneurs, officials and their families, missionary groups—ensured that law and jurisdiction would remain fractured and hierarchical. On the one hand, varied economic considerations induced a plural legal order in the frontier hills, while, on the other, this same plural order helped consolidate colonial sovereignty by the colonial state's strategic negotiation of custom and jurisdiction.

The manner and degree to which colonial laws were imposed in the frontier hills was multiple and varied. The augmentation of British economic interests required redesigning laws. Jurisdiction over European subjects also required enhancements to existing legal systems.[8] The development of a legal identity that was shared by all those who inhabited the hills was impossible for two reasons. First, the judicial structure was itself quite inchoate, especially in the first half of the nineteenth century. The relationships between the British courts in Bengal and Assam, the office of the political agent in the Khasi hills, the politico-judicial *durbars* run by Khasi chiefs or *Syiems*, and jurisdictional powers enjoyed by the local juridical heads or *Dollois* in the Jaintiah hills remained vague and contentious. Second, as several historians have pointed out, there was an inherent contradiction in the framework of colonial jurisprudence. The 'rule of law' was formulated not so much as to enable uniform justice, but rather to strengthen colonial power by spelling out racial and civilizational hierarchies between natives and Europeans.[9] Judicial

---

Mylliem for *Myllim*, *Khyriem* for *Khyrim*). Furthermore, I have abbreviated East India Company as EIC, District Commissioner as DC, and Chief Commissioner as Chief Commissioner.

[8] Lauren Benton, *Law and Colonial Cultures: Legal Regimes in World History, 1400–1900* (Cambridge: Cambridge University Press, 2001), 123.

[9] For a more recent formulation of the 'rule of colonial difference' in the judicial realm, see Elizabeth Kolsky, *Colonial Justice in British India: White Violence and the Rule of Law* (Cambridge: Cambridge University Press, 2010). For an elaborate breakdown of the plural judicial framework in British India, see Benton, *Law and Colonial Cultures*, 127–166.

developments in the frontier hills reflect a complex interdependence of jurisdiction and custom that was undergirded by concerns about private trade monopolies in the hills.

Mid-century Reforms

A. J. M. Mills, a judge of the *sudder* court in Calcutta, was sent on a deputation to the Khasi-Jaintiah hills to enquire into anomalies in the colonial judicial establishment in 1853. Mills prepared a one-hundred and twenty-three page-long report following his consultation of archived colonial correspondence, administrative and revenue reports, *pattas* or leases on land and natural resources, and judicial cases from 1826 onwards. Using these sources, he examined the anomalies in colonial jurisdiction in the Bengal frontier which had led to severe and persistent jurisdiction disputes between Sylhet and the hill districts. The report is significant because it led to several important changes in the judicial structure of the colonial state in the frontier zone encompassing Sylhet and the Khasi hills. It also provides insights concerning ideas about the legal status of non-British subjects, the relationship between the colonial government and private European enterprises, and the shifting British ideas of property and sovereignty in territories defined as non-British.[10] The report acquired especial importance after 1857 as part of a move to reformulate earlier agreements that had been signed with the Khasi *Syiems*. This report along, with the revenue report of 1858 by W. J. Allen, became important points of reference for colonial officials in the following decades.

The changes recommended by this report (and the discussions around it) informed the subsequent actions of the government—both in the immediate and in the long term. The immediate judicial reforms included efforts to delineate the precise judicial functions of the colonial government in the hills, and to establish a hierarchy of accountability within the colonial administrative structure in the north-east frontier. The long-term effects that unfolded over the rest of the century included administrative reshuffling and the consolidation of colonial notions of property, jurisdiction, and sovereignty in the hills. The report revealed what was

---

[10] Mills, *Report*, 10.

at stake for the colonial office in this complex frontier legal landscape. Pointing towards the necessity of reform in judicial administration, the report stated the following:

> In Cherra Poonjee there are numerous Europeans, both in and out of the services-coal mines are worked, lime is quarried, and other speculations engage attention.... [M]any disputes have, in connection with trade, sprung up and formed the subject of suits in the court, and that great complaint is made, and not unreasonably, I think, in which justice is administered. It is therefore time I think, that the administration of the territory in which the political agent exercises the powers of a magistrate, collector and judge should be placed on a more satisfactory and intelligible footing; that magistrate should know what law he has to administer, and the subjects should know under what they have to live. It is, I think, very doubtful whether Europeans are even amenable to the Political authorities in civil matters in consequence of Act XI of 1836 not extending to the Khasi hills.... I would suggest the enactment of a complete set of rules and procedure suited to the usages and institutions of the country.[11]

This extract from the report captured in a somewhat modified form crucial concerns that led to a reformulation in political relations with the Khasi polities. These included the centralization of power in the office of the magistrate, the unintelligibility of administrative scope of the colonial state in the hills, and execution of justice. In addressing some of these issues, the colonial government formulated an idea of a legal subject. Yet the report itself was unclear about who this subject was, nor was it clear as to whom the judicial reforms were directed. Direct references were made only to British subjects including officials, traders, and soldiers. The report largely ignored questions regarding the legal status of non-British subjects and the juridical authority of chiefs.

Another important aspect of the report was that it prompted the colonial government to re-evaluate the *Syiems* roles and responsibilities. The *Syiems* in the Khasi polities were instrumental for the commercial success both of private traders and of the colonial government. Their position as

---

[11] Ibid.

co-signatories had been essential for the very existence of trading agreements and leases. The economic value of the hills, mines, and quarries leased by private traders, and jointly managed, by the Company underwrote the drive for judicial reform. The governor summarized the relationship between the colonial office and the autonomy of Khasi polities in the following terms:

> the improvement in the condition of the inhabitants of the Khasi hills, the extension of cultivation, the development of mineral resources, the result of missionary education, the increase of traffic, and the cessation of all disturbances, both as among the Chiefs themselves and as between them and the inhabitants of the plains, afford evidence of the advantages that have attended the arrangements of 1835, whereby the Khasi hills was taken under the management of a British Agent, and a practical control exercised in a greater or less degree over the several Chiefs who were at that time either subdued or gave in their adhesion to the British Government.[12]

Despite the intended rearrangements, *Syiems* in the Khasi hills and *Dollois* in the Jaintiah hills continued to hold considerable economic and political influence, and the amplification of their authority was crucial for the smooth operation of colonial governance and trade. The governor general indicated that the judicial reforms meant that the Khasi hills were to be treated as a British territory so far as the 'rule of law' was concerned.[13] The place of the 'rule of law' in this complex relationship between the government and the political heads in the Khasi hills needs to be further understood in light of the presence of private traders and missionaries as influential economic, social, and political actors.[14]

Not long after Mills' report was published, another deputation was sent to the Khasi-Jaintiah hills, this time by the Revenue Department. It immediately followed the transfer of power from Company to Crown rule.

---

[12] Ibid., 114.

[13] Ibid., 111–112.

[14] The manner in which the colonial state in the hills engaged with missionaries, captured eloquently by Andrew May in his book, clearly shows that far from simply being colonial agents, missionaries were often considered recalcitrant road blocks to imperial sovereignty. See Andrew J. May, *Welsh Missionaries and British Imperialism: The Empire of Clouds in North-East India* (Manchester: Manchester University Press, 2012).

The report, dated 14 October 1858, was prepared by W. J. Allen who was a member of the Board of Revenue. The governor of Bengal revised and sanctioned the recommendations in March 1859.[15] The most significant parts of this report concern the discussions over private trade in the hills: particularly that of Henry Inglis.

Henry Inglis was the son of George Inglis a private trader and proprietor of a joint-stock company that owned leases in limestone quarries in West Khasi hills in early nineteenth century. Inglis's company was involved in boundary disputes between Nongstoin and Langrin polities before David Scott charged with colonial legal contracts shored up jurisdictional authority for the EIC.[16] The intimacy between British commercial interests and colonial law and jurisdiction manifested in Henry Inglis's role in negotiations with *Syiems* following the rebellion of 1829.[17] With the establishment of Political Agency in Cherrapoonjee, Henry Inglis, also known as Harry Saheb, became assistant magistrate of the Khasi Jaintia hill district under Captain Lister his father-in-law.

The unchecked influence and power of Henry Inglis and his growing private trading enterprise had been a sore point for the company government. However, the advantages of his influence among *Syiems* outweigh the transgression of rules disallowing public servants to carry out private trade. It was in the second half of the nineteenth century that the colonial government took action against Inglis' monopoly due to increasing numbers of complaints in the courts against him.[18] Private traders unrelated to Inglis's company were threatened, intimidated, and thereby discouraged from working in the hills.[19] After being acquitted of all charges following the Dunbar Enquiry in 1948 Inglis was required to step down from his post as magistrate. A jurisdictional dispute between Assam and Sylhet in which a private trader was attacked on his journey to Cheyla from Sylhet drew the attention of the government of Bengal. The influence of Henry

[15] Home Political, 29 April 1859, nos. 75–79, NAI.

[16] May, *Welsh Missionaries and British Imperialism*, 200–201. See also Rita Dorothy Dkhar, *The Inglis and Company and the Lime Trade in the Khasi Hills* (PhD Thesis, Shillong: North Eastern Hill University, 1987): 303–330.

[17] Letter from T C Robertson C E Trevelyan, 28 February 1984, IOR/4/1506/59036, no. 38.

[18] Letter from Rev. Thomas Jones to Halliday, Secretary to the Government of Bengal, 9 October 1949, IOR/P/143/39, 24 October 1949, No.128; Petition 8 September 1948, IOR/P/143/30, 14 MARCH 1849; Petition 18 September 1948, IOR P/143/30, 14 March 1949, No.68.

[19] Mills, *Report*, 114.

Inglis over the *Wahadadars* of Cheyla was obvious.[20] Cheyla was rich in limestone and was jointly ruled by four *Wahadadars*, who belonged to one of four clans in the polity.

The Board of Revenue supported Allen's recommendations for judicial reform and found it necessary to curb the monopoly and political influence enjoyed by private traders such as Henry Inglis. In the interest of the colonial government, it was decided that different competitors seeking to lease lime quarries in the Khasi hills would be allowed and encouraged to trade. An earlier order 'prohibiting "aliens" entering the Cheyla district without the consent of the Wahadadars' was rescinded by the Commissioner of Assam, and the *Wahadadars* were to be informed that 'all persons in peaceful pursuits must be admitted without let or hindrance and that they will themselves be strictly responsible for any interruption of free intercourse between traders or travellers from other places or the inhabitants of the district'.[21] It was also stated that agreements for government-owned lime quarries that were due to be renewed in 1861 would be offered for lease at moderate rates, and unworked quarries would be leased out to traders unrelated to the firm of Henry Inglis.

An important political precedent that allowed the colonial government to curb the authority of local rulers and private traders alike followed in the wake of this report. A decision was made to not renew Henry Inglis' lease in Cheyla after its expiration in 1865. In addition, the colonial government pointed to its role as an intermediary between the subjects of the polity of Cheyla and the *Wahadadars*.[22]

Concerns raised by Allen continued to haunt the colonial government, and they resurfaced in a memorandum by S. C. Bayley, Chief Commissioner of Assam in 1879.[23] By curbing private trade, the memorandum stated, 'the whole difficulty of our obligations to the *Syiems* would come upon us at once in an aggravated form'.[24] The government had to find a way to negotiate both its commercial interests and its sovereignty. Monopolies possessed by Inglis and Co. created political and economic insecurity on the one hand, yet, on the other, curbing private trade

---

[20] Ibid.
[21] Ibid.
[22] Home Department, Political Branch, 29 April 1859, nos. 75–79, NAI.
[23] Foreign Department, Revenue A, 1879, nos. 23–25, NAI.
[24] Ibid.

entirely was not considered to be a commercially viable option. The situation in Cheyla generated elaborate discussions on the nature of colonial presence in the hills.

In 1883, different departments and tiers of the colonial government honed in on the *legal questions* that were at the heart of trade, property, and political relations in the hills. The Revenue, Foreign, and Legislative departments entered deliberations in which it was stated,

> It is needless to discuss the question as one of pure law. The Wahadadars are a treaty-making power, and except for the pressure which we can put on politically, are not subject to our civil jurisdiction. But nonetheless we can scarcely, in regulating our own action in the matter, altogether repudiate the legal aspect of the engagement.[25]

The *Wahadadars* were only connected to the colonial state through treaties and were thus outside of its civil jurisdiction. Further, the government was concerned about the legal liabilities arising out of the nonrenewal of the lease to Inglis and Co., as well as the implications of the transfer of the right to manage quarries away from the *Wahadadars* and to the colonial government.

The Revenue Department was unable to trace records of agreements or leases between the three parties involved. Additionally, the law, at least according to earlier precedents, could not enforce the terms for nonrenewal of the lease. The Revenue Department proposed opening up the quarries to free trade and lifting restrictions on the use of the lime quarries for purely governmental requirements. The Legislative Department reiterated that the treaty signed in 1829, a copy of which was said to be missing, gave the EIC the right to extract unlimited quantities of lime from the Cheyla quarries. However, according to a separate agreement with Henry Inglis, the government had agreed not to use its rights to extract lime from the leased quarries, and this was in exchange for regular payment of four thousand rupees. Records of these payments were found.[26]

---

[25] A-Revenue-E, May 1883, nos. 1–7, NAI.
[26] Ibid.

New agreements were signed between the government, the *Wahadadars*, and Inglis and Co. This gave the government rights over the management of the quarries, with payments of half the profits made to the *Wahadadars*. The quarries were leased to Inglis and Co. under terms described as 'prohibitory'. The government stated that they did not 'expect or intend' for Inglis and Co. to accept the renewed lease and its prohibitory terms at the expiry of their contract with *Wahadadars* in 1883.[27]

Private trade monopoly in the hills was at odds with colonial sovereignty, and the state found legal ways to renegotiate the relationship between the government, companies such as Inglis and Co., and the *Wahadadars*. Debates over jurisdiction between 1859 and 1883 demonstrate the intersecting strategies used by the colonial state to maintain its supremacy over private traders and over local authorities. The following sections will demonstrate how the renegotiated relationship was further consolidated. Notions of property, custom, and the customary rights of the *Syiems* were formulated within parameters defined by and enforced by colonial jurisprudence.

Custom and Jurisdiction

Local rulers in the different Khasi polities—*Syiems, Wahadadars, Sirdars,* etc.—were legally recognized as treaty-making powers. Their presence both legitimized and undercut colonial governance in the frontier hills. In the aftermath of 1857, an increase in conservatism in colonial governance produced a greater regard for local customs and for indirect rule. At the same time, colonial governance was more deeply entrenched across the entirety of the colony. Faced with several challenges to their sovereignty and legitimacy owing to powerful private monopolies in trade, or to rogue missionaries, the colonial government focused on reconstituting the role and status of local rulers. In this section, I examine the changes in the local structures of political privilege, shedding light on the complex relationship between Khasi *Syiems* and colonial authority.

The Queen's Proclamation of 1858 stated,

---

[27] Ibid.

we know and respect the feelings of attachment with which the Native States of India regard the lands inherited by them from their ancestors and we desire to protect them in all rights and connected therewith subject to the equitable demands of the State, and we will wish that generally in framing and administering the law, due regard be paid to the ancient rights and usages and customs of India.[28]

By upholding custom, the colonial state emerged as a paternalistic but dominant political authority. For instance during the codification debates in Punjab utilitarian principles of law we sidelined. Colonial administrators showed a concern for collective rights in land and property, and they emphasized that among agricultural communities in Punjab, customs were embodied in practices not ancient texts. As Neeladri Bhattacharya has demonstrated, in Punjab custom and cultural pluralism was the new rhetoric of colonial power and legitimation.[29] In Bengal, on the other hand, the liberal discourse of custom was used as an umbrella term that connected capital, labour, and property. Pro-ryot advocacy was an outcome of the deeper entrenchment of colonial governance within agricultural communities. Customary practices were identified as liberal and politico-economic.[30]

Both Punjab and Bengal were directly-ruled territories and important political and economic centres. The frontier hills in the north-east were important too, but neither the conservatives nor liberals had that much of a stake in defending either indigenous rulers or colonial conquest, not least because, officially, the Khasi hills were a non-British territory. In the Khasi hills where customs were never codified, the loosely defined relationship between British courts in Sylhet and Assam, the office of the Political Agent in the Khasi Hills, and the politico-judicial forums headed by the chiefs produced specific forms of governance and relations of authority. The following section will discuss the jurisdictional disputes between the heads of different polities in the Khasi hills.

[28] Brian Bonhomme and Cathleen Boivin, eds., *Milestone Documents in World History: Exploring the Primary Sources that Shaped the World, 1839–1941*, vol. 3 (Dallas: Schlager Group, 2010), 1004–1005.
[29] Neeladri Bhattacharya, 'Remaking Custom: The Discourse and Practice of Colonial Codification', in *Tradition, Dissent and Ideology: Essays in Honour of Romila Thapar*, eds. R. Champakalakshmi and S. Gopal (New Delhi: Oxford University Press, 1996), 20–51.
[30] Sartori, 'Liberal Discourse'.

A dispute between the *Syiems* of the Rambrai and Nongstoin polities at the border of the Khasi and Garo hills provides an excellent example of the interstices of colonial jurisdiction and the role of local rulers. According to depositions given by villagers, records indicated the existence of practices such as the payment of tributes to one or the other *Syiem* interchangeably, in intervals of several years depending on which of the *Syiem*'s agents came to collect.[31] This indeterminacy was neither a sign of ignorance nor of a lack of knowledge as to their own jurisdictional authority. The vagueness concerning who was the precise juridical head was a result of interchangeable, or sometimes shared, local authority.[32] The failure to identify a single sovereign was dismissed as 'conflicting', and boundaries that were imposed were favourable for mapping colonial jurisdictional and sovereignty.[33] Kar's study of contracts between joint-stock companies and tribal communities is useful here. Although *posa* was not a term used in the Khasi hills to describe the various forms of tribute obligations between the state and communities, Kar's analysis of *posa* is useful for pushing further an understanding of the complex landscape of political economy, governance, and custom in the Khasi hills. To use Kar's words, the 'general economy of contracts' was set in motion in the Khasi hills by David Scott early in the century. In addition, the presence of men like Henry Inglis blurred the lines between private trade and colonial governance, despite efforts by the EIC government to separate the two.

In the second half of the nineteenth century, the reformulation of contracts and the specific focus on custom and customary authority offers an insight into the varying strategies of the colonial state to maintain a stronghold in the frontier hills. In the following pages, I will discuss three instances of disputes that were extensively debated by the colonial government. These cases contain clues as to how to understand the nature of authority and ruler-subject relations subsumed under colonial law.

Mylliem was a polity in the Khasi hills into which the colonial station of Shillong was carved. It was split into two jurisdictional polities— Mylliem and Khyrim—following the rebellions that began in 1829.

---

[31] Board of Revenue Papers 48, file no. 8/100, ASA.

[32] Sanghamitra Misra has explored how the 'ascending and descending' nature of sovereignties facilitated shared jurisdiction in the district of Goalpara in northern Bengal. See Misra, *Becoming a Borderland*, 19–41.

[33] Board of Revenue Papers 48, file no. 8/100, ASA.

A long-standing dispute between these two polities reached the offices of the Viceroy and Governor General of India in 1876 for final deliberations.[34] A petition from the *Syiem* of Mylliem pointed out that certain villages at the border of the two polities were rightfully under his jurisdiction, but that they had been forcibly taken under the control of Khyrim. *Syiem* Han Manik Sing of Mylliem wrote in his petition that the disputed villages had been under the jurisdiction of Mylliem since the 1820s when *Syiem* Bor Manik had signed the first agreement with the EIC on behalf of the polity. These villages, the petition stated, were later entrusted to the *Syiem* of Khyrim as the result of an order issued by the Political Agent. Han Manik Sing's petition thus reveals an interesting jurisdictional puzzle: the villages in question had enjoyed periods of independence from both Khyrim and Mylliem.[35] The petition by the *Syiem* was written in English, and it was probably drafted by a *mukhtiar* or advocate, or transcribed and translated by a British official or one of the *Syiem*'s associates. The legal language and tenor of the petition, at any rate, indicated that the *Syiem* had received legal advice from an advocate (presumably one that he employed).[36]

The DC Khasi hills were the first to receive the petition, following which he ordered that the villages remain under the control of Khyrim. The petition was then forwarded to the Chief Commissioner of Assam who stated that the two *Syiems* had been in conflict over their respective jurisdiction for over twenty-five years, and the government did not have enough records to reach a final decision.[37] According to the Chief Commissioner, 'their jurisdictions varied from time to time, according to the personal influence of the respective chiefs'.[38] The written historical evidence, according to him, was conflicting, and the only source of customary opinion was oral evidence, which he described as 'all hearsay and of no value'.[39] He thus came to the conclusion that 'if the Syiem of

---

[34] Letter from Secretary to the Chief Commissioner of Assam to the Secretary to the Government of India, May 1876, Foreign General B, June 1876, nos. 197–200, Foreign Department, NAI.

[35] Petition from Hain Manick, Sing Syiem of Mylliem to the Government of India, Foreign General B, June 1876, nos. 197–200, Political Department, Simla, NAI.

[36] The *Syiem* must have been in contact with and associated with several legal representatives in the British station of Shillong, which had been carved out of his chieftaincy.

[37] Foreign General B, June 1876, nos. 197–200, NAI.

[38] Ibid.

[39] Ibid.

Mylliem has lost one or two villages, to which he had apparently nearly as much right as his rival, he has ... retained those which villages, which from their position surrounding the station of Shillong, will grow rapidly, and become in the future valuable property.[40] The Chief Commissioner pointed out his final decision to uphold the DC's orders was made to ease the functions of the colonial police in the British station of Shillong.[41] Importantly, he asserted that he based his decision on his personal judgment, and not on historical or customary grounds.

The confusion around this case was compounded by the fact that Mylliem and Khyrim had been a single polity until the 1829 rebellions, as discussed earlier. The Chief Commissioner stated that,

> the truth appears to be that Myllim and Khyrim were in former times nominally one state, the ruler of which was called the Rajah of Khyrim. But this Chief held joint sway with another Chief, who ruled immediately over that portion of the State now known as Khyrim. The Myllim Chief overshadowed the lesser Chief of Khyrim, and the former was perhaps more influential, and the acknowledged head of society. But the lesser Chief of Khyrim held an *imperium in imperio*, and in the course of the years the interests of the two Syiems became more and more defined.[42]

The lack of written records regarding the boundaries between the two states of Mylliem and Khyrim during the time of their split was considered to be a serious setback for the colonial officials in establishing jurisdictional divisions. The DC's proceedings noted,

> there are no records nor is there any evidence to establish who was the last sole ruler, nor the exact period at which a separation took place.... What the respective jurisdiction of Seims of Khyrim and Myllim may have been in former times, it is impossible to determine; and I consider it not an unreasonable thing to assume, that at first in the primitive era

---

[40] Ibid.
[41] Ibid.
[42] Letter from Secretary to the Chief Commissioner of Assam to the Secretary to the Government of India, May 1876, in Foreign General B, June 1876, nos. 197–200, Foreign Department, NAI.

of the Khasi mountaineers, which may with safety be reckoned to have obtained previous to the advent of the British government which dates from 1826, the rulers were not divided; but held a joint sway and this in a erasure accounts for Bor Manik having been styled Syiem of Khyrim, for he was evidently the only ruler in the country called Khyrim which included Myllim, who was known in 1829 to the British Government, his brother ruler [sic] the ruler of Khyrim proper remaining then in the background.[43]

In his enquiries the DC revealed that the 'rule of the Chief has extended to the subject rather than to localities' and this made 'questions connected with jurisdiction ... difficult of solution'.[44] Subjects' allegiance rather than territorial limits thereby defined the extent of Syiem's influence. This was at odds with the entire infrastructure of colonial sovereign jurisdictional authority defined by territorial boundaries.

The DC claimed to have compared written documentation, oral testimony, and 'strength of suffrages' to arrive at his decision.[45] Numbers, graphs, and maps were used as additional evidence. The number of inhabitants in the villages was not recorded. However, a show of hands in favour of one *Syiem* or another was recorded. Oral testimonies and interviews were reflected only sparingly in the official proceedings. Answers that did not fall within either/or category were not included in the record.[46]

In his petition, the *Syiem* of Mylliem argued that complexities arising from the plurality of jurisdictions justified his claim over the villages in question. The petition used a combination of customary and colonial legal logic to argue that the judgment that ascribed the villages to Khyrim was wrong. To prove his claim he stated,

[43] Proceedings of the Deputy Commissioner, Khasi Jaintiah Hills Shillong, 9 September 1875, Foreign General B, June 1876, nos. 197–200, Foreign Department, NAI.

[44] Ibid.

[45] Oral testimonies in the borders of Khyrim and Mylliem give ample proof of the absence of the idea of an indivisible sovereign. The depositions give evidence of shared and interchangeable allegiances. The villagers whose total number is not mentioned were gathered, and based on a show of hands, it was determined which side of the jurisdictional boundary they belonged to. Many such boundaries were established based on oral testimonies and on what was described as 'suffrage'.

[46] An interesting point that emerges from the evidence is that with the creation of the British station of Shillong, many labourers from Khyrim settled in the disputed village of Malki. Forming a majority in Malki, these inhabitants wanted the village to be transferred to Khyrim.

The six poonjees which the Deputy Commissioner has pronounced to
have belonged to Khyrim from older times were not so, can be proved
thus: that when some case of arson took place in the Maolenrie and
Mowshubuid poonjees the Seim of Khyrim Sing Manik who was then
independent should have decided them instead of the Political Agent
taking them up. In proof of this appellant produced a Bengali Roobokari
dated 1848. On the face of this the Dy Commr detached the poonjees
on the statement of some unfriendly inhabitants from appellant's jurisdiction to that of Khyrim. This is referred to in Dy Commr's decision
at page 15 copy enclosed .... Appellant grants that it is the custom in
the Hills to appoint Seims on the consent of the Ryots but if it be made
another custom to separate poonjees belonging to one Seimship from
time immemorial to another merely on the statement of some inhabitants, as has been done in the present case by the Dy Commr, great
confusion will arise. Any one Seim can induce a portion of the Ryots
to express some dissatisfaction against their rightful Seim and go to
another.[47]

The *Syiem* or the advocate he employed had found legal records that
showed that colonial jurisdiction and administrative interference had
punctured customs 'from time immemorial'. The *Syiem* of Mylliem thus
sought the interference of the colonial government to override custom to
defend his jurisdiction over the villages in question. He thus argued that
although there was a custom of ryots choosing their *Syiem*, in this case
only some—not all—of the villagers had been taken into consideration by
the Deputy Commissioner. This was a winning argument for the *Syiem*.

The Government of India ordered the retransfer of the six villages
from Khyrim to Mylliem's jurisdiction. The final decision by the government reinforced the argument made in the *Syiem*'s own petition quoted
above: that despite the customary rights of ryots or ordinary subjects
to choose their ruler, they could not be trusted to make the correct decision. The DC argued that he based his decision on customary usage in
which subjects had the right to choose their ruler. Conversely, the *Syiem*'s

[47] Petition from Hain Manick Sing Seim of Mylliem to The Government of India, Political
Department, Simla, Foreign Department, May 1876, in Foreign General B, June 1876, nos. 197–
200, NAI.

petition to the Viceroy and Governor General argued that his jurisdiction could be validated based on the physical location of the disputed village. At the highest level of colonial decision-making, the *Syiem's* argument was found to be more acceptable than the evidence presented by the DC.

The dispute settlement revealed that the rhetoric of custom was fluid and strategic for both the colonial government and local rulers. The proceedings showed that neither physical location of the villages alone nor the custom of subjects right to choose their ruler was deemed enough in determining the jurisdictional dispute between Mylliem and Khyrim. Ultimately it was the judgment passed by the colonial courts that determined jurisdiction. Although custom was not codified in the hills, the presence of colonial courts for the adjudication of civil disputes set precedents that became norms. If custom was praxis, the presence of colonial courts affected its texture, form, and applicability.

It appears from the petitions and correspondence that the Syiem's authority over inhabitants of villages in the polity had been contestable and shifting. Colonial jurisdiction superseded the flexibility in ruler-subject relations clearly visible in the dispute. The indeterminate and changing positions and allegiances of the villages to one or the other *Syiem* were not so much about shared sovereignty as it was about a relationship of accountability and flexibility in allegiance. The discussions reveal that it was acceptable for villages to choose their allegiance to both, neither, or one or the other of the *Syiems*. Yet following the colonial jurisdictional infrastructure, flexibility was overturned in favour of fixed jurisdictional boundaries over the course of the nineteenth century.

In a case recorded in 1877, a village called Marbisu, made up of many smaller villages, renounced its allegiance to the chief of Mylliem and sought independent status. Marbisu was described as a village made up of many small villages. According to a government order, Marbisu was given three years to determine whether it wanted to be under the *Syiems'* jurisdiction or preferred to be under the direct management of the British government, to which it would pay taxes. At the end of the three years, the villages reaffirmed their demand for independence. A plebiscite was held by the District Commissioner 'with the result that 149 votes were recorded in favour of the village remaining under British management and 39 votes in favour of the village becoming again subject to Syiem of

Mylliem.[48] The *Syiem* once again used the British courts to petition for restoration of 'his sovereignty over his revolted subjects'.[49]

In a letter to the Foreign Department, the Chief Commissioner stated that he could not 'contemplate a return to the primeval barbarism of separate independent villages'.[50] The focus of both the colonial government and the *Syiems* fell on revenue and jurisdiction, and not upon the customary rights of their subjects. The nature of the decision-making process in the colonial office suggests that locally constituted customs and usages could be completely ignored or suppressed by the practical imperatives of jurisdiction and revenue. In a letter from the Foreign Office to the Chief Commissioner, it was argued that although there were independent villages in the hills, there were not any that were so close to the station of Shillong. Further, they stated that there was no reliable evidence that Marbisu had ever owed allegiance to the *Syiem* of Mylliem. Thus, it was decided not to enquire into the matter further, and instead to offer the *Syiem* monetary compensation.[51] In the case of Marbisu, the colonial state's ruling not only dismissed the rights of the villagers who demanded independent status, but also those of their former chief who had been responsible for collecting customary levies. The location of Marbisu was close to the colonial station of Shillong and directly administering it would be easier than the other independent villages scattered across the hills. Administrative convenience was considered more important than different customary claims.

In a separate dispute over ten villages at the border of the Khasi hills and Assam, the focal point was the location of villages along the hill-plain frontier. Between 1855 and 1856, ten villages were placed under the jurisdiction of the *Zamindar* of Kamrup in Assam. The DC of the Khasi-Jaintiah hills stated that 'many of them [the villages] in former times were

---

[48] From Secretary to Chief Commissioner to Assam to Secretary to Government of India, 4 July 1877, in Foreign Department Political Branch, October 1877, nos. 301–304, Foreign Department, NAI.

[49] Ibid.

[50] From the Chief Commissioner of Assam to the Secretary to the Government of India, Foreign Department, 4 July 1877, in Foreign Department, Political Branch A, August 1877, nos. 295–296, NAI.

[51] From the Under Secretary to the Government of India, Foreign Department to Chief Commissioner of Assam, Foreign Department, Political Branch A, nos. 295–296, NAI.

included in the Khasia Hills, to which they geographically belong.[52] The Khasi *Syiem* who claimed jurisdiction over these villages wrote a petition that highlighted numerous complaints made by the inhabitants of the disputed villages against the fact of their attachment to Kamrup in Assam. The *Syiem* emphasized two points in his petition on retransferring these villages to his jurisdiction. First, the inhabitants of the villages were ethnically Khasi; and second, the *Syiem* feared that because of the trouble faced by ryots under the jurisdiction of Kamrup, the inhabitants of the transferred villages would leave to work in other parts of the Khasi hills.[53]

Correspondence between officials of the Revenue Department in 1865 showed that there were several more complaints against the Zamindar of Kamrup, a man who was described as 'grasping and avaricious, and under the influence of his dependents'.[54] The colonial government found evidence against the *Zamindar* for oppression and extortion. This led to the annulment of his lease, and the villages were transferred back to the Khasi hills jurisdiction. This decision authorized the *Syiem* to regain the powers that had been appropriated by the *Zamindar*: namely, taxation and the right to manage labour.[55] The order sanctioning the transfer from the Government of India stated that 'the tract now in question has been for some years administered as part of the Kamrup District, a bona fide doubt exists as to whether it is really included in that district. Looking into its geographical position, *its physical features and the race of its inhabitants*, it is evidently part of the Khasi Hills'.[56] Geography and ethnicity overlapped in the order to justify the transfer of these villages to the Khasi hills.

It is to be noted that in 1875 Khasi hills had been included within the administrative province of Assam. The Legislative Department pointed out that the government's most pressing problem with respect to this

[52] Letter from DC of the Khasi-Jaintiah Hills to Assistant Secretary to the Chief Commissioner of Assam, 4 June 1875, in Home Judicial A, September 1875, nos. 209–211, Foreign Department, NAI.
[53] Petition from N. Shillong Sing, Seim of Nongpoh, January 1862, in Home Judicial A, September 1875, nos. 209–211, NAI.
[54] Letter from Deputy Commissioner of Revenue to Commissioner of Revenue, Assam, dated 20 February 1865, in Home Judicial A, September 1875, nos. 209–211, NAI.
[55] Ibid.
[56] Letter from Secretary to the Government of India to the Chief Commissioner of Assam, dated 15 September 1875, in Home Judicial A, September 1875, nos. 209–211, NAI (emphasis added).

case, and numerous others like it, was the 'confusion of law in force in the two districts and the differences in those laws'.[57,58,59]

In a letter to the Foreign Department in 1877, the Chief Commissioner of Assam noted, 'Lord Dalhousie's government in 1853 declared that it was not the intention of Government to extend its interference in the affairs of the petty Khasia chiefships'.[60] The different cases discussed above demonstrate that colonial non-interference in 'customary affairs' was neither practical nor desirable. The susceptibility of customs to change was as much a political imperative for both the colonial state and local authorities. The frontier hill inhabitants did not feature in colonial correspondence as legal subjects of the British Empire. Yet, their voices were crucial to changes in legal and jurisdictional governance. As protestors, petitioners, lobbyists, voters, and disruptors inhabitants were central actors in the shifts that induced reformulation of authority and ruler-subject relations in the Khasi hills.

The influence and reach of colonial courts in Cherrapoonjee, Sylhet, and Assam pervaded deep into the remote villages in the hills. The forms of engagement included consultations with rulers and village elders, depositions and interviews of village inhabitants, and the survey and military operations. The courts were flooded with petitions from frontier inhabitants who brought various complaints and disputes that were unprecedented in the first half of the nineteenth century. The court in Cherrapoonjee received numerous petitions on disputed successions of chiefs not only from the *Syiemship* of Cherra, but from other Khasi polities as well, where the political agent previously did not have a role in terminating a succession dispute. This change is examined in the next section. First, the section shows the change in contracts signed with *Syiems* that underpinned the role of the colonial state in succession disputes. This is followed by an exploration of different disputes about customs of succession and their outcomes.

---

[57] Ibid.
[58] Home Department, Judicial Branch, November 1875, nos. 68–69, NAI.
[59] Legislative department to Home department, 18 August 1875, in Home Department Judicial Branch A, September 1875, nos. 209–211, NAI.
[60] From the Chief Commissioner of Assam to the Secretary to the Govt. of India, Foreign Department, 4 July 1877, in Political Branch A, August 1877, nos. 295–296, Foreign Department, NAI.

Changing Contracts, Rulers, and Customs

The interference of colonial magistrates, officials, and judges in jurisdictional and boundary disputes discussed earlier shows the ways in which the colonial authority was overdetermined in dispute resolutions that involved more than a single polity or independent villages. The contractually and ritually defined hierarchy between the colonial government and the *Syiems* in a context where no other polities were involved was achieved strategically through succession disputes. In the second half of the nineteenth century, the colonial government introduced a new form of contract that enabled the involvement of the colonial state in the customary and civil disputes in polities, even when no bilateral conflicts were involved. Mills's and Allen's reports set the tone and provided the legal framework that underpinned the revised contracts, or *sanads*. Redefining the rights of the *Syiem* in relation to subjects of the hills was one such way. The *Syiem*'s property and land rights, rights to issue taxes, and his other political and judicial functions all came under scrutiny. The non-existence of land tax, for instance, was earmarked.[61] The emphasis on the quasi-judicial and non-proprietary nature of the *Syiem*'s authority gave an impetus to colonial sovereignty in the hills.

Property rights on land, rights to issue taxes, and other political and judicial functions exercised by the *Syiems* were examined by W. J. Allen in his report, discussed in detail in an earlier section. The Government of Bengal responded to Allen's report by claiming it had the right to dispense 'wastelands' in the hills that had been ceded by the British. Stating that it was necessary 'to prevent Cossyah Chiefs, Sirdars, elders and other village authorities, from alienating large tracts of land in their Districts in favour of Europeans or other persons not being Natives of the Hills without the knowledge of the Officers of the Government'.[62] Accordingly, the 'Chiefs and people of the semi-independent and dependent states' were notified by the district official 'that the Government will not recognize the grant of any land in any of those States without his [colonial] sanction'.[63] This

---

[61] Home Political, 29 April 1859, nos. 75–79, NAI; his source for this information was named as the Political Agent to the north-east Frontier, Captain Lister.

[62] W. J. Allen, *Report on the Administration of the Cossyah and Jynteah Hill Territory* (Calcutta: Bengal Hurkaru Press, 1858).

[63] Home Political, 29 April 1859, nos. 75–79, NAI.

particular response to Allen's report made a significant departure with respect to interference in civil disputes and customary practices of succession alongside the reformulation of property in the hills.

Introduced in 1875, the new form of agreement or *sanad* signed between the *Syiems* and the colonial state formalized the shift in the status of the *Syiem* from a political sovereign in his own right, to the elected, nominal head of a polity without any proprietary rights to land in that polity. Paragraph three of the new standard *sanad* stated,

> in the case of my using any oppression or of my acting in a manner opposed to established custom, or in the event of my people having just cause for the dissatisfaction with me, the Chief Commissioner of Assam may remove me from my Chiefship and appoint another Chief in my stead.[64]

The revised *sanad* stated that the *Syiems* were to be accountable to the Chief Commissioner of Assam. Further, that the *Syiems* must act according to custom.

No formal act or regulation was issued to introduce the new *sanads*. A succession dispute provided the necessary opportunity for the government to change existing contracts to suit the colonial project. The precise definition of the role of the *Syiem* became a point of contention in 1866 when the chief of Mawiong (spelt variously as Mowiyam or Mauwiong) was murdered, leading to riots in that polity. According to the existing agreements, the British could not interfere in civil or criminal jurisdiction in situations involving only the subjects of a single Khasi state. The Sessions Judge of Sylhet dismissed the case on grounds that Mawiong was not in his jurisdiction. The Lieutenant Governor of Bengal, however, believed the District Commissioner stationed in Cherra had the right to adjudicate this case as per a separate agreement with the *Syiem*. This agreement gave the Governor of Bengal the right to interfere in cases between the *Syiem* of Mawiong and his subjects, as well as the power to remove him if his subjects were dissatisfied with his rule.[65] This case set

---

[64] Foreign Political B, January 1875, nos. 166–167, NAI.
[65] Letter from Secretary to the Government of Bengal to the Officiating Registrar, High Court of Judicature, Fort William, 13 September 1866, no. 2166T, in Foreign Political, Programmes for October 1866, ASA.

a precedent whereby the colonial state emphasized its right to remove a *Syiem* on the grounds of his subjects' dissatisfaction. This new *sanad* served as the template for future agreements that would be made not only with Mawiong, but with all *Syiems* on their succession.[66]

The new *sanad* was first formulated for Mawiong before it was applied to other Khasi states.[67] In exchange for tributes, revised arrangements offered *Syiems* 'an income which they could not have themselves realised', in addition to 'protecting them from the arts of unscrupulous speculators'.[68] The new form of agreement also included the 'cession of limestone and other minerals, and of waste land'.[69] The *sanads* were officially instituted from 1875, a year after the passage of the Scheduled Districts Act that consolidated non-regulation areas across the colony under provisions. The Act allowed for local governments to extend any law in existence in British India to the hill districts as deemed necessary. The legal reorganization of so-called backward areas went hand in hand with revisions in the terms of contractual relations between erstwhile autonomous rulers of the region.

---

[66] From the Secretary to the Government of India, Foreign Department, to the Junior Secretary to the Government of Bengal, January 1867, no. 189, in Foreign Political Programmes for March 1867, no. 13, ASA. Additionally, this letter specified that the term Raja be substituted for *Syiem*. Nomenclature particularized the *Syiems'* role, distinguishing them from the Rajas who held proprietary rights and were often defined as sovereigns. This distinction was particularly noticeable because the letter attempted to define the *political* status of the DC vis-à-vis the *Syiems*.

[67] The previous agreement executed with the chief of Mawiong contained no such a clause, but the agent to the north-east frontier stated that there was a separate agreement in which these terms had been agreed upon, a copy of which was supposedly misplaced and unavailable to the officers. A different agreement that had been made with another polity was therefore used as an example. Separate agreements signed with different polities usually contained different clauses. This fact was glossed over in the assertion to gain the rights to Mawiong's mineral resources. After deliberations between different departments, the government revised the arrangements in order to satisfy both the *Syiems* and the colonial state. The *Syiems* were offered an income which they could not have themselves realized, and were offered protection from private traders. In exchange, the government would collect tribute, which it believed would increase over the years, and contribute towards administering the hills and public works. See, Letter from the Agent to the Governor General, North-East Frontier and Commissioner of Assam to the Secretary to the Government of Bengal, dated May 1867, no. 171, in Foreign Political, August 1867, no. 25, ASA; the same topic is discussed again in a letter from the Secretary to the Government of Bengal to the Secretary to the Government of India, Foreign Department, August 1867, no. 240T, in Foreign Political, August 1867, no. 25, ASA.

[68] From Agent to the Governor General, North-East Frontier, and Commissioner of Assam, to the Secretary to the Government of Bengal, May 1867, no. 171, in Foreign Political, August 1867, no. 25, GSA; the same subject is also discussed in a letter from the Secretary to the Government of Bengal to the Secretary to the Government of India, Foreign Department, August 1867, no. 240T, in Foreign Political, August 1867, no. 25, GSA.

[69] Ibid.

The new *sanads* stated that succeeding chiefs were no longer permitted to 'alienate the property of the state'.[70] This clause was supported on the grounds that the *Syiem* 'is elected for life or during good behavior. He is not even entitled to land revenue'.[71] The *sanads* thus strengthened the position of the government against private trade monopolies and placed legal restrictions on *Syiems*' right to state and negotiate the terms of engagement with private traders. As elaborated at the start of the chapter, private trade monopolies and the influence of private traders on local rulers were heavily discouraged in earlier decades. The new contracts would thus ensure security against the ambitions of private traders and their local allies.

The historical role of the *Syiem* in the different polities had been much more expansive before being circumscribed by the new *sanads*. In the early nineteenth century, they had led armed rebellions against the Company, made diplomatic decisions, oversaw trade, and headed local judicial and legislative councils. Official colonial literature from the period, including statistical accounts, descriptive and historical accounts, scientific literature on physical and political geography, early treaties and correspondence, and oral histories all account for the political role of the *Syiems*.

Between the middle of the nineteenth century and the first decade of the twentieth century, the absence of proprietary rights in land became a focal point for the colonial government in determining the *Syiem's* political status. According to the social structure that was ordered through a matrilineal kinship structure, land was either communally owned by one or more clan groups (*Ri raid*) or owned by the clan members (*Ri kynti*). Under such a system, a *Syiem's* power was not based on—nor was it understood as a product of—models of individual proprietorship. The new meanings invested in political authority by the colonial state, and the disputes that led to those meanings, informed, and reshaped ruler-subject relations that had hitherto been based on kinship obligations and matrilineal descent.

---

[70] Letter from L. Johnson, Secretary to the Commissioner of Assam to Secretary Government of India, Foreign Political B, January 1875, nos. 166–167, NAI.

[71] L. Johnson, Secretary to the Commissioner of Assam to Secretary Government of India, NAI.

Colonial records on succession disputes in Khasi polities provide a glimpse into the relationship between property and authority, the naturalization of a gendered authority, and the strategic malleability of custom. Succession of *Syiems* in different polities produced many disputes settled by colonial law. It demonstrates the way in which law and law courts were instrumentalized by local elites in their battles over succession to *Syiemships* and the strategic use of custom. In the official correspondence on succession disputes and petitions from competing heirs, one finds inflections of the contested nature of customs, and the malleability, and marginality of certain customs over others. The following pages show this fraught relationship between custom, customary authority, and colonial governance.

An unprecedented number of petitions on succession disputes poured into British courts from the mid-nineteenth century onwards. W. S. Clarke, DC Khasi-Jaintia hills, was given the task in 1878 to hold official enquiries into issues of succession after his predecessor Col. Bivar's actions were reported, which involved changes in procedures such as introduction of popular elections.[72] Clarke was asked to report on several aspects of succession eligibility, such as the candidate's residence and family, the candidate's specific relationship to the preceding *Syiem*, and whether female candidates were eligible for election.[73] He collected information from all *Syiems* except Rambrai. He noted,

> according to one and all of them, the office of the Syiem is not elective, but hereditary, going in regular succession to the senior nearest male relative, not being a son or a nephew, the son of a brother, or a cousin on the fathers [sic] side, but the brother by the same mother, or, failing brothers, the son of mothers [sic] sister, or son of a sister or failing heirs male, to the senior nearest female relative on the mother's or sister's side.[74]

---

[72] Colonel Bivar, the DC of the Khasi-Jaintiah hills in the 1860s, conducted popular elections in which all adult males voted to elect the *Syiem* U. Hajon Manik. See, Foreign Political, October 1878, no. 1337, NAI.

[73] Foreign External A, February 1902, nos. 88–110, NAI.

[74] From W. S. Clarke, Deputy Commissioner of the Khasi-Jaintiah Hills to the Secretary to the Chief Commissioner of Assam, dated 15 October 1878, no. 1337, sub-enclosure 5, enclosure 3, prog. No. 108, in Foreign External A, February 1902, nos. 88–110, NAI.

Furthermore, he stated that the candidates 'must be of a native state for which he stands, must be a blood relation of the last Syiem, and that females are eligible for the office of Syiem'.[75] Clarke emphasized that although the elective system was not customary, in many polities elections were held to ascertain candidates' eligibility.[76] In the Chief Commissioner's opinion, 'too much stress was laid on the remark by Captain Clarke' about the existence of popular elections. Although Clarke's report emphasized the hereditary nature of the line of succession, a second report emphasized instead the role of the *darbar*, backed by the Chief Commissioner, in electing a new *Syiem*. According to this second report, popular election was only held on the request of the *darbar*, which, along with the *Syiem*'s family, nominated the *Syiem*.[77] The varied opinions presented in the correspondence and reports throughout the second half of the nineteenth century as to what really was the custom of succession points to the role played by colonial governance in establishing the scope of custom, as well as in directing its malleability.

A particular succession dispute in the state of Cherra led to the government instituting a formal codification of the procedures for the appointment of a *Syiem*. After disturbances and riots broke out following the election of U Chandra Singh, who succeeded as *Syiem* of Cherra in 1901, the British government grew anxious to disentangle the complex principles and practices—political and customary—surrounding the role of the *Syiem*. The fact that the military had been deployed to settle the

---

[75] Ibid.

[76] In another dispute, educational qualifications provided the grounds for electing a *Dolois* of Nartiang in the Jaintiah hills. A petition from the contender who had received a higher number of votes than the elected *Dolois* claimed that the customary law of elections should prevail over the new law. The petition threatened the colonial office that encroaching upon the civil rights of the inhabitants would lead to the British government losing the favour of the people. The government dismissed the petition and upheld the decision of the local authorities, with a side note that although the governor general agreed that some degree of educational qualification was useful, it was nevertheless not necessary in areas such as the frontier hills. The approval of the *darbar* was considered to be more important. However, in order not to subvert the authority of the Chief Commissioner and other local officials, the Governor General dismissed the petition while at the same time acknowledging its validity. See, Memorial from U. Kat Sardar of Nartiang to the Viceroy and Governor General of India in Council, in Foreign External A, April 1886, nos. 189–197, NAI; and Letter from Assistant to the Government of India, Foreign Department to the Chief Commissioner of Assam, dated 29 March 1886, in Foreign Department External Branch A, April 1886, nos. 189–197, NAI.

[77] Extract from the Proceedings of the Chief Commissioner of Assam in the General Department, no. 3189-P, dated 21 July 1901, in in Foreign Department, External A Branch, February 1902, nos. 88–110, NAI.

disturbances caused concerns among the higher echelons of the colonial office, whose members continued to describe the Khasi polities as 'native states'.[78] This particular dispute attracted the attention of parliamentarians in the House of Commons as late as 1912, long after the issue had been settled in 1903.[79] A British parliamentarian asked the Secretary of State for India to explain why,

> the practice of electing the Syiem of the Cherra state in the Khasi and Jaintiah hills district ... was abrogated in the election of the present Syiem, and has caused dissatisfaction among twelve clans in the district; and whether, having regard to the immemorial custom among the people of the Cherra State to elect their chief by the votes of the representatives of the twelve clans, there is any reason why this custom should not be allowed in future?[80]

His question was shot down with an assertion that the government of India was satisfied that the method of election was 'in greatest accordance with the ascertained usage of the people'.[81] This was not wholly accurate: customs were being selectively applied to circumstances, and local colonial officers played a large role in that process.

The Cherra dispute started in 1901, and can be traced through the various reports and official correspondence that the case elicited, as well as through the records of engagements and discussions with the heads and elders of the villages and localities in the polity. The Chief Commissioner of Assam had overruled the order of the DC of the Khasi hills to appoint Roba Singh as *Syiem* who had been nominated by the *darbar* (comprises the heads of twelve clans). Instead, the Chief Commissioner ordered the appointment of another contender, U Chandra Singh. The Secretary of State to the Government of India in his turn then ordered the annulment of U Chandra's appointment following public outcry and protests, as well as extensive debate within the colonial government. The Chief

[78] Correspondence between Viceroy Lord Curzon, Secretary to the Government of India H. S. Barnes, and J. B. Wood, Military Department, December 1901, in Foreign Department, External A Branch, February 1902, nos. 88–110, NAI.

[79] Foreign General B, February 1912, nos. 356–357, NAI.

[80] Foreign General B, NAI.

[81] Ibid.

Commissioner who had authorized the appointment insisted, however, that a reversal of the decision and the ensuing re-election would weaken colonial political authority. He wrote,

> in dealing with a rude and uncivilized tribe like the Khasias, it is dangerous to weaken the hands of the controlling authority with whom they are brought into immediate contact. It is highly dangerous to afford such a people any inducement to believe that an order of the Chief Commissioner can be set aside by persistent intrigue backed by a display of force.[82]

In his statement, the Chief Commissioner referred to the informal but steady support given by the influential missionary John Roberts to Roba Singh, who, along with his family faction, had converted to Christianity. In the Chief Commissioner's view, protests by inhabitants of Cherra against U Chandra overlapped with political intrigues, at whose heart were groups of Christian converts. The fact that the inhabitants had protested very specific actions of the *Syiem* U Chandra was sidelined.

An emphasis on custom in colonial discourse led to debates on questions about past precedents and their validity. The role of the heads of twelve clan members in electing the *Syiem* from among the nominees became a point of contention.[83] Defending his appointment of U Chandra Singh, the Chief Commissioner argued that DC Captain Herbert had acted in haste by appointing U Roba Singh.[84] He argued that the council or the *darbar* which had elected U Roba Singh had not been summoned by the colonial government, and therefore, its proceedings were invalid. In these debates, the focus in the correspondence moved ever farther away from the root cause of the protests against U Chandra.[85]

Petitions brought by groups of inhabitants of the Cherra polity indicate several causes for the protests. They were not convinced of the *Syiem*'s

[82] Foreign Department, External A Branch, February 1902, nos. 88–110, NAI.

[83] H. S. Barnes, Secretary to the Government of India, Foreign Department, December 1901, in Foreign Department, External A Branch, February 1902, nos. 88–110, NAI.

[84] Letter from Chief Commissioner of Assam to the Secretary to the Government of India, Foreign Department, December 1901, in Foreign Department, External A Branch, February 1902, nos. 88–110, NAI.

[85] Foreign Department, External A Branch, February 1902, nos. 88–110, NAI.

ability as a political and spiritual leader.[86] Another petition—reportedly signed by two thousand people—argued that the male elders of the villages were the best judges of their ancient rights and established custom, and they should therefore be consulted before any final ratification of the said appointment was made.[87]

The demands of petitioners and protesters in the riots were not discussed in the official correspondence. One of the petitions claimed that U Chandra had not held a single *darbar* to consider public questions or to try cases since his appointment, thereby neglecting his political duty as a *Syiem*. Instead, he demanded a poll tax of one rupee from each male adult, and that he would impose a fine of fifty rupees and a pig on those who would refuse to pay the poll tax, and this would serve as a punishment against those who had not wanted him elected. In addition, men employed by the *Syiem* threatened the dissidents with torture and the forfeiture of their properties.[88] They stated that the *Syiem* introduced taxes on trade and 'exorbitant market tolls ... contrary to the usual practice'. The petitioners further claimed that he had re-instituted gambling houses for his 'personal enjoyment, and with a view to obtain money by unlawful means'.[89] The *Syiem* had also placed restrictions on the use of forests, only allowing his followers to cut wood freely from the reserved forests. The petitioners also claimed that the *Syiem* had disrupted religious ceremonies, and had engaged with witches and sorcerers, thereby devising means to offend the religion of those who opposed him and to bring about their ruin.[90] Yet official correspondence circumvented the political nature of the protests and debates over the political role of the *Syiem* so that the entire conflict could be framed in terms of custom and religion.

---

[86] Petition from R. Lumsyntiew, Mantri of Vougrum Clan and Other Inhabitants of Cherra to the Viceroy and Governor General of India in Council, dated 20 October 1901, in Foreign Department, External A Branch, February 1902, nos. 88–110, NAI.

[87] Memorial from the People of Cherra to George Curzon, Viceroy and Governor General in Council of India, in Foreign Department, External A Branch, February 1902, nos. 88–110, NAI.

[88] Petition from R. Lumsyntiew, Mantri of Vougrum Clan and Other Inhabitants of Cherra to the Viceroy and Governor General of India in Council, dated 20 October 1901, in Foreign Department, External A Branch, February 1902, nos. 88–110, NAI.

[89] Ibid.

[90] Lumsyntiew, Mantri of Vougrum Clan and Other Inhabitants of Cherra to the Viceroy and Governor General of India in Council, NAI.

The government viewed custom as a set of rules.[91] Although the Chief Commissioner tried to assure the officers at the central level that the protests were of no significance, they remained adamant and questioned his conflicting opinions on long-established customs. Viceroy Curzon insisted that in order to avoid the recurrence of disputes of this nature, the uniformity of custom should be ensured and local authorities should determine the exact procedures to follow, both in regular and in disputed successions.[92]

By ordering an immediate re-election in which Roba Singh was declared the new *Syiem*, the government placed a temporary check against rising public opinion surrounding the appointment of *Syiems* and the nature of their political role.[93] The DC however emphasized a significant breach in custom. His point was reinforced by the Foreign Office during their final deliberations: U Chandra Singh was the heir to the deceased *Syiem* U Hajon Manik. But the legitimacy of this deceased *Syiem* was itself under dispute. According to colonial correspondence U Hajon Manik had refused to perform the cremation rituals of his predecessor which was considered a breach of custom. Moreover, 'thirty villages did not consider him Syiem'.[94] The Foreign Office used this argument to invalidate U Chandra Singh's claim as U Hajon Manik's successor. Ironically, the final orders of the Viceroy upheld the principle of popular election—i.e., the method that had brought U. Hajon Manik into office in the first place.

In 1903, the same year that Roba Singh was appointed by re-election as *Syiem* of Cherra, a compendium of customs related to succession in every Khasi polity was published. *The Report on Succession to Syiemship in the Khasi States* by Captain D. Herbert, DC of the Khasi-Jaintiah hills, became the official guide for determining all the principle rules and differences across twenty-five Khasi polities.[95] What had begun as a debate

---

[91] Letter from Chief Commissioner of Assam to the Secretary to the Government of India, Foreign Department, dated December 1901, in Foreign Department, External A Branch, February 1902, nos. 88–110, NAI.

[92] From Governor General and Viceroy George Curzon to H. S. Barnes, Secretary to the Government of India, Foreign Department, dated February 1902, in Foreign Department, External A Branch, February 1902, nos. 88–110, NAI.

[93] Letter to the Chief Commissioner of Assam, no. 328 E. B, dated 11 February 1902, in Foreign Department, External A Branch, February 1902, nos. 88–110, NAI.

[94] Foreign Department, External A Branch, February 1902, nos. 88–110, NAI.

[95] The five principle points that Captain Herbert formulated in his report emphasized the uniformity of procedures and ascertained the specific procedures to follow in cases of dispute. In his report, the DC circumvented the political functions of the *Syiem* by strictly maintaining the customary nature of the procedures and the constitution of the office. The report was produced by

with the potential to increase public accountability and a broadening of the principles for electing *Syiems* eventually led to the codification of rules and practices in all Khasi polities that were based on selective usage and generalizations.[96] Significantly, the use of British judicial procedures and courtrooms as forums for debate and discussion inadvertently marginalized the role of women in positions of power, whether that role was to help determine a succession or serve as *Syiems* themselves, or even their very presence in the *darbars*.

The systematic marginalization of customs that emphasized the role of women in political and religious aspects of Khasi society can be traced in the extensive correspondence on a succession dispute in the Khyrim polity that took place between 1905 and 1906. Petitions poured into the colonial offices following the election of a *Syiem* who was a 'remote heir', but was nonetheless elected by a majority of the clan heads or *myntris* because other heirs had been disqualified for various reasons. Petitions from the disqualified candidates as well as from the *myntris* give access to several customary procedures that do not otherwise appear in the standardized principles published by Captain D. Herbert.

In 1905, the Assam government forwarded two memorials from two Khasi men, U. Shemuel and U. Borgusain, to the Secretary of State for India. Their petitions showed the preference that was given to some customs over others, and also contained clues as to why specific customs were sidelined. U. Shemuel was disqualified as an heir because he had converted to Christianity, while U. Borgusain's disqualification was for

collating information collected at *darbars* that were summoned in all the different *Syiemships* in the presence of the DC. The report noted an increase in what it defined as the electoral body. The number of *lyngdohs*, or priests, who could dismiss the *Syiem* only on religious grounds was reduced so as to include gradually a larger number of male representatives from the different clans. The increase in the electoral body varied in different polities. A further step towards 'strengthening the public will' came with the introduction of popular elections in which all adult males voted. The report maintained that the British government had the 'right of refusing to accept a person as Syiem whose appointment would be undesirable for any serious reason'. In support of this point, the Secretary to the Government of India stated, 'It must ... be clearly understood that the Government, as a Parliament Power, reserve an absolute discretion to reject any nominee, and that no succession is valid and complete until it has been expressly approved and confirmed by Government'. Thus, the report contained caveats to undermine the very same customary principles that it stated. See Foreign External A, July 1903, nos. 59–61, NAI.

[96] It is important to note that D. Herbert's published report continues to be referred to in the Khasi hills where the institutions of *Syiems* and *darbars* exist to this day. The report privileged some customs over others, and introduced some new ones.

the reason that he was not the most closely related individual to the last *Syiem*. Both petitions complained that Captain Herbert's findings on succession in the Khasi polities were incomplete and glossed over important aspects of custom.

U. Borgusain stated a number of defects in the official enquiries, and he pointed to that fact the last *Syiem* had persuaded Captain Hebert to restrict the line of succession to matrilineal descendants and to the descendants of his fourth sister, whose son was appointed as the next heir.[97] The petition stated that the *Syiem* did not have the right to choose a *Syiem*-priestess, who in this case was his sister. He wrote,

> in most Khasi states there are Syiem-priestesses who have similar functions as those exercised by the Syiem priestesses in the State of Khyrim and they are always the senior female members of the houses of the ruling Syiems, but in the course of the enquiry of Major Herbert into the custom of succession in those States, the status and functions of the Syiem-priestesses were not introduced and no mention was ever made of them as succession is always traced from the ruling Syiems on the female side and not in a converse way from the Syiem priestesses who are appointed from the house of the ruling Syiems and not the latter from the house of the former. An artificial importance was given to the position of the Syiem-priestesses in the succession enquiry of the Khyrim State, as without it, the late ruling Syiem could not achieve the object he had in view.[98]

This petition is important because it brings within the field of debate the role of the women in the family in determining succession. Borgusain pointed out that personal grievances and factional differences within the family had produced a distortion of custom. He wrote,

> When it is borne in mind that in the social custom of the Khasis an importance is given to female descent and female authority, the senior female members being regarded as the head of the household, the

[97] Memorial from U. Borgusain to the Secretary of State for India in Council, in Foreign Department, External Branch A, May 1906, nos. 35–38, NAI.
[98] Ibid.

position of the Syiem-priestesses and the functions discharged by them can easily be understood.[99]

Although Borgusain rejected the role allotted to the *Syiem*-priestess in Khyrim because it restricted the eligibility of the heirs from the extended family, he inadvertently revealed the significance of women in electing the *Syiem* in all Khasi polities. Yet official correspondence did not address women's role in the Khasi political structure at all.

From the outset, the colonial legal order precluded the recognition of female *Syiems*, and ignored the centrality of women in a socio-political system framed around matrilineal kinship. In discussions about custom, women's role was relegated to matters of descent and of the household. Colonial conceptions of property, rights in land, and political authority in the colony were formulated and developed through the agreements with the male elites of directly ruled provinces. Colonial legal order in the Khasi hills was established by identifying male heads who could serve as the signatories of the initial treaties. Further, innovations in customs concerning succession, such as the adult male franchise, undercut the socio-politico-religious authority of women in the Khasi hills. Borgusain's petition is evidence of the procedural marginalization of women during the nineteenth century.

Borgusain's petition invoked 'ancient custom' whereby clans were understood to be joint families, sharing in collective temporal and spiritual concerns and responsibilities. Confining succession to a particular house he believed only served to 'split up the clan, destroy its communal [sic] and create divisions in it as has proved now to be the case'.[100] He wrote,

All kinds of objections of any version of custom supported by evidence should have been admitted and a decision after a full consideration of all facts should have been given and appeals against the same allowed ... the authority of the ancient custom has been wholly repudiated by the introduction of distasteful innovations creating thereby

---

[99] Ibid.
[100] Ibid.

party factions and discontent among the members of the Syiem's family and the people of the state.[101]

In contrast, supporters of U. Shemuel indicated the need to reform customs, and to introduce changes, such as allowing the election of a Christian *Syiem*. A large number of inhabitants who were, presumably, themselves converts demanded that democratic principles be considered when electing the *Syiem*. Both petitions did not yield their desired results. The Government of India was satisfied with the initial decision that had been backed by sixteen *myntris*, namely that a third claimant named U. Dakhor had been rightfully elected. Religion—i.e. non-conversion— was declared to be an essential criterion for eligibility to the *Syiemship*.

The selective use of custom and the ability to exploit the malleability of custom gave the colonial state extensive control over the Khasi hills. There were two instances of succession disputes—one in Maharam and another in Cheyla—where the colonial government used their discretion to overhaul completely the existing structure of political authority.[102] Existing practices of multiple *Syiems* were overturned in order to make way for a single political head, even though Maharam traditionally had two *Syiems*, and Cheyla had four *Wahadadars* who were jointly elected to represent four respective clans. Was custom a rhetoric of colonial legitimation? Which customs served the political and economic security of the colonial state? If custom was praxis, what happened to it when it was selectively applied in different contexts by colonial and local rulers?

Laws governing property and succession were topics of extensive debate and legal analysis by political theorists and administrators throughout the nineteenth century.[103] Questions of property and jurisdiction, law and custom were integral to the ideological underpinnings of 'indirect rule' that was used as a strategy of governance in several princely states across the colonies.[104] In the second half of the nineteenth century,

---

[101] Ibid.

[102] Foreign Department, Political Branch A, May 1878, nos. 60–68, NAI; Foreign Department Political Branch A, August 1877, nos. 303–308, NAI.

[103] Sandra den Otter, 'A Legislating Empire: Victorian Political Theorists, Codes of Law and Empire', in *Victorian Visions of a Global Order: Empire and International Relations in Nineteenth-Century Political Thought*, ed. Duncan Bell (Cambridge: Cambridge University Press, 2007), 89–112.

[104] Karuna Mantena notes that Henry Maine's fears of the inevitability of the 'radical undoing of customary basis of village community under imperial rule' that would be the result of

Henry Maine's formulation of indirect rule was employed by colonial administrators as a methodological foundation to accumulate ethnographic information, and as an explanatory tool for customary bases of indigenous institutional frameworks. Clearly as this chapter demonstrates indirect rule was also a mode of organizing power, fragmenting resistance, and creating, conserving, and subordinating tribal political institutions.[105] In the Khasi hills indirect rule meant that law and custom were inextricably tied together through the operation of colonial courts and contracts, reports and enquiries, and mutual legitimation. Neither law nor custom represented liberal rights of frontier inhabitants. Together they formed pertinent tools of indirect rule.

atomized private property, led to his formulation of an alternative strategy, a solution in the form of indirect rule. See Mantena, *Alibis of Empire*, 135.
For a broad overview of the colonial policy of indirect rule in the princely states, see Barbara Ramusack, *The Indian Princes and Their States* (Cambridge: Cambridge University Press, 2003).

[105] See Mahmood Mamdani, *Citizen and Subject: Contemporary Africa and the Legacy of Late Colonialism* (Princeton: Princeton University Press: 1996).

5

'Tribes of Trees' and 'Economical Geology'

Narrating Space and People

In the frontier hills the movement of colonial law and the Christian civilizing mission in the early nineteenth century relied on discourses of primitivism.[1] Introduced in cartographic representations of the frontier and culminating in disciplinary studies on tribal anthropology, primitivism was not a singular theory but a shifting and varied ideological set of assumptions. The longevity of primitivism as a framework across centuries needs repeated emphasis to identify the tropes, assumptions, and ideas that continue to hold significant popularity. In this chapter I argue that an association between people and landscape characterized all forms of colonial knowledge on the Khasi hills throughout the nineteenth century. Ranging from universalist to culturalist articulations the primitive was a spatial-temporal trope of colonial knowledge ordering.[2] Together these ideas formed the racialized core of governance and domestication of the frontier hills. By centring the questions of knowledge production this chapter provides an important link between the politico-legal aspect

---

[1] Primitivism as a movement date back to the sixteenth century and was based on a logic separating people spatially and temporally. I don't intend to trace the genealogy of primitivism in the frontiers of colonial India or map its shifts. I identify the ways in which the discourse of primitivism informed colonial law and knowledge leading to the emphasis on certain forms of representation. Primitivism has been described a type of liberal ideology with four identifiable stages of development according to Uday Chandra. He argues that the Scheduled Districts Act 1874 was the first formal articulation of this ideological trend in policy to bring all tribal areas under a singular legal framework. My understanding of primitivism as it operated in colonial ordering of the north-east frontier hills differs from that is Chandra's. While Chandra's emphasis is on the category of the universal abstract primitive, I show how currents of the long-standing ideology of primitivism were differently deployed by administrators and knowledge makers throughout the nineteenth century. See Uday Chandra, 'Liberalism and Its Other: The Politics of Primitivism in Colonial and Post Colonial India', Law and Society Review, 47, no.1, 2015, pp. 135–166.

[2] See Prathama Bannerjee, *Politics*, 40–81.

Placing the Frontier in British North-East India. Reeju Ray, Oxford University Press. © Reeju Ray 2023.
DOI: 10.1093/oso/9780192887085.003.0005

of spatialization that forms the core of the book so far and the intricacies of lived experience through place-making discussed in the following chapters.

Ideas of the savagery of tribes provided justification for extra territorial jurisdiction in non-British territories of imperial India as shown in Chapters 2 and 3. After the 1857 rebellion ideas of primitivism were tied to a rhetoric of custom. As demonstrated in Chapter 4 the conservative focus on custom and indirect rule in fact created a more intrusive and fastidious approach to governance in the hills. Decades before the justification of empire involved an emphasis on governance through native institutions, discourses of primitivism informed colonial administrative and popular writing on the frontier hills. Through many variations primitivism informed a range of different governmental policies and disciplinary colonial knowledge that bound together space and people. The impact of the knowledge produced in the nineteenth century within this framework is resonant in the postcolonial hills to this day.

Colonial knowledge on the frontier hills represented the landscapes, plants, rocks, and people as quantifiable data. The hills provided rich 'fields' for scientists, botanists, geologists, anthropologists, and linguists. Scientifically mapped primitivism connected local knowledge with global circuits of knowledge, rendering space and its people as marginal and abstract.[3] The chapter illustrates efforts to domesticate the frontier hills by analysing the shifting foci of imperial knowledge over the course of the nineteenth century from geography, geology, and botany in the first half of the nineteenth century to ethnography and anthropology in the second half. I describe the links between these disciplines to show their commensurability in producing a frontier imagination. The conditions in which these treatises, journals, and reports were produced bear witness to the deeply local and contingent nature of the ideas that they converted into seemingly scientific and objective interpretations.

This chapter further underscores the entanglements between conquest through law and colonial knowledge production. The first chapter

---

[3] Charles Darwin is credited with conceptualizing the temporal evolutionary chain in which the primitive was connected to the modern. However ideologues of primitivism were not all Darwinists. Botanist Dalton Hooker was a friend of Darwin and disagreed with him in many respects. His work is studied in this chapter and provides a glimpse of the vast and varied forms in which primitivism was employed as an analytical framework.

has discussed in detail the travel narrative of Sir Henry Walters, a judge of the Sylhet sessions court. He travelled the Khasi hills in 1828 at the peak of the treaty-making exercises led by David Scott. His travel narrative was published in Asiatic Researchers in 1832 and used an amalgam of geographical technologies, geological study, and personal observations. He used maps, figures, and sketches to supplement his informative text. Walter's account is an excellent example of overlapping roles of colonial officials in the frontier—a judge with military training could sometimes be a geographer and dabble in geology as well as ethnography. Thomas Fischer's military and cartographic surveys used repeatedly in jurisdictional disputes have also been discussed earlier in the book. Colonial officials had multiple interchangeable roles—military officers, administrators, ethnographers, and anthropologists contributing to commissioned or non-commissioned production of a vast amount of literature on the frontier hills.

Literature on the Khasi hills with varied foci, whether a botanical treatise by Dalton Hooker or Thomas Oldham's geological study, characteristically provided information on inhabitants in rich ethnographic detail.[4] In addition to a reliance on local knowledge, these studies reflect a large amount of cross-referencing. For instance, a botanical study drew from ethnological accounts, a geological study included elements of missionary work on language and grammar, and an anthropologist relied on comparisons with communities in Europe and archaeology. Such overlap implied that the relationship between writing about botany, geology, language, or geography was one that similarly located the people as analogous to 'tribes of trees' or as part of 'economical geology'. Such accounts could be commissioned or non-commissioned but together informed colonial governance and policy.

The colonial geographic imagination readily made associations between landscape and the status of colonial sovereignty—defined by law and jurisdiction. In this imagination, landscape and people were defined

---

[4] Chandra points out that ideologues of primitivism such as Edward Tuite Dalton, Henry Lewis Morgan, and Fustel de Coulanges were keen on separating and locating the non-Aryan or pre-Aryan among the 'wild' in Asia, Africa, and Americas. They were keen on safeguarding these primitive islands in the sea of modernity and at the same time improve their economic and educational standards. Colonial administrator-anthropologist Edward Tuite Dalton was the author of the much-cited *Descriptive Ethnology of Bengal* published in 1872 considered to be a classic example of primitivism.

in tandem by such corresponding geographical and legal discourse.[5] The hill tribal was thus produced as a spatio-temporal category. The association between geographical and legal discourse informed other disciplinary discourses such as botany, geology, ethnography, and anthropology. The mosaic of inhabitants in the north-east frontier of Bengal, among others, was represented as hill tribals, a category defined by the relationship between people and the landscape and location.[6] These were inhabitants of forests and hills stretching into the Sylhet plains. As some scholars have suggested, such settlements were products of territorialization of pre-colonial and colonial states.[7] Colonial spatiality produced tribal spaces by processes of land reclamation and settlement in Sylhet marking the hills as outside (before) and plains as inside (after) of colonial law.[8] Hence, the association between land, location, and people was both product of historical processes that bound people to land, and a

---

[5] See Lauren Benton, *A Search for Sovereignty: Law and Geography in European Empires 1400–1900,* (Cambridge: Cambridge University Press, 2010), 1–39.

[6] As I have stated earlier, the colonial construction of 'tribe' itself varied across the colony. The category 'tribal' has been examined by several scholars. For instance, James C Scott argues that tribes were 'barbarians by design' and evaded imperial and civilizational forces as a political response. Tribes, he points out, were not genealogically or culturally homogeneous units but created as such by the colonial state in order to exert control over them. See James C Scott, *An Upland,* 209; Scott's idea of a coherent anarchist community of tribes has been rejected by many scholars. In directly administered and agricultural areas tribes were idealized as aboriginals and sedentarized for agricultural labour and revenue. See K Sivaramakrishnan, *Modern;* Also see Kavita Phillip, *Civilising;* Prathama Bannerjee, *Politics;* The image of the 'noble savage' was invoked in Ootacamund and other hilly areas where colonial stations were built and a resolution for creating European enclaves demanded such definitions. See Judith Kenny, 'Climate'; In the north-west frontier province, tribes were characterized as inherently aggressive, trained in warfare since childhood, fanatical, and brave. See Sameetah Agha, 'Inventing a Frontier: Imperial Motives and Sub-Imperialism on British India's North West Frontier, 1899–98', in ed. Sameetah Agha and Elizabeth Kolsky, *Fringes of Empire,* (2009) pp. 94–114; Radhika Singha has pointed out that the colonial state attempted to create an encompassing typology of tribal and incorporated diverse groups like the Thugs, Pindaris, Bhils, and others. Such classification enabled distinguishing between the productive revenue yielding subjects and the non-revenue yielding subjects. More significantly, such classification enabled legalized coercive measures against certain groups, culminating in the Criminal Tribes Act of 1871. Sangeeta Dasgupta has pointed out in her most recent book that even the lasting classificatory category of tribe was informed by changing meanings and ideas of both colonial and colonized including members of the tribes. See Dasgupta *Reordering.*

[7] David Ludden, 'Investing', 64–94; K Sivaramakrishnan, *Modern;* Sumit Guha, *Environment and Ethnicity in India 1200–1991,* (Cambridge: Cambridge University Press, 1999).

[8] K Sivaramakrishnan has argued that the production of 'tribal places' informed representations of communities as inextricably tied to their lands. Curbing shifting cultivation, regulating patterns of settlement and production, and extending colonial control over forests confined communities in the Nilgiris to terrains of 'backward agriculture'. K. Sivaramakrishnan, 'Geographies of Empire', in *Historical Anthropology,* ed. Saurabh Dube (New Delhi: Oxford University Press, 2007): 298.

representational strategy of colonial spatiality. The following sections will demonstrate the interconnections between centralized and decentralized, official and unofficial, commissioned and improvisational, colonial and indigenous forms of knowledge.

Geography, Botany, and Law

The characterization of Khasis as hill tribals was a product of colonial territorialization and legal imperatives that began in the late eighteenth century to control raids in the frontier of the newly formed collectorate of Sylhet in 1778.[9] The creation of a discriminatory terminology and notions of criminality to inhabitants of the frontier hills of Garo, Khasi, and Jaintia was directly linked to the discourse of primitivism. Differences and shifts in characterizations did not preclude the underlying racialization through tropes of primitivism. While several official sources into the late nineteenth century continued to use characterizations such as 'barbaric' and 'marauders' among others to define the 'hills tribal', there were a few sources that distinguished the specifics groups of Khasis as possessing 'independent disposition' and having 'high moral character'.[10] In Bengal and central and southern India, historians have argued that tribal communities were identified as resources vis-à-vis the productivity of their lands and their labour.[11] Inhabitants of the Khasi hills were neither legal nor revenue subjects of the British in the early nineteenth century, whereas resources of land and forest were highly prized as capital. Through contractual agreements with local Chiefs and rulers, both land and labour were converted into resourceful commodities without the need to establish direct rule.

In the nineteenth century scientific and non-scientific imaginaries produced these hills as mysterious yet inviting, outside of British political territory yet constituting resources of the Empire. The Khasi hills were incorporated in large-scale scientific projects in the mid-nineteenth century such as prominent British botanist Joseph Dalton Hooker's study

---

[9] See Chapter 1.
[10] See Walters' characterization of the inhabitants of the Khasi hills as towering morally over the neighbouring people of the plains. In H Walters, 'Journey' ,501; also discussed in Chapter 2.
[11] See Kavita Phillip, *Civilising*; Also, see K Sivaramakrishnan, *Modern*.

of natural science of the Himalayan mountain ranges. The hills were included in this study due to its location, as both the lower and easily accessible ranges of the Himalayan mountain chain, and because of Company stations like Cherrapoonjee and Shillong that were deemed safe and salubrious for Europeans. J D Hooker published his study in two volumes of *The Himalayan Journal or Notes of a Naturalist in Bengal, the Sikkim and Nepal Himalayas, the Khasia Hills etc.* in 1854 and dedicated it to close friend and associate Charles Darwin.[12] He travelled between 1849 and 1851 to several places in the north-east frontier including Sikkim, the Sunderbans in Bengal, the Khasi-Jaintia hills, the Garo hills, and Cachar. His project was funded by the Crown, covered three years of his research travels during which he documented the flora and fauna in extensive detail. He also acquired collections of large numbers of botanical specimens that were brought back to England for the Royal Gardens at Kew.[13]

Joseph Hooker's work exemplifies the confluence of experience and epistemology in scientific narratives of travel. The representation of his travel and research appears sequentially as he travelled across the frontier hills within British territories and across frontier spaces. His narrative was not confined to botanical study only, as he described scenery, noted his impressions of people and places, and narrated strange and familiar encounters. He described the essence of his experience in the following way, '[throughout] our travels in India, we were struck with the undue reliance placed on native names of plants, and information of all kinds; and the pertinacity with which each linguist adhered to his own crotchet as to the application of terms to natural objects, and their pronunciation. It is a very prevalent, but erroneous, impression, that savage and half-civilised people have an accurate knowledge of objects of natural history, and a uniform nomenclature for them.'[14] His statement juxtaposed two important facets of colonial civilizational discourse that informed the

---

[12] J. D. Hooker, *The Himalayan Journal or Notes of a Naturalist in Bengal, the Sikkim and Nepal Himalayas, the Khasia Hills etc.,* (Kew, 1854), e-book.

[13] David Arnold has dedicated a chapter in *Tropics* to discuss the impact of botany to the construction of the idea of 'tropics' and focused largely on J D Hooker and his work *The Himalayan Journals.* According to Arnold the book represented one of the most accomplished examples of scientific travel narrative and also marked the decline of the disciple of botany and 'of the once prolific genre of travel writing about India, and the waning of travel's centrality to colonial science'. See David Arnold, *Tropics*, 185–224.

[14] Hooker, *Himalayan*, 450.

scientific and geographical framework of his work. One was the idea that local knowledge was inaccurate or simply dated as it was a product of 'half-civilized' and 'savage' communities. This understanding enhanced the significance of and legitimized his representations, inferences, and conclusions. Ironically, the second was a reliance on local knowledge to build, develop, and legitimize all forms of colonial knowledge that were crucial for the Empire. Hooker's narrative gives further access to the already established premise that new knowledge produced on this region was both imperfect and improvisational.

Hooker's narrative was informed by colonial geographical discourse and identified the places he visited including the Khasi hills with specific botanical discoveries, offering a particularity to the hills. This was also done by revising errors in botanical knowledge of plants found in the vicinity. For instance, he wrote, '[before] the geographical features of the country north of Silhet were known, the plants brought from those hills by native collectors were sent to the Calcutta garden (and thence to Europe) as from Pundua. Hence Silhet mountains and Pundua mountains, both very erroneous terms, are constantly met with in botanical works, and generally refer to plants growing in the Khasia mountains.'[15] A map that Hooker used was copied from an original submitted by him to the office of the Surveyor General of India in 1851 which showed his route along the Khasi hills. The copied map revised Hooker's original map by correcting names, and adding information in spaces left blank in the previous one.[16] It showed a triangulated cross-section of the hills marked by rivers, names of some polities and villages. The copied map focused on the route taken by Hooker and his major stops, prominent among them Cherrapoonjee a colonial centre and Mawphlang known for its sacred grove.

Geographical mapping of this botanical tour was also considered to be a study of history of the place. The origin and growth of botanical specimens were read as history of a particular place including England.[17] Making a botanical distinction between Indian flora and that found in the hills Hooker described it to be 'of Malayan character; by which is

[15] Hooker, *Himalayan*, 415.
[16] See Figures 5.1a and 5.1b.
[17] Hooker, *Himalayan*, 416.

meant the prevalence of brilliant glossy-leaved evergreen tribes of trees (as *Euphorbiaceae* and *Urticeae*), especially figs, which abound in the hot gulleys, where the property of their roots, which inosculate and form natural grafts, is taken advantage of in bridging streams, and in constructing what are called living bridges, of the most picturesque form.'[18] The 'tribes of trees' that Hooker identified were brought under the purview of science in the same way the tribes of people living in these hills were brought under the influence of civilization. The correlation between tribes of plants and people and the confluence of science and enlightenment was reiterated in Hooker's narrative. He pointed out the processes through which 'blood thirsty' Khasis were brought into submission by 'extreme penalty' and the *force of law*. Yet, he claimed not all local authorities were 'quiet under our rule' and as both a warning and an explication of his own vulnerable position there he emphasized that 'various parts of the country are not safe to travel in'.[19] This was not only an indication that his scientific enquiries were limited to the areas considered safe in the Khasi hills and the frontier in general. The regions considered safe were those under Chiefs who were in diplomatic agreements with the colonial government. The reliance on and assistance of local inhabitants and Chiefs was indispensable to Hooker's famous work.

J. D. Hooker's Route across the Khasi Jaintia hills

Scientific projects like Hooker's were weaved out of and were thereby reflective of the legal and political context of the places he visited within the Empire (see Figures 5.1a and 5.1b). Geographical discourse on frontiers was not tangential to such scientific enquiry but a central feature of it. Landscapes were identified as constituting not only unknown plants, but equally strange societies. The frontier landscape was thick with knowledge to be domesticated and consumed.

Although the underlying aim of the book for Hooker was to gain prominence as a botanist like his father, a large part of the narrative described different aspects of his travel including detailed descriptions of

---

[18] Ibid.
[19] Ibid.

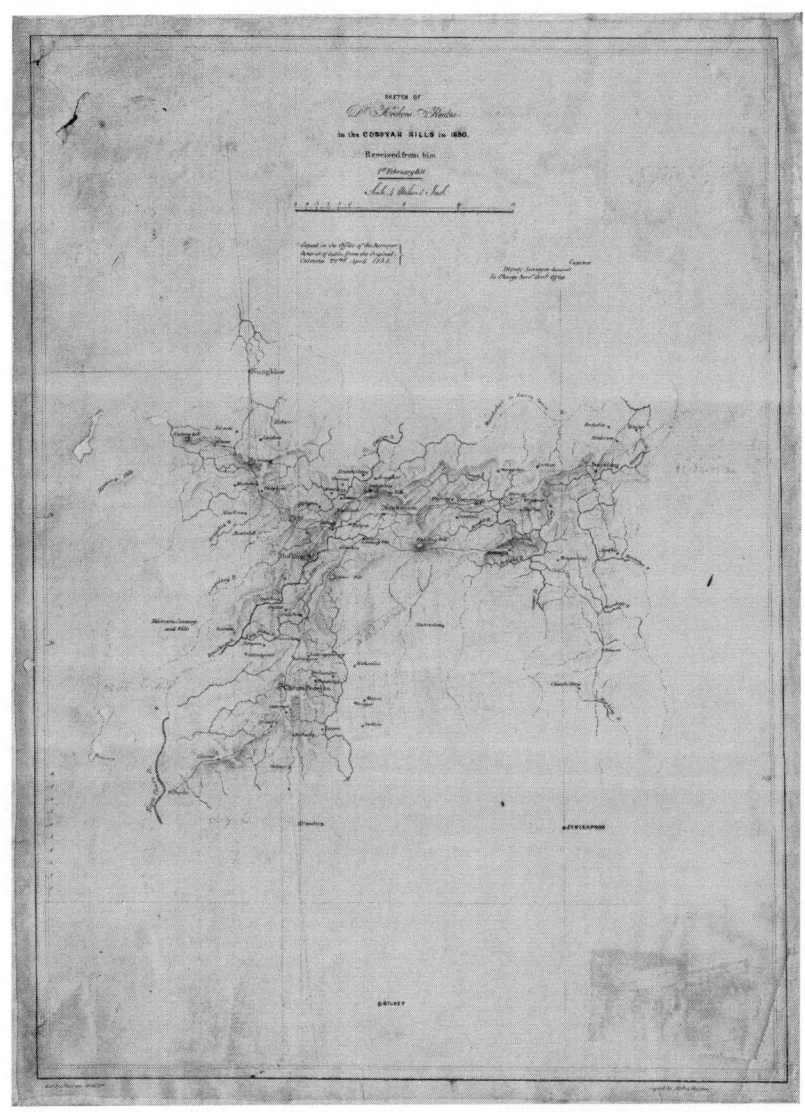

Figure 5.1a J. D. Hooker's Route across the Khasi Jaintiah Hills. National Archives of India.

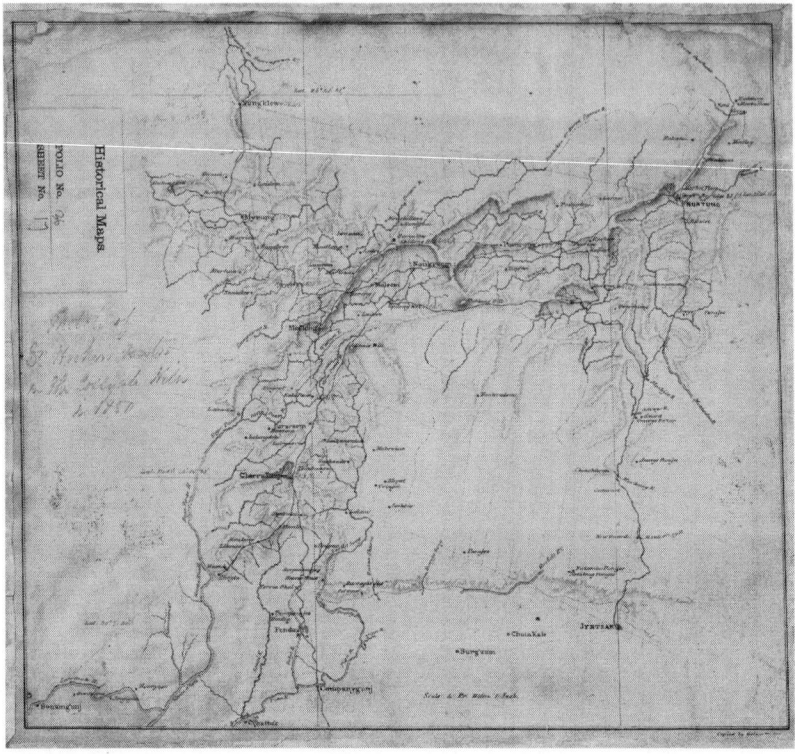

Figure 5.1b Revised map of J. D. Hooker's route across the Khasi Jaintia Hills. National Archives of India.

people and places.[20] Throughout the two volumes of Hooker's journal, names of places he visited were changed or spelt to suit the English reader. Toponymy is an important aspect to consider here because the local naming of different features of the landscape, rivers, and often villages carried meanings that were tied to a broader conception of peoples' relationship to these elements. Encounters with inhabitants of the hills and Hooker's impression of them reflected a racialized scientific classification. Hooker wrote:

---

[20] For a discussion of the personal context, achievements and goals of Hooker see Arnold, *Tropics,* 186.

The Khasia people are of the Indo-Chinese race; they are short, very stout, and muscular, with enormous calves and knees, rather narrow eyes and little beard, broad, high cheekbones, flat noses, and open nostrils ... We found the Khasias to be sulky intractable fellows, contrasting unpleasantly with the Lepchas; wanting in quickness, frankness, and desire to please, and obtrusively independent in manner; nevertheless we had a head man who was very much the reverse of this, and whom we had never any cause to blame.[21]

Racially embedded physiographic descriptions were juxtaposed with favourable and unfavourable 'personality' types—helpful, frank, unpleasant, intractable, and so on. This was followed by a description of their houses, clothes, and religious ceremonies. Historical landscape features such as large and small monoliths spread across the Khasi and Jaintia hills were divorced from their relevant context and described only in relation to Stonehenge in Britain. Such comparisons are found in many accounts of the hills, and their emphasis confirmed the universality of primitive societies and their crucial link in the civilizational chain.

Hooker's map shows his travel into the Jaintia hills. Just as in the Khasi hills, Hooker's stops included significant political centres such as Nartiang. In describing Nartiang he once again noted the presence of 'impressive stone monuments' and emphasized how these stones were as relevant to the landscape as to the social norms of the inhabitants. He wrote that Nartiang, 'contain[ed] a most remarkable collection of those sepulchral and other monuments, which form so curious a feature in the scenery of these mountains and in the habits of their savage population.'[22] He described the precise location of these stones such as within a 'grove of trees, occupying a hollow' but glossed over the social and political relevance of such ritual centres. Half-hearted ethnographic notes were complemented with brief descriptions of the nature of the stones. 'The flat slabs', he noted, 'were generally of slate or hornstone; but many of them, and all the larger ones, were of syenitic granite, split by heat and cold water with great art. They are erected by dint of sheer brute strength, the

---

[21] Hooker, *Himalayan*, 419–420.
[22] Ibid., 429.

lever being the only aid. Large blocks of syenite were scattered amongst these wonderful erections.'[23]

In another commonly found trope of primitivism, Hooker claimed that the Khasis did not have a religion but believed in a supreme being and deities of groves, caves, and streams. He described his visits to sacred peaks of Shillong and Mawphlang, and important religious and political centres like Khyrim in which he compared local practices as paganism. He described the renowned village of Mawphlang in a narrative style reminiscent of early travellers in the hills:

From a hill behind Moflong bungalow, on which are some stone altars, a most superb view is obtained of the Bhotan Himalaya to the northward, their snowy peaks stretching in a broken series from north 17 degrees east to north 35 degrees west; all are below the horizon of the spectator, though from 17,000 to 20,000 feet above his level. The finest view in the Khasia mountains, and perhaps a more extensive one than has ever before been described, is that from Chillong [sic] hill, the culminant point of the range, about six miles north-east from Moflong bungalow. This hill, 6,660 feet above the sea, rises from an undulating grassy country, covered with scattered trees and occasional clumps of wood; the whole scenery about being park-like, and as little like that of India at so low an elevation as it is possible to be.[24]

In his description of locations across the hills, Hooker pointed to marked differences with the rest of the colony. Instead he pointed to particularities of unknown botanical species and comparisons with an earlier time in Europe. The hills were particularly significant in Hooker's study because they represented that transitional and subtle overlap of temperate and tropical climate, flora, and landscape. David Arnold has pointed out that Hooker employed a scientific approach 'to trace through changes in temperature, humidity, elevation, and aspect the subtle shift from tropical to temperate ... The changing moods of the sky, the brilliant colours of the landscape, the taste and smell of exotic fruits—these were too important to be left to poets or painters.'[25] Yet, unmoved by

---

[23] Ibid., 429.
[24] Ibid., 429.
[25] Arnold, *Tropics*, 200.

Darwin's evolutionary perspective on temperate plant species finding their way into tropical climates, Hooker maintained that the tropicality of genera was sustained in the highest elevations, thereby emphasizing the tropicality of the Himalayan hills.[26] This project, like most other scientific and non-scientific, colonial, and imperial accounts of the hills, offered a dual perspective. On the one hand it emphasized difference, and on the other served to incorporate the hills of the universal evolutionary civilizational fold.

Racial characterizations of inhabitants of the hills complemented the description of their habitation and surroundings inscribed with reference to civilizational hierarchies. Scholars like Prathama Bannerjee and K Sivaramakrishnan have differently argued that the production of tribal spaces through colonial spatialization imposed a temporal backwardness to those places.[27] Prathama Banerjee has demonstrated that temporality was superimposed on territoriality and through this 'an-other land could be understood as an-other time'.[28] For colonial administrators, policy-makers and knowledge creators re-presentation were the only means by which those occupying another time and place could be included in the narrative of modernity. In the process, the construction of people as 'primitive' and 'backward' transformed them from being subject-agents of different histories to being objects of a totalizing representational knowledge.[29] Sivaramakrishnan has demonstrated that representations achieved consistency by colonial intervention in the production of social space through botanical surveys, tea plantations, timber conservancy, etc.[30]

---

[26] Ibid., 201.
[27] Banerjee has employed Hegel's philosophical articulation of 'spatialized temporality' to understand the founding moment of colonial modernity. Prathama Bannerjee, *Politics*; K Sivaramakrishnan, *Modern*, 34–119.
[28] Prathama Banerjee, *Politics*, 7.
[29] Ibid.
[30] K Sivaramakrishnan, 'Geographies', 298.

'Economical Geology', Language, Ethnology

The production of knowledge was concomitant with the ordering of landscape and simultaneous representation of inhabitants.[31] The hills were rich in mineral resources. The colonial government, private traders, and joint-stock companies were invested in the hills through agreements with various local authorities. There was no estimate available to colonial administrators of the extent of coal, lime, iron, and other products available for extraction. The second half of the century saw an intensification of extractive uses of natural resources in the hills and swift transformation in definition of sovereign authority in the hills in terms of property.[32] The hills, constituting its land, mineral resources, timber, pasture, and even roads and rivers were reconstituted as property. This is evident not only in the centralized politico-judicial processes discussed in the last chapter, but in commissioned and decentralized research and knowledge production.

One such specific study commissioned by the government was Thomas Oldham's *On the Geological Structure of Part of the Khasi Hills, with Observations on the Meteorology and Ethnology of That District* (see Figure 5.2). The sub-title boasted an encompassing scientific study of the land, skies, and people, and intentionally or not pointed towards what Khasi cosmology comprises. This study was conducted by the Superintendent of the Geological Survey of India beginning in 1851 and published in 1854. In his words the study examined 'the principal facts in the physical structure of these hills, and to indicate some of the more important economical considerations springing from this structure.'[33] The area that this study covered was limited to the Sohra chieftaincy and around the station of Cherrapoonjee and certain parts of the Jaintia hills.

This study drew upon Dr Mc Clelland's study of rocks and fossil shells of these hills in 1835 and discussed further the location of deposits, the age of the rocks, and its quality. Oldham declared that his study was an

---

[31] This process was sharply evident in the north-east frontier into the postcolonial period and is at the root of several conflicts between national and provincial identities.

[32] See Chapter 4.

[33] Thomas Oldham, *On the Geological Structure of Part of the Khasi Hills, with Observations on the Meteorology and Ethnology of That District* (Calcutta: Bengal Military Orphan Press, 1854), 2.

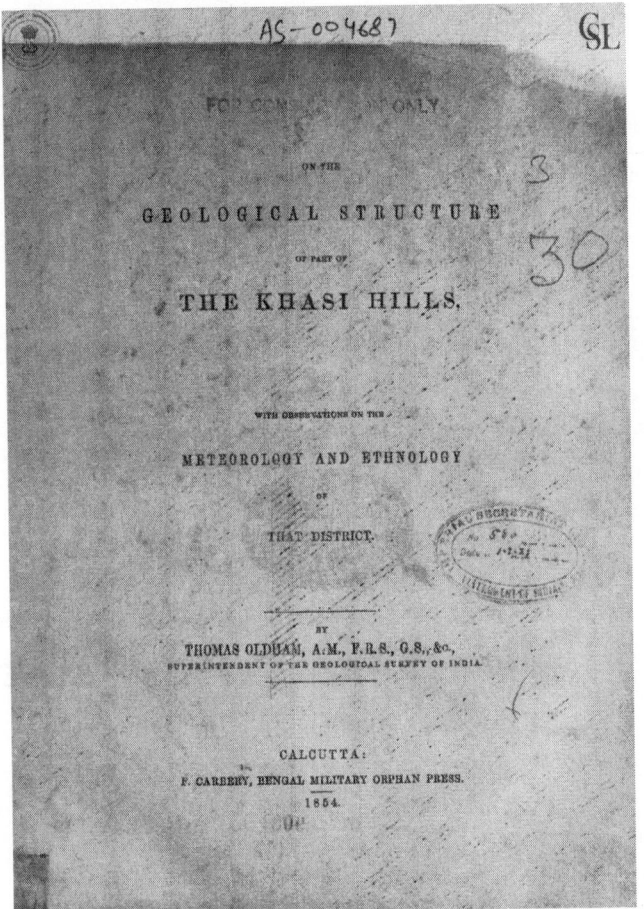

Figure 5.2 Thomas Oldham, On the Geological Structure of part of the
Khasi Hills, (Calcutta: Bengal Military Orphan Press 1854).

'economical geology' with double significance. First the importance of
this work in scientific research. Second its implications for revenue generation. He wrote about the importance of locating 'the great source of
supply for the large demand of Calcutta and other markets.'[34]

Oldham's project was published years before W J Allen's report that
raised alarm at the monopoly of Inglis and Co. on the entire range of lime

---

[34] Ibid., 53.

quarries along the base of the hills. His calculations of the quantity of limestone potentially available for extraction and trade were very useful for the colonial government. Curtailing the monopoly of European traders and enhancing government revenue were motivated by this kind of information. Oldham's work was crucial in attracting multiple investors and challenges the monopoly of Inglis and Co.

The study of 'economical geology' also focused on the most cost-effective means by which coal could be transported from mines in the higher hills to the Sylhet plains. Oldham followed up on a study conducted in 1842 on the same subject and noted that nothing was done to facilitate the transport of coal from Sorah thereafter. He pointed out that coal was carried down the hills by coolies on their back. The estimated profits from the amount of coal traded or used would not be enough to justify the undertaking of setting up a mixed transit system using trucks for half of the way and machinery for the other. Yet, he maintained that the coal found in the Sorah was of superior quality compared to coal in mainland India especially for the manufacture of gas. He also stated that '[the] manufacture of iron appears to have been carried on in these hills from time immemorial; and by all the tribes inhabiting them'.[35] The long history of iron manufacturing in the hills was found to be rare. The extensive employment of women labourers in iron manufacturing was also given a special nod. Oldham wrote, 'the manipulative skill of some of the Khasi women, acquired by long practice in these operations, is very great; and a very small proportion of the ore is lost in the washing'.[36] Oldham's account incorporated the figure of the local inhabitant as extractor of resources, imbued with local knowledge of production and as central to 'economic ecology'.

Concluding his discussion Oldham reiterated two of the goals underlying this publication. He wrote,

if this outline should lead to further investigations, and tend to direct the attention of any to this district, and so increase the number of its visitors, I am satisfied, that whether profit may be derived from such investigations or not, much pleasure will result from a sojourn amidst the

[35] Ibid., 70.
[36] Ibid., 72.

lovely scenery and among a people presenting many interesting points for study, and many excellent traits of character; and in a most salubrious climate.[37]

Attracting European travellers and investors to these hills was clearly one aim of this book. But just as in Hooker's botanical study, Oldham's geological treatise included ethnographical descriptions. People as objects of knowledge were inextricable to the scientific nature of the landscape. Sivaramakrishnan has noted that, in analysing the objectifying gaze of colonialism, scholars have mostly examined separately consequences of colonial spatialization and ordering of bodies. The confluence of people and landscape classification he demonstrates were dual processes found in other designated tribal areas such as the Santhal Parganas of Bengal and in the Nilgiris in Tamil Nadu. In the Khasi and Jaintia hills the representation of a tribal became inextricably tied to frontier imagination. This imagination was based on interdisciplinary cross-referencing.

Evident in accounts discussed in this chapter and others is the large amount of cross-referencing. For instance, a botanical study drew from ethnological accounts, a geological study included elements of missionary work on language and grammar, and an anthropologist relied on comparisons with studies on groups and communities in Europe, on archaeology, and on travelogues. Such overlap implied that the relationship between writing about botany, geology, language, and geography was one that similarly located the people as analogous to 'tribes of trees' or as part of 'economical geology'.

Oldham's study included three appendices each highlighting distinct colonial interests. The first marked the different elevations above sea level of various localities in the Khasi hills. The second further demonstrated the use of measurement devices including barometers, hygrometers, thermometers, pluviometers and anemometers. In this section he discussed the climate and meteorology of Cherrapoonjee and Sorah polity overall. Oldham was asked to add to discussions on British sanatoriums in the north-east and in his opinion by virtue of excessive rain Sorah was deemed less suitable than other stations in the hills.[38] At the same

---

[37] Ibid., 77.
[38] Thomas Oldham, On the Geological Structure of Part of the Khasi Hills, ix.

time Oldham Cherrapoonjee was preferable to Darjeeling because of the scenery and location. It was convenient to travel into the interior, as well as in either direction towards Sylhet in Bengal or Guwahati in Assam.[39] In his opinion a station in the interior of the Khasi hills would be most favourable. He wrote in another report that was published in 1852, '[p]laced geographically between the great plains of Assam and of Sylhet, and accessible with ease from either side, the Khasi hills would seem to have been indicated by their position as the place for a convenient hill resort common to the inhabitants of both, although at present the station is placed on the extreme Southern verge of the district.'[40] His opinion found its way into official circles where the decision was made to construct Shillong as the frontier hill station in the second half of the century.

In the third appendix Oldham discussed language and ethnology of the Khasis. Typical of colonial literature on tribes, linguistics offered explanation of origin and civilizational connections. Linguistic differentiation of tribes was used by administrator-anthropologist PRT Gurdon discussed in the next section. Interestingly Oldham's reference to the first published write-up on Khasi language in 1831 in a journal called *Gleanings in Science*, pointed to the monoliths and clusters of rocks found in the Khasi hills. Oldham stopped short of suggesting that the 'monumental stones' strewn across the hills were inscriptions in themselves. The inclusion of the stones in a discussion of Khasi language and ethnology leaves a curious impression of what nineteenth-century accounts did not incorporate. In representing the newly discovered aspects of the frontier landscapes and translating the local information into colonial knowledge, some aspects were emphasized over others. The stones were of interest to ethnologists, and every travel account, whether official or unofficial, referred to the stones.

One such official study is found in an article dated 1874 published in *The Journal of the Anthropological Institute of Britain and Ireland* by C B Clarke called, Stone Monuments in the Khasi Hills. This article documented the types and purposes of the stone monuments and emphasized the significance of such sites for 'all modern treatises of Archaeology and

---

[39] Ibid., xxi.
[40] Ibid., xxi.

Anthropology'.[41] This account, like those that preceded it, emphasized the location of these stones within a civilizational model by juxtaposing Khasi society and primitive European societies as Hooker had done. They failed to note that the stones possessed greater significance than as memorials and sepulchres. The dominance of knowledge in written form evaded knowledge which was performed, inscribed on land, or transferred orally. The stones and hill landscape in general were framed within a discourse of ancient civilizational history.

A written script was introduced in the Khasi hills in the early nineteenth century. The official Khasi language recognized today was chosen among many variations in dialect and standardized by missionaries of different denominations starting with the Welsh. Early legal documents used the Bengali script while the Roman script was introduced to ease missionary work. It also served to distinguish Khasi identity from the neighbouring Bengalis. A series of compendiums of Khasi words and grammars were produced from 1830s onwards as initiatives by mostly Welsh missionaries. Cherrapoonjee was a centre of proselytization in the hills, and the missionaries learnt the local language in order to translate religious literature. Hence dialect chosen by the missionaries was from this area. The first set of books published in Khasi using the Roman script included the following: A translation of *Mother's Gift* by Thomas Jones (1842), *A Scriptural Catechism* by Thomas Jones (1845), A translation of the *Gospel of Matthew* Thomas Jones (1846), *A Primer in Khasi by Thomas Jones, A Small Scriptural Cathechism* by the Rev. W Lewis (1848), a small hymn book compiled by Lewis (1850), *Khasi Primer* published by Calcutta School books society (1852).[42]

Oldham attempted to revise several erroneous deductions made in such works from the earlier decades. He provided an account of the structure of the language or dialect spoken in Sorah and a list of vocabulary. The diversity of dialects in the Khasi and Jaintia hills was erased in the process of standardizing Khasi grammar. The creation of a homogenous Khasi language was a product of books written and published by missionaries like Thomas Jones and Reverend Lewis Pryse discussed in the next

---

[41] C B Clark, Stone Monuments of Khasi hills, *The Journal of Royal Anthropological Institute of Britain and Ireland*, 3 (1874), 482.

[42] For a discussion of these publications see Clarence Calhoney, *Language and Civilization Change in South Asia Vol. 11* (Leiden: E J Brill 1978), 170.

chapter. Pryse's comprehensive account of Khasi language and grammar was produced using Thomas Jones' unfinished work on Khasi grammar.[43] In an article published in U Khasi Mynta in 1902 an anonymous contributor quoted the Chief Commissioner of Assam in a report from 1884 stating that the use of roman characters in Khasi language was not only wrong but the transliteration was 'barbarous' and 'uncouth'. The heavy influence of Welsh in Khasi language and grammar caused several disparaging opinions by some colonial officials.[44] The prevalence of multiple dialects and variations in customs and practices in the different polities of the Khasi hills was identified in colonial reports. Yet most publications on language relied on the official, standardized form of Khasi.[45]

Anthropology as History Writing

PRT Gurdon, author of *The Khasis*, the first anthropological monograph on the Khasis published in 1909, recognized five different groups that inhabited the hills (see Figure 5.3).[46] He categorized the inhabitants into Khasi, Pnar (Jaintia), War, Bhoi, and Lyngam.[47] Anthropology emerged as a professional discipline by the early twentieth century and drew upon previous disciplines of ethnology and ethnography and their scientific and scholarly focus on tribes.[48] Gurdon's book was part of a project initiated by the Chief Commissioner of Assam, Bampfylde Fuller in 1903 with an aim to produce a series of monographs on the tribes and castes of the north-east frontier. Gurdon served as Deputy Commissioner in eastern Bengal and Assam as well as Superintendent of Ethnography in

[43] Clarence Calhoney, *Language*,170–171.
[44] Ibid., 170.
[45] Indrani Chatterjee has pointed out that the term Khasi was a Tibetan word for lay and ordained disciples of monastic orders. The word Cosseah or Cusseah was used by colonial officers to describe the individual heads. See Indrani Chatterjee, *Forgotten*, 95–96.
[46] Gurdon, *Khasis*.
[47] Gurdon first mentioned the different groups in the third section on law and custom when the different customs of the groups are described. This was preceded by two sections on 'general' characteristics including physical features, and another on social and economic practices. See Gurdon, *Khasis*, 62.
[48] See Sangeeta Dasgupta's discussion on *The Tribes and Castes of Bengal* by Herbert Risley census commissioner and director of the ethnological survey of the Indian Empire. Risley drew upon research methods used by European anthropologists distinguishing himself from earlier works in the colony. In Dasgupta, *Reordering*, 72–86.

Figure 5.3 Images from P R T Gurdon's The Khasis.

Assam. He spent a large amount of time travelling in the Khasi hills and learnt the standardized Khasi language as part of the required anthropological methodology. He reproduced and accounted for information he gathered during his travels. He acknowledged the role of missionaries in providing him information on folk tales of the Khasis and other colonial agents for providing help in putting together the monograph. No local inhabitant was acknowledged for contributing to his findings. Further, his study made no note about the century-long Christian proselytization in the hills.

Gurdon's book described in detail most aspects of the lives of the inhabitants, including the politico-economic structure, social formation, religious rituals, landscape, and other ethnographic information. The narrative reads as an interface between personal observation and scientific account. Referring to Henrika Kuklick's work, Kavita Phillip writes that anthropology was defined by colonial discourse as apolitical, as technical expertise, scientifically grounded and 'value neutral'. Yet, it was

employed to identify and provide solutions to social conflict 'thus transforming political issues into administrative ones'.[49] The correspondence
between political and administrative functions facilitated the frontier.
His book provided the scientific account of Khasis as 'hill tribals', as fixed
in time and place. Socio-political activities were reduced to unchanging
cultural forms, and life experiences including Christian conversion, and
missionary education was erased from his account.

The anthropological literature on the Khasi hills formulated inhabitants as 'cultural' versus 'political'. Such apolitical representation was already visible in nineteenth-century jurisdictional debates on borders and
administrative discussions on customs. It carried over into anthropological accounts and was most apparent in the emphasis of tribal religion
as animism, typical in writings about tribe across the colony. In the introduction to the book by C J Lyall noted that '[all] forms of animistic religion make it their chief business to avert the wrath of the Gods, to which
calamities of all kinds—sickness, storm, loss of harvest—are ascribed, by
some kind of propitiation.'[50] Gurdon described the veneration of ancestors to be the foundation of tribal piety. Describing the method of divination to ascertain causes of misfortune or remedies to cure the same
Gurdon emphasized their religious belief as irrational, superstitious.
Once again, to explain belief systems and practices in the hills, examples
from the European ancient past were used. For instance, the practice described as 'extispicium' found among the Khasis was defined in correlation to similar practices known to have been present in Roman society,
and similarly the practice of 'egg breaking' known to diviners in ancient
Hellas. Primitivism turned the hill tribals as relics of history and connected them in the civilizational sequence from primitive to modern.

Gurdon's anthropological subject was a resource for labour. For instance, the matrilineal kinship system (described as 'matriarchy') is considered to adversely affect the population increase over a period of two
decades. In the census of 1891 data revealed 117 children under five to
every hundred married women between 15 and 40 and in 1901 it dropped
to 108. Gurdon wrote that the independence of the wife, and the facilities,

---

[49] See Kavita Philip, Civilising, 137.
[50] Gurdon, Khasis, xv.

which exist for divorce, lead to restrictions upon childbearing, and thus keep the population stationary.

Gurdon presented with fair detail an account of the 'state organization' in the Khasi hills. He described the main functions of the *Syiem* as head of state and the differences in election of *Syiems* in different polities. Once again, he avoided the significant changes and debates on the method of electing *Syiems* that occurred during and preceding his official tenure through severe interference of the colonial state. Property, which became central to debates on succession of *Syiems*, is ignored by Gurdon. Moreover, Gurdon's description of the state organization did not address the role of the colonial political agents in the hills. He was careful not to narrate the political shifts and history of the hills. Yet, he provided inferences on the shift in political role of the *Syiem's*. 'In the olden days', Gurdon wrote, 'the *Syiem* marched to war at the head of his army.'[51]

In the context of the Nilgiri hills, Philip has shown that scientifically grounded anthropological studies naturalized tribal practices around land and forest, stripping them of political meaning. This recasts the utilization of forest into binary terms: the colonial state's intended transformation of the landscape based on scientific and inherently progressive system of knowledge, against the pre-existing tribal methods of resource use, deemed unscientific and inherently backward.[52] In the Khasi hills forest management was not undertaken by the colonial government, but resource extraction was central to the colonial project. Anthropology performed similar but additional functions in the frontier hills. The functions are apparent through an analysis of colonial literature produced over the nineteenth century, culminating in Gurdon's monograph of the early twentieth century.

The construction of a geographical frontier landscape through scientific and disciplinary studies—on plants and trees, mineral resources and technology, people and their social formation—shaped discourse on the nature of colonial sovereignty in the Khasi hills. Early tropes of primitivism legitimized colonial law and violence from early nineteenth century when the colonial government assumed rights over criminal jurisdiction in the non-British territories. Gurdon's book was a culmination

---

[51] Ibid., 69.
[52] Kavita Philip, *Civilising*, 137.

of nineteenth-century colonial discourse on tribalization of non-British territories and non-British subjects.

Within the reconceptualized landscape produced by colonial geographical imagination, geological and botanical descriptions and anthropological objectification, Khasis were located, not in isolation but alongside other tribes across the colony and in similar frontier spaces in the north-west. The comparisons were informed by and validated by the evolutionary and civilizational models used by colonial administrators, missionaries, anthropologists.[53] Dasgupta has shown that ideas about a shared aboriginal linguistic history originating from Dravidian language were revised after the 1854 when Bishop Robert Caldwell pointed out that there was more than Aryan and Dravidian origins and included a third of the Munda or Austro Asiatic linguistic group.[54] Comparative studies of languages and linguistic research traced origins and migratory patterns of tribal groups.[55]

Ethnography and linguistic study shared a fraught history in British India. The publication of the Linguistic Survey of India in 1894 and ongoing work on census took place within a context of much debate and discussion about the relationship between language and race.[56] Simpson points out that the Khasi language posed a problem for colonial ethnographers because it was markedly different from other frontier languages. Gurdon reiterating the new linguistic and ethnographic research stated in his monograph that Khasis were distinct from other tribes like the Garos who belonged to a 'Tibeto-Burman stock'. Superintendent of the Linguistic Survey of India George Grierson traced Khasi origin to the linguistic family of Mon Khmer and remnants of Indo-Chinese migrants in the region. Although Gurdon pointed out that there remained a gap in knowledge about the origin and migration patterns of Khasis.[57] I have argued in Chapter 3 that an overlap between linguistic and racial categories was part of the jurisdictional process of boundary making in

---

[53] For a detailed investigation into the various intellectual traditions that informed colonial anthropology see George Stocking, *Victorian Anthropology* (USA: Free Press, 1991).

[54] Dasgupta, *Reordering*, 54.

[55] Javed Majeed, *Colonialism and Knowledge in Grierson's Linguistic Survey of India* (Abingdon: Routledge, 2019), 78–81.

[56] Simpson, *The Frontier*, 178.

[57] Gurdon, Khasis, 10–18.

the Khasi and Garo hills that the emphasis on a standardization of languages and linguistic forms enabled colonial administrators in creating jurisdictional boundaries. This invariably led to the characterization of bordering villages and communities as uncharacteristic anomalies. For instance, in order to separate Khasi and Garo hills in terms of ethnicity meant that many who spoke separate dialects in the villages bordering the jurisdictional divisions fell through the cracks of ethnic categories. The 'mixed-race' of Sylhetis and Khasis in the lower hills and plains was identified as demonstrating the worst traits of both groups. Histories on this region have reproduced colonial spatial and ethnic assumptions ignoring communities that present interruptions to the colonial spatiality and knowledge.

Although historians like Dasgupta and Simpson in recent studies have argued that ethnographic works were shifting and unstable, my interest in demonstrating cross-referential and overlapping tropes in knowledge on the Khasi hills is to highlight their pervasive and lasting impression. Gurdon's book is a classic example of primitivism as a signature of colonial frontier narratives. The 'hill tribal' was a cultural artefact of representational knowledge and a spatio-temporal trope. The domestication of frontier tribals Gurdon's book shows required the erasure of their political identity.

If the primitive marked a civilizational boundary, to be modern and civilized was also to consume the primitive aesthetically, scientifically, and intellectually.[58] The knowledge thus produced was not only deemed important for colonial governance in the hills. It informed the emerging public sphere in the Khasi hills from the late nineteenth century examined further in the following chapter. A reconstitution of conceptions of the self and surroundings inevitably and sometimes violently accompanied processes of knowledge production. The pervasive use and reference to colonial publications like Gurdon's since its publication with repeated references in national and local histories of the region presents a conundrum. It raises the question of how to understand the overlap and

---

[58] See Satadru Sen, *Encyclopedia of Anthropology.*

separation between colonial and postcolonial representations of self and identity. It also compels one to think about decolonization not simply as academic theory or political rhetoric but as systematic change, with all its attendant danger of appropriation by majoritarian Hindu ideologues. This point guides the discussion in the following chapter.

6

Narratives of Continuity

Imperial knowledge, whether officially sanctioned scientific information or unofficial accounts of travel and life, was written and published
to create an archive of verifiable and referential documents argued in
the last chapter. This chapter examines the development of knowledge
through education, literacy, writing in the Khasi hills as components of
place-making.[1] Place-making is understood as heterogeneous articulations, including material and imaginative processes, that shape identity, livelihood, and belonging in the hills. In this chapter processes of
place-making appear in narratives of continuity with a pre-colonial past.
I argue that the published writing by Khasi men in the late nineteenth and
early twentieth century demonstrates colonialism's 'irreversible process
of transmutation' that impact notions of place in the hills. Missionary
evangelical work in the frontier hills was the primary vehicle for English
education, the production of standardized vernaculars, and the crystal-
lization of ethnic categories.

The chapter shows that certain English-educated Khasi men writing
in the nineteenth century were part of what Skaria has called an 'interpretive community' within the public sphere. They emphasized pre-
colonial continuities in writings on history, identity, and indigenous
knowledge on the one hand, and demonstrated an allegiance to imperial
frameworks and disciplines of knowledge on the other. English-educated
Khasi men drew upon multiple spatial frameworks to represent the hills
and its people including those of colonial law.[2] Even within the public
domain created by published books, newspapers, and journal articles, the

---

[1] Place-making is further examined the next and final chapter.
[2] Skaria shows how Dangi narratives captured an understanding of self, time, and space that
exceeded the colonial. The colonial was present but not Ajay Skaria, 'Writing, Orality and Power
in the Dangs, Western India, 1800s–1920s', in *Subaltern Studies*, eds. Dipesh Chakrabarty and
Shahid Amin, vol. 9 (New Delhi: OUP, 1996), 13–58.

Placing the Frontier in British North-East India. Reeju Ray, Oxford University Press. © Reeju Ray 2023.
DOI: 10.1093/oso/9780192887085.003.0006

assertion of Khasi religion and identity played a significant role in challenging a strictly colonial spatial imagination of place and its people.

The chapter further demonstrates the linkages between the development of literacy through English education and the constitution of a gendered ethnic identity within a legal-customary space. Despite the presence of local educated male elite within dominant colonial spaces, either as the missionary-educated elite or as government servants, their position remained marginal within the public sphere. Differential access to the public sphere in the nineteenth-century Khasi hills also affected how women were allowed to negotiate 'spatial [and social] boundaries for themselves and for other subjects'.[3] Probing into the gendered form and content of the public sphere in the hills, the vestiges in the present-day debates on issues of gender and ethnocentrism become apparent. This further allows a historical examination of feminist-materialist place-making in the next chapter. The following two sections lay out the historical conditions and processes of place-making through literacy and writing. This chapter concludes with a discussion of the overlap between gendered spatial relations and social relationships in the frontier hills.[4]

Missionary Education

The Charter Act of 1813 and the English Education Act of 1835 were combined factors in the expansion of English education in the frontier hills of Bengal. While the 1813 Act allowed the entry of missionaries into India, the Education Act was considered to be a milestone in the movement towards liberal, utilitarian reform in the colony. Whether it was Thomas Macaulay's push to create an English-educated colonized workforce to run the empire, the influence of romantic philosophy and philological

---

[3] Sara Mills, 'Gender and Colonial Space', in *Feminist Postcolonial Theory: A Reader*, eds. Reina Lewis and Sara Mills (New York: Routledge, 2003), 692–721; see also, Henrietta L. Moore, *Space, Text, and Gender: An Anthropological Study of the Marakwet of Kenya* (Cambridge: Cambridge University Press, 1986).

[4] An overlap between linguistic and racial categories was part of the jurisdictional process of boundary-making in the Khasi and Garo hills discussed in Chapter 3. The emphasis on a standard linguistic form separating Khasis and Garos ethnically meant that many who spoke separate dialects in the villages bordering the jurisdictional divisions fell through the cracks of ethnic categories. The 'mixed-race' of Sylhetis and Khasis identified for the particularly worst traits of both groups were also victim to the dominance of regional languages.

science, or Missionary zeal to save the heathens, the advance of education was a common thread. Across the British Indian colony, missionaries, colonial administrators, intellectuals, and local elites alike supported the emphasis on language learning. Standardization of what was identified as regional language, or a 'mother tongue', was one of the outcomes of this education project.[5] State patronage shifted away from the practice of using multiple languages for a variety of official and unofficial purposes, and was concentrated instead upon increasingly standardized vernaculars. Linguistic standardization was aided by a growing print and publishing industry in the second half of the nineteenth century. As Jayeeta Sharma states: 'a circular set of processes appeared: local languages responded to the new "civilizing" and "ordering" imperatives; realizing these imperatives, in turn, seemed to depend upon the transformation of language'.[6] The educational and linguistic transformations can be tracked in the Khasi hills by looking at the work undertaken by different sets of Christian missionaries. By the early twentieth century, missionaries of the Welsh Presbyterian Mission, the Baptist, and the Catholic Missions were all operating in the hills.

In 1813 William Carey a Baptist missionary based in the Danish territory of Serampore near Calcutta sent one of his converts, Krishna Chandra Pal to Pandua an important market centre in the foothills of Sohra polity. With the assistance of the first few converts in Pandua including two Khasi men, U Dewan and U Anna, Christian evangelical missionary work gained ground in the frontier hills of Bengal. The Serampore Mission press published the first Khasi translation of the New Testament in 1831 using the Bengali script.[7] Andrew May points out that William Carey at first commissioned a *pundit* to help with the Khasi translation because he was believed to be 'the only one in that nation who could read and write'.[8] However, there were different accounts of inhabitants from the Khasi hills including the widow of a Syiem, and Khasi men studying at Serampore college and Fort William College in Calcutta who could have helped with the translations. May suggests that due to the use

---

[5] Jayeeta Sharma, *Empire's Garden: Assam and the Making of India* (Durham and London: Duke University Press, 2011), 178.
[6] Sharma, *Empire's Garden*, 180.
[7] May, *Welsh Missionaries*, 53–56.
[8] Ibid., 54.

of Bengali script and the Shella (Cheyla) dialect that was not known to inhabitants higher in the mountains including Cherrapoonjee, the translated texts did not make an impact.[9]

Alexander Lish, a student of Serampore College, was another early missionary in the Khasi hills, and worked there between 1832 and 1837. He is credited with starting several schools in the hills in places including Cherrapoonjee, Mawsmai, and Mawmluh.[10] There was an existing notion that evangelical work among inhabitants in the frontier will be successful because they were neither Hindu nor Muslim. Lish wrote a racialized account of the inhabitants of the hills, and emphasized the need to civilize them through education and religion. He wrote,

> They have no sense of duty they owe as creatures to the Creator, they have no form or place of public worship, nor do they seem sensible that God requires this worship of his creatures. They are literally 'led captive by Satan at his will', 'without God and without hope in the world'.[11]

The Welsh Calvinists arrived in the hills after the Serampore Baptist missionaries.[12] The Welsh mission began a sustained effort to standardize the Khasi language. Thomas Jones of the Welsh Mission first used the Latin script to write translated extracts from the Bible in Khasi. The dialect he chose was the one spoken in his vicinity in Cherrapoonjee and Sorah. Jones had a clear purpose when he arrived in the hills. He wrote, 'I had to come here to learn their language, and then make books for them.'[13] Jones relied on two Khasi men who had been instructed in English by Lish. U Dewan (one of the first converts of Krishna Chandra Pal) and U Juncha helped Jones translate and compile an alphabetical list of Khasi words, as well as longer sentences.[14] Employed by Jones these

---

[9] Ibid.

[10] Ibid., 55.

[11] Alexander Lish, 'A Brief Account of the Khasees', *Calcutta Christian Observer Vol. VII* (1838), 140–141.

[12] For a detailed account of the engagements and disagreements between different denominations and missionary groups like the Welsh Calvinist Methodists and the London Missionary Society for instance, see May, *Welsh Missionaries*, 13–58.

[13] Letter from Thomas Jones to John Roberts, 28 July 1842, Y Drysorfa, October 1842, Quoted in May, *Welsh Missionaries*, 135.

[14] In May, *Welsh Missionaries*, 136, Thomas Jones was caught in several legal and social scandals that led to his eviction from the Mission Church, but he continued to work in the hills until his death.

Figure 6.1   Images of Khasi language books. By Tarun Bhartiya.

men were crucial to the formation of standardized Khasi, forgotten in the celebration of Jones as the 'bringer of the book', and 'father of Khasi literature'.[15] The loss of literacy in the hills was recounted in missionary and colonial accounts, and local legend. A sacred book containing legal prescriptions was lost in a flood which was the reason the societies in the hills relied on oral knowledge forms. It was thus propagated that the missionaries brought back both literacy and the word of God.

While the relationship between the Company government and the evangelicals was not always smooth, the two were connected through mutual interests and dependence.[16] Political Agents David Scott and his successor Francis Jenkins were the first among company administrators to encourage missionary work in the hills.[17] Government-sponsored missionary schools were opened in the Garo hills in 1829.[18] Educational

[15] May, *Welsh Missionaries*, 135.

[16] The Charter Act of 1813 allowed the entry of missionaries into the colony. Separation of state and church belies the mutual dependence of the two in an imperial context. However, there were also disagreements and conflicts between the government and missionary societies, as well as individual missionaries like Jones.

[17] *American Baptist Missionary Society Records 1817–1959* (Microfilm, Nehru Memorial Museum and Library, New Delhi).

[18] Scott, *Memoirs*.

work was further supported with government grants made to schools run by Welsh missionaries from 1854 onwards. The Government was able to outsource its responsibility for education at relatively little expense.[19]

F. S. Downs has argued that until 1880, the Christian community in the hills grew very slowly and opposition to proselytization remained strong.[20] Downs draws a correlation between large-scale conversion and natural disasters, such as the great earthquake of 1897. By the end of the century, there was a rapidly growing Christian community based on a large educational system run by missionaries. According to official estimates, between 1891 and 1901, the number of native Christians in Assam increased by 28 per cent.[21]

In 1855, Rev. William Pryse published *An Introduction to the Khassia Language*, which became the official handbook for officials and missionaries alike.[22] It provided a guide for English speakers to learn Khasi. The standardized Khasi chosen by Pryse was the dialect spoken in Sorah. Pryse wrote,

This little compilation originated in the desire of the compiler to learn that dialect, with a view to try and disseminate a little elementary knowledge amongst the tribe.... It is hoped that such an unpretending performance may render some assistance, not only to those Europeans and others, who may desire to acquire the dialect through the medium of English, but also to those Khasis who having acquired some knowledge of English, may be desirous of composing elementary books in their own language.[23]

Rev. Pryse included a description of Khasi grammar and different usages of similar words, and he also recorded statements made by the inhabitants of Cherrapoonjee on topics such as the 'transgression of law', the 'reconciliation of a quarrel', 'concerning the creation of man', 'thanks offering to the goddess', among others. The book also included previous translations

[19] Downs, *Christianity*.
[20] Ibid., 2.
[21] B. C. Allen, *Assam District Gazetteers: The Khasi and Jaintia Hills, the Garo Hills and the Lushai Hills*, vol. 10 (Allahabad: Pioneer Press, 1906).
[22] Rev. W. Pryse, *An Introduction to the Khasia Language: Comprising a Grammar, Selections for Reading and a Vocabulary* (Calcutta: Calcutta School-Book Society's Press, 1855).
[23] Pryse, *Introduction to Khasia Language*, 7.

of religious sermons by Rev. Thomas Jones, Khasi translations of prayers in the Bengali script, and catechisms for children in the missionary schools in Cherrapoonjee that were written by Rev. Alexander Lish. The aim of such a book was to create a foundation for learning standardized Khasi that could be used both by the inhabitants of the Khasi hills and by colonial agents.

Another book of Khasi grammar was published later in the nineteenth century by H. Roberts, and its title clearly explained its purpose: *A Grammar of the Khassi Language: For the Use of Schools, Native Students, Officers and English Residents.*[24] Over the course of the nineteenth century, missionary schools and evangelical efforts led to extensive English-language education among inhabitants in certain Khasi polities like Sohra and Cheyla. This in turn led to the emergence of a class of English-educated Khasi men who were employed in government service, and who also became influential voices in the articulation of a modern subjectivity for inhabitants of the hills.

By the end of nineteenth century, men with a Western missionary education articulated a modern Khasi identity in a newly forming public sphere. Their works, to different degrees, present the complex aspirations of a modern tribal subject in the decades leading up to the creation of India and Pakistan. Colonial knowledge and a missionary education connected the inhabitants of these frontier hills to a universal abstract primitive on the one hand, and invested new cultural meanings to their location and identity on the other. Such combined articulations of culture and identity formed the basis of ethnic definitions across colonial space and, later, that of the nation-state.

The Public Sphere and Writing Culture

The Khasi, Jaintia, and Garo hills in the late eighteenth and early nineteenth centuries were non-literate societies in which orality was the dominant form of knowledge transmission and dissemination. Yet, treaties and agreements signed between the Company and political heads across

---

[24] H. Roberts, *A Grammar of the Khassi Language: For the Use of Schools, Native Students, Officers and English Residents* (London: Kegan Paul, Trench Trubner and Co., 1891).

the frontier hills, contracts with private traders, petitions, and a wide corpus of official texts including surveys and maps all demonstrate the problem with an anthropological emphasis on orality as the primary mode of knowledge during the colonial period. The importance of oral knowledge notwithstanding, written culture dominated all modes of legal and political communication, negotiation, and engagement from the early nineteenth century onwards. Ajay Skaria problematizes the works of Jacques Derrida, Michel de Certeau, Walter Ong, Jack Goody, and Ranajit Guha among others, to develop a framework that avoids both 'the reification of the distinction between orality and literacy, and the historicist closure of the argument with the valid but limited point that the meanings of writing varied in different contexts'.[25]

In his study of the Dangs in Western India, Skaria points out that writing assumed dominance through its extensive and consistent use during the colonial period. Like in the frontier hills of Sylhet, writing was an important tool of colonial domination among the Dangs. Agreements with colonial authorities assumed a fixity and unalterability, while lists and written genealogies helped in the recognition of Chiefs and of succession practices through male primogeniture. Specific forms of writing, such as surveying and mapping, demarcated territory and zones of control, and thereby created a new geography. Skaria states that writing was not just a technology, but it was also an ideological tool that valorized written over oral communication in the functioning of administrative and jurisdictional processes. Skaria defines the 'rhetoric of fixity' as

> the notion that meanings once inscribed in writing, were more stable and less arbitrary than those embodied in oral traditions or precolonial forms of writing. From this perspective the inscription of colonial laws substituted a regular and ordered world for a personal tyrannical and arbitrary one. This understanding extended to the necessary fictions surrounding the contract or the written word. The principle of inviolability of the written agreement, the assertion that it bound both parties to stipulated and unchangeable rights and obligations, was the cornerstone of the written agreement. If signatories failed to adhere to the stipulations of the agreement, they left themselves open, within the

---

[25] Skaria, 'Writing, Orality and Power', 18.

terms of colonial ideology, to legal measures, punitive sanctions, and delegitimization.[26]

Despite this fixity, the colonial state was able to manipulate written documents by means of several strategies. Attention to these strategies can help us understand the processes at play when rendering certain documents invisible, or when overruling existing documents if necessary, including land deeds and settlements, agreements with deceased Chiefs, etc. Through processes of negotiation, a new consensus could be created between the colonial government and the Chiefs that sought to override previous agreements. The most important of these strategies, according to Skaria, is the reinterpretation of inviolable texts by a limited and exclusive interpretive community.

Not all missionary-educated Khasi men were able to claim a seat within the interpretive community, but they could engage in confrontation with that community in the public sphere.[27] The majority of non-literate and literate inhabitants of the hills, however, remained outside of this interpretive sphere. This is because writing required an acceptance of norms of validity about knowledge and proof. Within the heavily policed interpretive sphere, the presence of an English-educated Khasi middle class demonstrates a crucial shift in the way that writing superseded orality as the valid, reliable, and dominant source of knowledge in the hills.

The colonial government employed men with multilingual skills as interpreters; such figures were officially called *dubhashis*, which meant speakers of two languages. *Dubhashis* were indispensable for the smooth functioning of the colonial government and gained influence and prestige, among both the colonial state and local society. Let us look at Figure 6.2 in some detail. Jeebon Roy Mairom joined on to work for the East India Company in 1858, serving as a *dubhashi* for the District Commissioner of the Khasi hills. Roy was a prolific writer, entrepreneur, and co-founder of the Khasi Young Men's Association renamed the Seng Khasi organization. After his retirement from government service, Roy became involved in the lucrative limestone trade in Cherrapoonjee.

---

[26] Ibid., 37.
[27] U Khasi Mynta and Nongphira.

Figure 6.2 Babu Jeebon Roy

In 1895, Jeebon Roy established a printing press called the Ri Khasi Press. The press contributed to the emergent public sphere in the Khasi hills and in the dissemination of knowledge about *Niam* Khasi—the consolidated religious beliefs of the inhabitants of the Khasi polities who had not converted to Christianity, Hinduism, or Islam. *U Nongphira* (watchmen), a monthly publication started by Jeebon Roy, also promoted *Niam* Khasi, and positioned itself firmly against the practice of Christian proselytization. Another significant publication in the late nineteenth century was the journal *U Khasi Mynta* (The Khasi of Today), started by

U Hormu Rai Diengdoh in 1895. The readership of the newspaper was at the time limited to those educated in the English and Khasi languages in missionary schools.[28] Khasi intellectuals such as Roy took an interest in multiple religions, including Hinduism and the Brahmo religions, writing about them and translating their tenets for a wider audience.[29]

Jeebon Roy's *U Niam Jong Ki Khasi*, compiled and published in 1897, was the first collection written in the Khasi language that described customs and social norms (see Figures 6.3a and 6.3b). It comprised fourteen chapters, and included descriptions about the structure and relationship between different clans; specific customs and rituals associated with marriage, birth, and death (and the variations within such ritualized events); customs to follow while constructing a house; norms and taboos during pregnancy; and teachings of the elders. One of the chapters was entitled '*Shaphang kaba ki knia ki khasi*', which literally translates as 'rituals and rites that constitute a Khasi identity'. A thread running throughout the chapters was the significance attached to clan lineage, and thus much discussion was devoted to describing practices that were essential in maintaining clan membership. *Sang* or prohibitions prohibited marriage between two clans that were believed to be intimately related not by marriage, but by lineage. Kinship structured through marriage and descent was seen as foundational to Khasi identity by the English-educated men who are credited with codifying Khasi custom. A number of the English-educated men writing about *Niam* Khasi were members of the Seng Khasi organization.

Founded in 1899 by sixteen prominent men with English education, the Young Men's Association or the Seng Khasi organization was informed by the ideas of the Brahmo Samaj.[30] Among its members were influential writers such as Radhon Singh Berry Kharwanlang, who is known to have helped set up a Brahmo Samaj mandir near the colonial station of Shillong, in the polity of Mylliem (see Figure 6.4). The Brahmo Samaj was a modernist reform movement that began in Bengal in the early nineteenth century, and its nomenclature developed in stages in 1823, 1829, and 1843. Challenging the orthodoxy of Hindu doctrine, the Brahmos

---

[28] Gurdon, *Khasis*, 111.
[29] Jeebon Roy Mairom, *Ka Niam Jong ki Khasi* (1897; Reprint, Shillong: Ri Khasi Press, 1994).
[30] It was not until the 1940s that a women's wing of the Seng Khasi was formed.

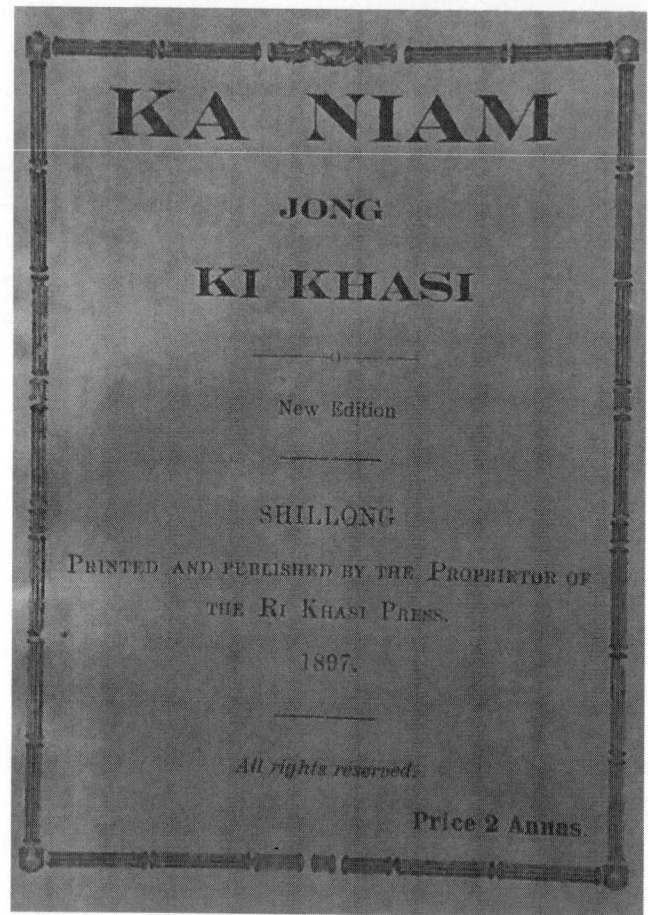

Figure 6.3a　Ka Niam Jong ki Khasi by Jeebon Roy, 1897

emphasized the need for social reform and gender equality. Membership
was dominated by the intelligentsia of the Bengali urban elite, who combined Western notions of scientific enquiry and rationality with spiritu-
alism. While early Brahmos were influenced deeply by 'rational faith and
social gospels of nineteenth-century British and American Unitarianism',
there were others who seemed ambivalent towards reform, and who
displayed a growing suspicion of Western dominance and emerging

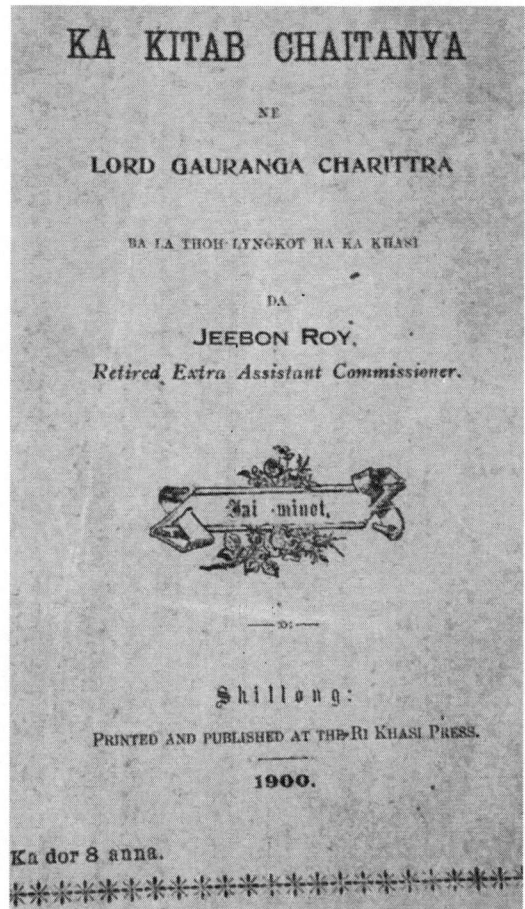

Figure 6.3b Lord Gauranga Charitra, Translated
into Khasi by Jeebon Roy

anticolonial nationalism.[31] Among several segments that emerged from
the larger umbrella of Brahmo thought, the modernizing consciousness
of the English-educated Khasi intelligentsia in the late nineteenth century was rooted in and expressed through an assertion of preserving indigenous Khasi religion.

---

[31] David Kopf, *The Brahmo Samaj and the Shaping of the Modern Indian Mind*
(Princeton: Princeton University Press, 1979).

Figure 6.4 Radhon Singh Berry

Radhon Singh Berry, along with Jeebon Roy, published *Ka Kitab Pule Nyngkong*, which was a compilation of the Khasi alphabet and corrected spellings of words. Radhon Singh Berry is most known for writing *Ka Jingseng Tymmen*, published in 1902. The continued popularity of this book is because Berry consolidated orally transmitted instructions, morals, and beliefs. The ideas in the book reflected the influence of Calvinist thought, Brahmanism, and highlighted strict codes separating the role and behaviour of men and women. Another prominent Khasi intellectual at the turn of the century was Rabon Singh Kharsuka. He presented a detailed description of the Khasi religion, first published in 1889, in a Khasi monthly paper entitled *U Nongkit Khubor*. He also wrote *Ka Kitab Niam Khein Ki Khasi: la pyniasoh bad ki ain ki adong, bad ka rukom hiar pateng* in 1911, which further explained the rules and customs of *Niam* Khasi.

At the same time as when a prolific Khasi intelligentsia was writing about indigenous faith and custom, the colonial administrator P. R. T. Gurdon was working on his anthropological treatise about the Khasi hills, discussed in the previous chapter. Gurdon described Khasi religious beliefs as animism and as,

a vague belief in a God or creator, *U Blei Non-thaw*, although this deity owing, no doubt, to the influences of the matriarchate, is frequently given the attribute of the feminine gender, cf., *Ka lei Synshar*. The Khasis cannot, however, be said to worship the Supreme God, although it is true that they sometimes invoke him when sacrificing and in times of trouble.[32]

Gurdon's descriptions further clarify the introduction of Christian concepts into Khasi thought. For instance he wrote,

Tradition amongst the Khasis states that in the beginning (mynnyngkong ka sngi) there was no sin, heaven and earth were near each other, and man had direct intercourse with God. How man fell into sin is not stated, but it is certain that he did fall. Experts at 'egg healing' never forget to repeat the formula 'nga briw nga la pop' (I man have sinned). The cock then appears as a mediator between God and man. The cock is styled 'u khun ka blei wuba kit rydang ba shah ryndang n aka bynta jong nga u briew', i.e the son of god who lays down his neck (life) for me man.[33]

This statement can be read as a confluence of Christian ideas and local beliefs as recorded by Gurdon.

[32] Gurdon, *Khasis*, 105.
[33] Ibid., 117.

In the twentieth century historians and social scientists who have written on the Khasi hills extensively engage with Gurdon's ideas. While most have read his work as historical record, some have noted their disagreements. H. Onderson Mawrie, a prominent member of the Seng Khasi movement, wrote scathing critiques of colonial and anthropological readings of Khasi religion in several of his books in the decades that followed independence from colonial rule. *The Khasi Milieu* was translated into English in 1982, and remains one of the most prominent and widely used books on Khasi religion. Mawrie asserted that *Niam* is

[a] relationship between man and God and this relationship is governed by two factors, namely, Ka Nia and Ka Jutang (reason and covenant) . . . . The covenant is an agreement which should be executed by two parties. When man needs an agreement with God, the word of approval of God is necessary and it must come from Him.[34]

Mawrie read *Niam* as a 'covenant', 'commandment or law' by which it was necessary to abide in order to attain protection.[35] Mawrie's work, when juxtaposed with Gurdon's, provides important insights into the practices, usages, and rites that made up the Khasi religion. However, Mawrie himself rejected the influence of other religions and ideas on Khasi society. The ideas of reason and covenant resonated deeply with Christian teachings and with Western enlightenment philosophy. Further, the contractual relationship described in the passage above was synonymous with the relationship between the colonial government and the Syiems. Mawrie's work was an attempt to rescue Khasi thought, religion, and values from the framework of primitivism. Yet it resonated at once with the attempt to catch up with the 'enlightened'. Mawrie derived his framework for the Khasi religion based on the same principles of Christianity and formulated this framework by using the civilizational logic of Western modernity. For instance, Mawrie distinguishes the Khasi religion from the other religions of the subcontinent, such as Hinduism, Jainism, and Buddhism, while at the same time, he emphasizes the similarity between Khasi *Niam* and Judaism.[36] It is important to note that he

---

[34] H. Onderson Mawrie, *The Khasi Milieu* (New Delhi: Concept Publishing, 1981), 35.
[35] Mawrie, *Khasi Milieu*, 35–36.
[36] Ibid., 24.

presented notions of reason and enlightenment as inherent qualities of Khasi religion.

In historian David Ludden's work the emergence of Khasi religion is located within a longer period of movement of ideas and people in the Himalayan borderlands. He pointed out that several religious thoughts and practices collided in the frontier hills because of processes of sedentary agriculture and territorialization. According to Ludden Khasi religion was a product of socio-political and economic changes produced by waves of territorialization first in the 1600s and then again in 1800.[37] Ludden's analysis is a welcome addition to our understanding of the nature of change in the frontier of Bengal from the late eighteenth century onwards. It is relevant historically to consider the longer duree religious ideas in the Himalayan borderlands.[38] It is also important to consider the historical ideas that came together through practices and usages, which emphasize the locality and particularity of place of the Khasi hills. *Niam* can be understood as located in and emerging from the particularity of place as conceived by its inhabitants, while at the same time being limited, codified, and standardized in texts from the late nineteenth century onwards.[39]

English-educated elite Khasi men were not only writing about Khasi identity through the topic of religion. The wave of anticolonial nationalism that swept across the colony also reached the hills, and significant changes were visible in the engagement between different Syiems across different Khasi polities.[40] In an essay entitled 'Whiter the Khasi hills', David Roy (1884–1966), a government official and prominent intellectual, voiced the anxieties of a section of elite Khasi men in the hills. Written in 1946, this essay echoed the aspirations of those Khasi elites— largely Christian converts and English-educated men in government

---

[37] Ludden, 'Investing in Nature Around Sylhet', 5081.

[38] See Indrani Chatterjee, *Forgotten Friends*, for a discussion of various monastic orders that existed in the Himalayan borderlands creating a dynamic religious, social, and politico-economic space that was fragmented from mid-eighteenth century onwards with the onset of European colonialism.

[39] For a larger discussion of how personal and cultural narratives are linked to embodied, spatialized activity and articulated vis-à-vis place, see: Jeff E. Malpas, *Place and Experience: A Philosophical Topography* (Cambridge and New York: Cambridge University Press, 1999), 175–198.

[40] J. K. Tariang, *Ka Thup Jingkynmaw Ia Ka Khasi National Dorbar* (Shillong: Ri Khasi Enterprise, 2007).

service. They found the integration of the hills into the Indian union a feasible and welcome option.[41] The Khasi hills were located as a 'distinct entity in India'.[42] Prominent among those who joined the anticolonial rally for Indian independence and the integration of the Khasi states into the Indian Union was J. J. M. Nichols Roy. Nichols Roy stood firm in his rejection of the Federation of Khasi States that was formed in 1929 at a conference that had brought together Syiems of different polities together. He was also opposed to the colonial plan for an autonomous governance in the form of a hills agency in the north-east frontier.[43]

Poets from the early twentieth century, like So So Tham, on the other hand, reflected an ongoing undercurrent of resistance in the hills in an effort to protect a distinctive hill identity from being subsumed by a colonizing geography. He wrote in the prologue to his collection of poems,

> *Sa Shisien pat kin win ki khlaw*
> *Sa Shisien pat kin khi ki maw*
> Once more the forests will clamour
> Once more the stones will tremor.[44]

Tham's poems, particularly his collection *Ki Sgni ba Rim U Hynniew Trep (Golden Days of the Seven Huts)*, is a significant piece of Khasi literature from the early twentieth century; it combines stories from oral traditions with descriptions of the changes in the socio-political structure. His poems represent a particular articulation of place, at once infused with memory and shaped by upheavals of change. Tham's poetry is also integral to an understanding of the history of ideas in the hills. The ideas found in these poems are based on a sentient geography, historical memory, and everyday resistance to the currents of colonial transformation. The title spells out the emphasis on kinship and a better time in the

---

[41] David Roy, 'Whither the Khasi Hills', in *Discovery of North East India: Geography, History, Culture, Religion, Politics, Sociology, Science, Education and Economy*, eds. S. K. Sharma and Usha Sharma, vol. 7 (New Delhi: Mittal Publications, 2005), 1–8.

[42] Roy, 'Whither the Khasi Hills', 1–8.

[43] James J. M. Nichols-Roy, 'Hill Districts of Assam: Their Future in the New Constitution of India', in *Memoirs of Life and Political Writings of the Hon'ble Rev. J.J.M Nichols-Roy*, ed. O. L. Snaitang, vol. 1 (Shillong: Shrolenson Marbaniang, 1997), 13–14.

[44] U Soso Tham, *Ki Sngi Barim U Hynñiew Trep* (Shillong: P. Gatphoh, 1976). For Shlur Manik Syiem's translation of Soso Tham's work, see: Shlur Manik Syiem, *The Olden Days of the Seven Hut* (Shillong: 2006).

past. He identifies a rupture between then (pre-colonial) and now (colonial), with historical memory travelling across this divide. Myth and history also bleed and blend into one another.

Khasi-literate men were able to enter the heavily gated interpretive sphere and engage in the production of ideas around modernity, history, and identity. The written histories they produced catapulted the hill tribes into the discourse of colonial modernity. As the discussion above shows, Khasi intellectuals carved out spaces nestled within colonial state space wherein alternative discourse around tribes was possible. Kinship defined the bounds of that identity. Yet, the officially sanctioned status acquired by anthropological works such as P. R. T. Gurdon's, in contrast to the local publications by Khasi intellectuals clearly demonstrates the racialized hierarchies within this community. Writing one's history and codifying myths from oral to written forms, as Joy Pachuau argues, validated the sense of being a people and an ethnic group identity for the Mizos.[45] Just as in the Khasi hills, as we shall see in the next chapter, selective myths and ways of being that did not contradict the dominant Western epistemology were considered to be valid and historical. For instance, the process of writing one's history had to fit within linear and territorial schemas of colonial knowledge.[46] The varied genres that populated the public sphere in the Khasi hills split, reformulated, challenged, and derived from colonial frameworks of spatiality and civilization.

Identity and Gender

In this dialectical relationship between colonial and indigenous knowledge, certain voices were invisible or absent. The central role of women in religious rituals, and their importance in preserving kinship-based identities, was written about extensively. Yet, their voices remained unrecorded. The mission reports of the nineteenth and twentieth centuries

---

[45] Joy L. K. Pachuau, *Being Mizo: Identity and Belonging in Northeast India* (New Delhi: Oxford University Press, 2014), 110. See also Margaret L. Pachuau, 'Orality: Analysing Its Politics within the Domains of the Mizo Narrative', in *Modern Practices in North East India: History, Culture, Representation*, eds. Lipokmar Dzüvichü and Manjeet Baruah (New York: Routledge, 2018), 172–194.

[46] Pachuau, *Being Mizo*, 112.

repeatedly speak about local populations' resistance to the idea of educating girls.[47] Frederik Sheldon Downs, in his extensive study of Christian missions in the north-eastern frontier, points out that there was a systematic challenge to women's education. He writes about a Welsh missionary who attended the American Baptist Conference held at Nowgaon in 1886, and reported that while his mission ran many girls' schools in the Khasi-Jaintia hills, the education offered was limited; and those women who had been enrolled in the normal school in Cherrapoonjee 'did not turn out very well'.[48] Further, this report implied that converted inhabitants had opposed a mission proposal suggesting that a young woman should be sent to Calcutta to undertake medical studies.[49]

Downs states that missionary work 'became one of the important focal points of women's efforts to bring about change in their own status as well as that of their sisters around the world'.[50] Unlike the American Baptists, the Welsh Presbyterian Church did not form a separate woman's society, but they did send a large number of female missionaries to the north-eastern hills through their general society. The emphasis on education was considered to be the most effective means of improving the status of women; the education of other women was also an area where the missionary woman could establish a relatively autonomous sphere of work, since it was generally accepted that the education of girls and women was best entrusted to women, rather than to missionaries. Hence, from the very beginning, missionary wives and unmarried female missionaries emphasized education, whether it be education in regular schools, bible schools, or nurses' training programmes.[51]

In 1924, C. Becker wrote in his famous book, *Early History of the Missionaries to the North East*, that the position of women was a positive feature in tribal society because gender norms were more egalitarian. This was because according to Becker women participated during preaching

---

[47] Reported in *The Assam Mission of the Baptist Missionary Union Papers and Discussions* of the Jubilee Conference held in Nowgaon, December 1886, in Frederick S. Downs, *The Christian Impact on the Status of Women in North East India* (Shillong: North-Eastern Hill University Publications, 1996), 43–44.

[48] Downs, *Christian Impact*, 43–44.

[49] Ibid.

[50] Ibid., 29.

[51] Ibid., 42–43.

of the gospels and missionaries 'can bring the blessings of Christian religion to all'.[52] However, unlike the women's movement in the West, the question of suffrage or political participation was almost totally absent from the missionary engagement on the situation of women in frontier hills. The exclusion of women from decision-making processes in the public and private spheres was neither subject to critique nor was it even a subject of discussion. Missionaries in general, and female missionaries in particular, described the status of women as unsatisfactory, but did not indicate precisely why.[53]

Missionaries measured improvements in the status of women by reviewing the progress made in women's education as a result of their work. Neither Christian ideology nor the hermeneutic tradition could be challenged at a time when the church orthodoxy was stern (see Figure 6.5).[54] The importance of the Christian home was a point of frequent emphasis by the missionaries. Yet the education given to girls was different from that given to boys. In addition to the basic academic subjects, girls were also trained in how to be more effective homemakers; they received instruction on how to improve kitchen gardens, for instance, and on how to weave, sew, cook nutritionally, etc.[55] A typical example of the way in which girls were educated during the early missionary period is found in a report dated to 1921:

> The girls are busy all day. They are up at 5.30, cook and eat their rice, get ready for school and are in school from 7.30 to 12 o'clock. In the afternoon they sew or weave, or work in the garden, then they pound rice, bring wood and water, sweep their houses, clean lamps etc. we try to teach them to be better house-keepers than their mother's [sic] are.[56]

---

[52] Christopher Becker, *History of the Catholic Missions in Northeast India, 1890–1915* (Calcutta: Firma KLM, 1980), which was originally published as *Im Stromtal des Brahmaputra* in 1923, in Munich.

[53] James P. Alter has discussed the influence of the egalitarian ideology of the French and American Revolution among Evangelical missionaries working in nineteenth-century India in James P. Alter, 'Liberty, Equality, Fraternity: Themes in Anglo-Saxon Protestant Missions and the Church in the North India', *Indian Church History Review* 8, no. 1 (1974): 14–40.

[54] Downs, *Christian Impact*, 56.

[55] Ibid., 57.

[56] *Baptist Missionary Review, October 1921,* NMML.

Figure 6.5 Image of Khasi Christian Women, British
Library

As the number of missionary institutions that served girls and women
grew, the higher-level station schools increasingly devoted their efforts
towards training women to become teachers, doctors, or nurses. Higher
education was deemed as a success if young women, after receiving further education outside their local area, later came back to serve in their
local mission institutions. Conversely, their education was considered to
be a failure if the women then went into 'secular' work.[57]

Over the course of the nineteenth century the church became the
guardian of this ethnocultural identity. The church advanced patriarchal
norms, meaning that women were increasingly confined to lesser public
roles. Women—including female missionaries—were put in a subor-
dinate position. It was no contradiction that evangelism informed and

---

[57] Downs, *Christian Impact*, 58.

reinvigorated patriarchal authority, while a liberal education's emphasis on written culture allowed for specific voices to define the boundaries of an ethnocultural Khasi identity. The public sphere was even inaccessible to educated women in the hills, and this crystallized the practices of the exclusion and non-participation of women in political negotiations. The process of marginalization of women in the public domain can be seen from the early nineteenth century by considering the systematic governmental policy of identifying male heads or chiefs as the key signatories to agreements and treaties. The spatial dimensions of matrilineal kinship relations developed a colonial public/private dichotomy, which furthered a discursive separation in the roles of men and women. Yet women were not considered to be devoid of political power. In fact, even colonial sources, such as Gurdon's, give attention to the exercise of women's agency in political and religious contexts. For instance, in describing the roles played by the female priestess or *Ka lyngdoh*, who is believed to have assisted the *lyngdoh* or male priest, Gurdon states that the *lyngdoh* was in fact the deputy of the *Ka lyngdoh* while performing sacrifices.[58] Thus he writes,

The female soh-blei is without doubt a survival of a time when, under the matriarchate, the priestess was the agent for the performance of all religious ceremonies. Another such survival is the High Priestess of Nongkrem, who still has many religious duties to perform ... she is the actual head of State in Syiemship, although she delegates her temporal powers to one of her sons or nephews, who thus becomes Syiem. A similar survival of the ancient matriarchal religious system is the *Syiem sad*, or priestess, at Maysynram, who on the appointment of a new Syiem or Chief, has to assist at certain sacrifices.[59]

Despite the acknowledgement of the presence of women with political authority (Syiems and Syiem sad) in colonial texts as well as in myths and legends, the notion that women were excluded from participation in political affairs because of religious reasons became dominant.[60]

---

[58] Gurdon, *Khasis*, 121.
[59] Ibid.
[60] A story about the Syiemship family of Nongkhlaw refers to two Jaintia women captured by Khasi hunters who were 'anointed as the rulers of the new emerging State'. See Soumen Sen, *Khasi-Jaintia Folklore: Context, Discourse, and History* (Chennai: National Folklore Support Centre, 2004), 122–124.

The customary proscriptions laying out the non-participation of women in the public sphere, and in the judicial councils or *darbars* led by the Syiems, cannot be understood simply as relics of a pre-colonial past. The signatorial authority vested in the male heads of various communities across the hills from the early nineteenth century reaffirmed male privilege and representative authority. Kinship became an important reference point for colonial officials who supervised succession to Syiemships; kinship was equally important for jurists, administrators, and legislators who were engaged in resolving succession disputes between contending heirs. As mentioned in Chapter 4, petitions from contending parties in succession disputes invoked their proximity as relatives to particular lineages, or contested the importance given to one lineage over another.[61] Despite the varying positions of the respective claims in the Cherra succession dispute, the Syiems' legitimacy emerged from kinship and lineage. The processes of depoliticization and gendering of the Syiem's role, and the simultaneous recognition of his customary and non-proprietary authority over land, meant significant transformations in gender roles during the nineteenth century.

The hyper-sexualized colonial space further created strict gender boundaries which impeded women's participation in the public sphere. The colonial archive from the nineteenth century, as examined in the previous chapters, demonstrates that women were not only viewed as heiresses through whom claims of descent were made. Women held leadership positions in religious and ritualistic affairs; and they even held the power to confirm succession to Syiemships; worked in different trades, including iron kilns and agriculture. I am not tracing a form of matriarchal epistemology, and I am not suggesting that patriarchal gender norms are an invention of the colonial period. I argue that along with the introduction of missionary education and writing culture, the social and legal-customary space of the frontier hills became reconstituted through a male and patriarchal voice.

To work with a feminist-materialist understanding of place-making that will be elaborated in the final chapter, we have thus far examined the historical and material conditions surrounding the production of a

---

[61] Memorial from U Borgusain to the Secretary of State for India in Council, in Foreign Department, External Branch A, Cons., nos. 35–38, May 1906, NAI.

gendered ethnic identity embedded in spatio-legal, politico-economic, and socio-cultural relations. The creeping and insidious domination of written culture in the region was the product of legal power and of the supposedly inalterable nature of the written agreements made between the Syiems and the EIC from the early nineteenth century.

Written records, such as agreements, petitions, judgments, and reports on succession, among others, were repeatedly referenced and recalled, and thus informed the Khasi public sphere. Men trained in the English language, in schools run by missionaries, first articulated an indigenous ethnic identity that emphasized religion and the division of gender roles. The written and published words of colonizers, as well as of the English-educated Khasi men, produced compendia of Khasi grammar, written histories, accounts of norms and values, and studies of indigenous religion. There was a massive shift in the way that culture and identity were articulated among communities for whom orality was a prominent form and source of knowledge and of remembering the past.

The absence of women's participation in the public sphere in the late nineteenth and early twentieth centuries is stark. During this time, literature was published on women's roles and responsibilities. Matrilineal kinship was thus an important site of the struggle for power and for the assertion of gender identity. The discourse on a matrilineal kinship system was as diverse as the experiences of the women within it. Locating women within a spatiality of matrilineal kinship structure offers an understanding of the complexity and heterogeneity of female experiences in ways that defy singular ethnic considerations of gender roles. Alternative maps and spaces produced through material and imaginative processes offer a critique of colonial territoriality and knowledge. Expanding further on the above-mentioned points the following chapter will return to the dialectic between literacy and orality and discuss *other places* of the frontier hills.

7

Place-Making

Imperial geography enabled and augmented the production of the frontier as an abstract space.[1] Through this process the frontier hills were
included within the cartographic imagination of the empire, and the
region's inhabitants and landscape were incorporated as subjects of colonial law. The abstraction of people and places through categories of colonial legal spatiality violently marginalized multiple social formations,
inter-community links, ways of being, and forms of knowledge. The
dominant forms of knowledge that emerged in the nineteenth century
through literacy and writing eluded the experiential reality of frontier
societies. This chapter turns towards the embodied and situated experiences of frontier hill inhabitants by exploring their relationship to landscape, environment, and the changing spatiality of new jurisdictional
boundaries, lines of communication, enhanced economic mobility, and
politico-social architecture. The chapter highlights difficulties in accessing forms of knowing, remembering, and being that weren't refracted
through the experience of colonial violence. The chapter demonstrates
the importance of partial and complex conceptions of the past arguing
against notions of homogenous identity, and singular, authentic narratives of self, community, and belonging in the hills. By examining oral
histories and oral traditions this chapter centres the non-hegemonic notions of space and place found in the Khasi and Jaintia hills.

Social theorists including geographers, anthropologists, and legal
studies scholars have engaged with the dual concepts of space and place,
often understood in binary terms. The earlier chapters have demonstrated
that space is multidimensional and political. Space is produced through
governmental, and politico-economic practices, legal trajectories, and

---

[1] Daniel Clayton, 'Critical Imperial and Colonial Geographies', in *Handbook of Cultural
Geography*, eds. Kay Anderson, Mona Domosh, Steve Pile and Nigel Thrift (London: SAGE
Publications, 2003), 360. See also Derek Gregory, 'Imaginative Geographies', *Progress in Human
Geography* 19, no. 4 (December 1995), 447–485.

Placing the Frontier in British North-East India. Reeju Ray, Oxford University Press. © Reeju Ray 2023.
DOI: 10.1093/oso/9780192887085.003.0007

socio-political interrelations. This chapter will show how notions of place cut across and weave through spatial practices trajectories and interrelations. Place is not understood in opposition to space, or as an authentic locality. Instead, places are sites of negotiation and thereby non-essentialist. Places allow, 'to retain, while reformulating, an appreciation of the specific and the distinctive while refusing the parochial.'[2]

Place integrates the multidimensional aspects of space (abstract space, representational space, and lived reality), and highlights the experiential voices of frontier inhabitants. The positions, voices, visions, and imagination of place are heterogeneous, shifting, and partial. Heterogeneous and partial histories of place can be extracted from memory-archive can be sites of resistance to colonial and nationalist histories. A collective memory archive contains narratives of heterogeneous ways of inhabiting a place.[3] Kieth Basso has eloquently pointed out in relation to the western Apache societies that the 'ephemeral nature of contemplation' that places evoke as sites of memory, are not socially isolated experiences.[4] Similarly, in the Khasi hills oral traditions that imbue physical sites with life and history link land, community, and shared histories of inhabitants.

Place-making is essentially time-bound—whether linear, cyclical, or iterative. The heterogeneity of place and its narratives provide access to non-linear histories. Places offer an encounter between the past, present, and future; nearness and distance; temporality and spatiality. Places embody time in multiple ways reaching back into the years, touching simultaneous epochs and countless days widely separated from one another in time.[5] This chapter begins with a discussion of landscape and memory as intersubjective elements of place-making through megalithic

[2] Massey, 'Geographies of Responsibility', 5–18. See also Doreen Massey, *Space, Place, Gender* (Cambridge: Polity Press, 1994).

[3] Ajay Skaria has brilliantly argued that memories extracted from oral traditions are sites which continue to challenge cooption into any meta-narrative of history. See Ajay Skaria, *Hybrid Histories: Forests, Frontiers and Wildness in Western India* (Delhi and Oxford: Oxford University Press, 1999).

[4] Keith H. Basso, 'Wisdom Sits in Places: Notes on a Western Apache Landscape', in *Senses of Place*, eds. Steven Feld and Keith H. Basso (Santa Fe: School of American Research Press, 1996), 57.

[5] Basso, 'Wisdom Sits', 74. See also Jeff E. Malpas, 'Introduction', in *Place and Experience: A Philosophical Topography* (Cambridge and New York: Cambridge University Press, 1999); For an extensive theoretical study of place and space as binary categories, see Edward S. Casey, *The Fate of Place: A Philosophical History* (Berkeley and Los Angeles: University of California Press, 1997).

Figure 7.1 Monoliths and Mawbynna. By Tarun Bhartiya

record-keeping, sacred ecologies, and folktales. The chapter then turns to alternative geographies found in legends and social forms that contain interruptions to colonial spatiality and hegemonic power relations.

Kynmaw: Landscape and Memory

Kynmaw is the Khasi word both for stones and memories. *Kynmaw* dot the landscape of the frontier hills, and are variously known as menhirs, megaliths, or monoliths, in addition to their local names that vary across the hills (see Figure 7.1). Archaeologists have dated many of the megalithic monuments found across the subcontinent to as early as the Neolithic period.[6] Existing studies on these stone structures make ready

---

[6] According to archaeologists R. K. Mohanty and V. Selvakumar, 'these monuments lend these disparate peoples the common traits of what we know as megalithic culture, one which lasted from the Neolithic Stone Age to the early Historical Period (2500 BC to AD 200) across the world. In India, archaeologists trace the majority of the megaliths to the Iron Age (1500 BC to 500 BC), though some sites precede the Iron Age, extending up to 2000 BC'. See R. K. Mohanty and V. Selvakumar, 'The Archaeology of Megaliths in India: 1947–1977', In *Indian Archaeology in Retrospect*, eds. Ravi Korisettar and S. Settar, vol. 1 (New Delhi: Manohar, 2002).

comparisons between the prehistoric megaliths and living megalithic cultures found across South Asia.[7] Such continuities are anachronistic, and often coincide with colonial discourses and civilizational ideas of primitivism. Living megalithic cultures suggest an interrelationship between the use of stones to inscribe the landscape with memories, the recording of historical events, and communicating with an ancestral past. This section will use anthropological writings, as well as field interviews, about megalithic culture in Meghalaya to demonstrate the complex and intersubjective ways in which landscape itself can be imbued with sentience and history.

Queenbala Marak, in her study of living megalithic sites across northeastern India, has shown the wide and varied range of usages and meanings associated with the stone structures and the practices that take place around them. One of the sites she studies, Nangbah, located in the Jaintia hills, has over five hundred megaliths. While some stones clearly serve as sepulchres, and are thus associated with ritualistic practices surrounding death, other stones can also be associated with several other social and political activities. Different rituals that can be understood as oral traditions concerning important life moments, particularly death, along with various religious and cultural festivals, are conducted around the stones. Each type of event focuses on different kinds of stones, each with their own names.

The stones are gendered according to the position in which they are placed. Standing stones represent the maternal uncle and younger male members of the clan, while flat stones represent the clan ancestress or younger sub-clan ancestresses. The table stones marked as feminine using the prefix *Ka*, unlike the upright stones. The importance of oral tradition and of funerary rituals for clan members is an integral element in fostering clan unity, according to Marak. Death is considered to bind a person both to the land and to their respective clans; it does so by interring the deceased person's remains in clan sepulchres that are

---

[7] See S. Mendaly, 'A Study of Living Megalithic Tradition among the Gond Tribes, District—Nuaparha, Odisha', *Ancient Asia* 6, no. 9 (2015): 1–6; S. Chongloi and Q. Marak, 'Rang Taiba's Stone: A Study of a Megalith in Maram Khullen, Manipur, India', *Antrocom Journal of Anthropology* 11, no. 1 (2015): 97–104; Queenbala Marak, 'Megaliths, Types, and Its Living Traditions among the Jaintias of Northeastern India', *Journal of Indo-Pacific Archaeology* 32 (2012): 45–53.

physically embedded in the ground. Life, afterlife, and landscape are all connected through oral traditions that centre around these stones. As Marak writes that after the cremation ceremony remains of bones are placed first in individual family cists. She states,

> From these individual cists, the bones are collected in a year or even later and placed in a larger cist of the subclan/lineage. Thereafter some years when the clan members are able to gather sufficient money for the ceremony, these bones from family and sub-clan cists are gathered and laid to rest in the moobah. Thus, an individual born into a clan will likely travel thrice if not twice to reach its final resting place at the clan cist, even if it takes years to do so. The above ceremonies reiterate the importance of the clan system, and therefore a person born into a clan will likely remain in it even after death.[8]

This ritualistic journey of the deceased corresponds to a belief in the afterlife that is tied to land and lineage. Descriptions of the stones by interviewees during my fieldwork emphasized the relevance of ancestors and of their continued presence in spaces within and outside the physical landscape.[9] This can also be read in Gurdon's descriptions of these same stones. *Mawbyna* or *mawnam* were erected to commemorate deceased parents or ancestors and consisted of odd numbers of upright stones with flat table stones in front. The megaliths that made up these clusters represented different members of the family of ancestors, such as the maternal uncle, brothers, and nephews. Gurdon described these clusters of stones as follows: 'The table stone is called *ka iawbei tynrai* or *ka iawbei tymmen*, literally the grandmother of the root, or the old grandmother. These are different from *ka iawbei khynraw*, or *ka iawbei kpoh* (the grandmother of the family or branch of the family).'[10]

These anthropomorphic definitions of the stones in Gurdon's book, published at the turn of the twentieth century, highlighted the matrilineal kinship systems of frontier communities. The presence of two sets of flat table stones acknowledged the 'first ancestress'. Stones placed on

[8] Marak, 'Megaliths', 51.
[9] Sweetymon Rynjah and Tambor Lyngdoh, interviewed by Reeju Ray, June and July 2012.
[10] Gurdon, *Khasis*, 151.

the right signified *ka iawbei longkpoh*, who, according to Gurdon, was 'the grandmother of the clan to which the memorialists belong, or ka Iawbei khynraw, the young grandmother, i.e. the grandmother of the actual family to which the memorialists belong'.[11] Matrilineal kinship geography is an important place where resistance to colonial epistemology can be located. Yet, the kinship system was also deeply impacted through the consolidation of male authority, and gender codes and norms that crystallized in the nineteenth century. This is further discussed in the last section of this chapter.

A direct connection between megalithic culture and place-making is found in the names given to villages or different locales across the Khasi hills. Gurdon wrote of 'places in these hills as Maomluh, the salt stone (the eating of salt off the blade of sword being one of the forms of oath), Maosmai, the oath stone, Maophlang, the grassy stone, and others'.[12] Importantly, Gurdon expressed his difficulty in acquiring information about the stones because of the inhabitants' 'feelings of delicacy in revealing secrets of their religious system to a foreigner or through [*sic*] ignorance or apathy'.[13] The secrecy surrounding many oral traditions was a clear rejection on the part of locals of making known certain aspects of community life and place.

From Gurdon's limited sources, he divided the stones into the following categories: (1) *mawlynti* or *mawkjat*, which serve as 'seats for the spirits of the departed clans folk' when their remains are carried to the 'clan cromlech', (discussed in detail by Marak); (2) *mawbynna* or *maynam*, which are stones erected to commemorate a parent or some near relation, thereby suggesting personal inscriptions for commemoration; (3) *mawumkoi* are signposts for water tanks, where such water tanks were used in particular for the ritual cleansing of ashes and bones of those who died unnatural deaths; and (4) *mawshongthait*, flat table stones, often found alongside vertical stones found in market places and along roads to serve as seats for weary travellers. Interestingly, there is a correlation between seats for a traveller and seats for ancestors. *Mawshongthait* were not only seats for living persons travelling between two places, but also for spirits of the

[11] Ibid.
[12] Ibid., 144.
[13] Ibid., 149.

dead during their transportation to the clan sepulchre or *mawbah*.[14] Marak's study adds many other kinds of stone in the Jaintia hills, all of which demonstrate the varied uses and meanings of stones across different places in the hills.

The representation of landscape in colonial sources, such as Gurdon's book, was informed by the ideology of primitivism discussed in detail in Chapter 5. The emphasis on religion as nature worship was a pervasive feature of colonial anthropology and discourses on putative primitivism. Thus, the stones found in the Khasi hills were understood within the confines of religion. Gurdon also alluded to the possibility of human immolation on the stones rumours of which set in motion colonial military excursions in the Jaintia kingdom.[15] Gurdon's account of the landscape combined within a unified vision of a religious Khasi framework ideas about the importance of women through matriliny and female figureheads, the ritualistic significance of the stones, and the barbarity of human immolation.

Sweetimon Rynjah, a community elder and prolific writer on Khasi orality and history, suggested during a series of interviews I conducted with her between 2011 and 2013 that these stones contain secular functions that are often neglected by researchers. Her account contains descriptions of many types of megalithis which she interchangeably referred to as kynmaw during our conversations. Moving away from an emphasis on religious significance of stones Kong Rynjah described stones that were erected as part of obligatory ritual following the resolution of personal disputes and other social conflicts. Rynjah also pointed towards clusters of megaliths that have been erected in memory of deceased soldiers or *mawshyrwait* are quite common.[16] These stones record the death of many Khasi men who were part of the labour corps in the British Indian army during the world wars.[17]

---

[14] Sweetymon Rynjah, interviewed by Reeju Ray, July 2012.
[15] Gurdon, *Khasis*, 151–152.
[16] Sweetymon Rynjah, interviewed by Reeju Ray, June 2012.
[17] Ibid.; in the centre of Mawkhar in Shillong, near the now famous Iew or market, is a memorial dedicated to the Khasi labour corps who died in World War I.

Kong Rynjah's insistence on looking beyond religion in understanding megalithic culture in the hills is insightful in several ways. First, it presents a refusal of colonial tropes of primitivism and anachronistic linkages between prehistoric and living megaliths. This creates a necessary understanding that megalithic culture is informed by social and historical contexts and thus cannot be attached to any singular homogenous articulation of cultural identity or religious belief. Second, and relatedly it helps us contextualize why in instances of infrastructure development such as building highways one finds instances of uprooting megaliths. During the recent beautification efforts in the city of Shillong leading up to the commemoration of fifty years of statehood in Meghalaya, many neighbourhood entrances including mine were adorned with new *maybynnah*. This was a state government initiative in collaboration with neighbourhood councils.

The stones embedded in the landscape performed everyday functions, recorded memory, and served as sites where a community's relationship with its ancestors was rehearsed and remembered. The living environment and the practices of agriculture, labour, and boundary-making all formed part of a symbiotic relationship between inhabitants and the spirits that embodied the landscape.[18] It is important to note that the boundaries differentiating the uses of these stones— whether they were used for ritualistic purposes or practical use—were very blurred. While colonial geography relied on binaries of sacred and secular spaces, the use of the stones and their varied meanings point us towards the multivalence in how inhabitants might otherwise have imagined the hills. For instance, in another extended interview conducted in 2011, the conservationist Mr Tambor Lyngdoh emphasized the ritualistic, metaphysical, and religious aspects of the stone clusters found in the sacred grove of Mawphlang. Sacred ecology marked by megaliths in Mawphlang has played a significant role in enabling forest conservation in the state.

---

[18] In her study of Mongolian landscapes, Caroline Humphrey writes that the 'human relation to natural entities is analogous: their unpredictable energies and beneficial powers can be tamed by ritualized actions. People have their own relationship with particular mountains, cliffs, or trees which they feel to be especially influential in their lives'. See Caroline Humphrey, 'Chiefly and Shamanist Landscapes in Mongolia', in *The Anthropology of Landscapes: Perspectives on Place and Space*, eds. Eric Hirsch and Michael O'Hanlon (Oxford: Clarendon Press, 1995), 137.

Law Kyntang: Sentient Ecology of the Hills

Annual visits to the Mawphlang sacred grove in the Khasi hills, along with several other trips to sacred groves in Nartiang in the Jaintia hills during the years growing up in Shillong, created for me a sense of personal attachment and familiarity with these forests rich with myths and oral traditions. It was many years later when I re-visited these places as a researcher that I began to understand the intersection of statutory laws meant for protecting forests and tribal land, and regime of extractive economies the significance beyond the aims of conservation which began as colonial policy from late nineteenth century. Many of these groves are protected by law from deforestation while conservationists continue to lament the surreptitious felling of forests for timber trade, and degradation of ecology due to extractive mining economies. Sacred groves, forests, and community forestry are now part of the mainstream discourse on conservation.

The Meghalaya government website records one hundred and twenty-five sacred groves in the state. A total of 1000 sq. km of forest area is classified as sacred through a survey conducted by the National Afforestation and Eco-Development board and placed under the administrative control of the Autonomous District Councils.[19] Oral traditions and community practices are understood by the forest and environment department as religious beliefs and separated from methods used by inhabitants to care for and engage with ecology.

This process of transforming forest commons into abstract protected forest legally moved into the hills in late nineteenth century. Laws of forest management and conservation were extended to the frontier hills when they were attached to the administrative province of Assam in 1874. During this decade the colonial government articulated forest conservation/control through the Indian Forest Act of 1878. The act divided forests as reserved (fully under government control), protected (partially controlled), and village forests (local community control). Around the same time the colonial government became the largest beneficiary of timber trade. The public works department was the 'largest official

---

[19] See Meghalaya Forest and Environment Department, Government of Meghalaya, last Accessed on 25 January 2022.

consumer of timber.'[20] Forests were also repurposed for expanding agriculture, mining, and the construction of roads. Whereas colonial and postcolonial laws transformed landscapes into reserved and protected forests, ideas of environmental protection, natural resources and biodiversity have negatively impacted communities living in these places. As Shalini Randeira writes, 'carving out of ecologically and commercially valuable spatial zones and the policing of boundaries based on the impositions uniform global classificatory schemes and property regimes, which entail varying degrees of exclusion of local communities, have been pursued by more or less coercive measures, then as now.'[21]

In this section I will focus on local narratives of sacred ecology with an understanding that spaces like the sacred groves were validated through colonial law and knowledge which in turn gave legitimacy to the same.

Sa'ng, or injunctions forbidding people from disturbing any external element within the *law kyntang*, was about agency invested in sacred forests and groves. Interaction with nature through rituals further created an ongoing engagement and socio-cultural relationship with ecology and landscape. That such agency was invested in landscape is also clear from the names of places in the hills. *Nong*, which is a common prefix in place names, is a Khasi term for agent. Other place names in the Khasi hills use prefixes such as *Um* (water), *lum* (hill), and *maw* (stone). Communication with these agents, who are often referred to as spirits, took place within forests and groves known as *law kyntang* or *law Niam*.

In most colonial accounts, such as Gurdon's, the different elements of nature are described as having spirits—often identified as deities—who need to be placated. The word *ryngkew* translates as spirit and it is sometimes gendered. The main forest energy or spirit is *U Ryngkew U Basa* (masculine gender denoted by the prefix U), believed to have the power to harm anyone who injured the forest or disturbed it in any way. Any

[20] Arupjyoti Saikia, *Forests and Ecological History of Assam, 1826–2000* (New Delhi: Oxford University Press, 2011), 32.

[21] For a detailed discussion of the different aspects of the 'janus faced' policies of environmental protection and commercial extraction of natural resources, see Shalini Randeria, 'Global Designs and Local Lifeworlds: Colonial Legacies of Conservation, Disenfranchisement, and Environmental Governance in Postcolonial India', *Interventions* 9, no. 1 (2007): 17.
See also Madhav Gadgil and Ramachandra Guha, *This Fissured Land: An Ecological History of India* (Berkeley and Los Angeles: University of California Press, 1993); Richard H. Grove, *Green Imperialism: Colonial Expansion, Tropical Island Edens and the Origins of Environmentalism, 1600–1860* (Cambridge: Cambridge University Press, 1995).

person was allowed to enter the forest, but there were *Sa'ng* that prohibited against taking anything away from it or from corrupting it in any way. The most important of these injunctions is that no tree was to be cut down in these forests. Apart from the *ryngkew*, there are also other elemental energies in the forests. The forests not only provide a home to energies of the different elements of nature, such as *Lei Lum* ('mountain or hill spirits'), *Lei wah* ('river spirits'), *Lei Khlaw* ('forest spirits'), *Lei Wallang* ('spirit of the state'), *Lei Umtong* ('water spirits'), *Lei Mulluk* ('spirit of the state'). Also inhabiting these forests are the *rngai* (literally meaning 'shadow') of deceased ancestors.[22] Not every sacred forest was believed to contain multiple elemental spirits. In the sacred grove of Mawphlang, for example, only the *U Ryngkew U Basa* is placated through rituals and oral traditions.[23]

At the Mawphlang sacred forest, rituals only take place when the twelve founding clans feel that it is necessary to appease the ancestors and the *U Ryngkew U Basa*. The grove at Mawphlang is dated to be five hundred-year-old, and is under the care of the Hima Mawphlang *lyngdohship*. According to Tambor Lyngdoh, only during a time of natural calamity do the elders of the village initiate rituals to appease the *U Ryngkew U Basa*.[24] These various spirits represent the sentience and agency of the landscapes, like mountains, rivers, forests, water, and even of abstract entities such as the state. The sacred nature of these groves, and the complex and sometimes secretive rituals performed within them, made such spaces inaccessible to colonial governance or knowledge. The presence of protective and malevolent spirits, and oral traditions to placate forest deities point to community narratives and efforts to preserve the ecology.

Folk tales also recount several instances of the destruction of sacred groves, including *lum shyllong*, the now-famous tourist spot of Shillong peak. Bengt Carlson described the slow desecration of this once sacred grove, which began when one Francis Syiem leased the lands—including

---

[22] Rekha Shangpliang, *Forests in the Life of the Khasis* (New Delhi: Concept Publishing, 2010), 32. Shangplaing notes that there are two kinds of 'spirits'. Those with good intentions are called *lei* and are associated with welfare, wealth, water, villages, etc., whereas the malevolent spirits, which are called *skuid*, bring harm.

[23] Tambor Lyndoh, interviewed by Reeju Ray, June 2012; belonging to the Lyngdoh clan and the son of a traditional healer, Tambor Lyndoh is now involved with community-based projects centred on forest conservation.

[24] Tambor Lyndoh, interviewed by Reeju Ray, June 2012.

the sacred hill and forest—to a timber contractor.[25] Several sacred groves and forests have been destroyed over the centuries, particularly those in the vicinity of colonial stations like Shillong.[26]

Nartiang with its famous megaliths surrounded by a sacred grove was the political centre of the Jaintia Rajah. Nartiang's political importance grew once the Jaintia king was forced to abdicate his seat in the capital of Sylhet plains at Jaintiapore (see Figure 7.2). It is hardly surprising, then, that the mid-nineteenth-century rebellions against colonial taxation in the Jaintia hills broke out in Nartiang. The centre of Nartiang was important for several different activities, such as the succession of Rajas or for conducting judicial and administrative deliberations. The functionality of the Nartiang forest and monoliths cannot be understood by separating sacred ecology from the political significance of this place. Colonial geography was neither isolated from nor absent in these conceptualizations, but it was marginal to them. The oral traditions, myths, legends, and folktales that surround sacred ecologies in these hills contain political articulations of inhabitants. They also contain rich narratives about the modes of livelihood and political economy tied to a culture of orality.

Esther Syiem has argued that oral traditions in the Khasi hills were woven into and out of the sentience of ecology. In her study of

---

[25] In his interview with Lyngdoh Nongkrem (a traditional priest of the Khyrim polity), Bengt Karlsson learned of a folk tale about a deer: after trespassing into the forest, the deer was killed by the inhabitants of the corresponding village. Of the several interpretations for this folk tale, one that explained the cutting down of the sacred forest involved the analogous trespass by outsiders or by the British. The deer was killed for encroaching into the sacred forest, and then transformed into a sacred stream after the hill spirit had been moved by the cries of the deer's mother. Although the analogy is not quite clear, the overlap in themes of encroachment, violence, and a subsequent transformation of the landscape is clearly visible. Syiem Francis' sale of lands is dated to the 1980s, while the analogy used to explain this occurrence is situated in the early nineteenth century. What Lyngdoh Nongkrem was emphasizing is that transgressions, such as that made by Syiem Francis, resulted from the encroachment of the British, which caused the people to 'forget their culture and faith'. See Bengt G. Karlsson, *Unruly Hills: A Political Ecology of India's Northeast* (New York and Oxford: Berghahn, 2011), 4–6.

[26] Mawphlang is one of the surviving and better known of the sacred groves. It has recently come to international attention due to the work of conservationists, anthropologists, and the like. But not all sacred forests have enjoyed the same fate. Many have suffered rampant deforestation. The belief that a Hima (or Khasi state) must contain a sacred forest is no longer in practice, and its desuetude may be the result of colonial efforts to appropriate lands that were once sacred groves or forests, resulting in those lands being transformed into saleable property.

Figure 7.2 Sylhet Plains and Hills. By Tarun Bhartiya

the weaving communities of Khweng and Umtngam, in the Ri Bhoi District of Meghalaya, Syiem argues that to challenge dominant patriarchal and state narratives, it is vital to locate women's voices who are agents of political economy and oral culture.[27] The relationship between preservation of oral cultures and local political economy is an important intervention. It shows that orality is not a site to simply excavate an authentic past, but contains ecological codes and 'discourses of the future'.[28] The culture and practices of orality are therefore not simply remnants of a pre-colonial past marginalized through Western knowledge. Orality as in the case of weavers in Khweng and Umtngam, Syiem shows, is a women-centred community practice connected to livelihood. Such oral practices are actively political sites and contain narratives of place that are profoundly local with radical possibilities.

---

[27] See Esther Syiem, 'Negotiating the Loss: Orality in the Indigenous Communities of North East India', *India International Centre Quarterly* 43, no. 1 (2016): 80–89.
[28] Syiem, 'Negotiating the Loss', 80–89.

Places of Myth and Memory

History and memory do intersect to create, in Indira Chowdhury's words, a 'polyphony of dialogue'.[29] The myths and oral histories recorded by colonial anthropologists and codified in religious and sanctioned through state publications focus on the origin of U Hynniewtrep or the seven original clans that constitute the Khasi identity. I am not interested here in asking whether origin myths provide historical insight into the precolonial past. Instead, I want to draw attention to the kind of spatiality they represent, and the kind of narratives of place they produce.[30] Joy Pachuau has argued that the conflict over territory was central to the way colonial and indigenous represented tribal identity. The historical context of demographic displacement, movement, and contests over space, accompanied means of creating rootedness of identity even forcibly. The transition from orality to written narratives reflects the rootedness to space. Pachuau shows that Mizo meaning hill people also indicated the hill-plain boundary.[31] Joy Pachuau's rich and compelling analysis is helpful in understanding the centrality of origin myths in the Khasi hills.

In the decades following the publication of Gurdon's book, several anthropologists, historians, linguists attempted to locate and trace the origin of the Khasis. Such attempts to establish scientifically the 'vexed question' of Khasi origin led to Gurdon making several inferences.[32] Using various colonial and missionary interpretations as references, he suggested that the origins of the Khasis were unclear and ambiguous. These ranged from political connections with the Burmese, to nomadic 'wanderings' from somewhere in the north up to Sylhet. He also noted that the Khasis and other tribes were believed to be part of the 'Mon Anam family', which had occupied a large portion of the subcontinent. Among their many possible

[29] Indira Chowdhury, 'Speaking of the Past: Perspectives on Oral History', Economic and Political Weekly 49, no. 30 (2014): 39–42.
[30] For a discussion of origin myths as cultural construction, based on Satnami myths, see Saurabh Dube, 'A Contested Past', in Historical Anthropology, ed. Saurabh Dube (New Delhi: Oxford University Press, 2007), 173–190. For an analysis of origin myth as 'causation', see Gyan Prakash, Bonded Histories: Genealogies of Labour Servitude in Colonial India (Cambridge: Cambridge University Press, 1990), 34–81.
[31] See Joy L. K. Pachuau, Being Mizo, 100–110. See also Margaret L. Pachuau, 'Orality', 172–194.
[32] Gurdon, Khasis, 10. The published writing by Khasi intellectuals on Khasi identity has been discussed in Chapter 6.

origins that Gurdon discussed, one was that the Khasis formed part of 'the different irruptions of foreign peoples into Assam … from south east to north west as it was the case with the Ahom invaders of Assam who invaded Assam from their settlements in the Shan States via the Patkoi range, the different Burmese invasions, the movements of the Khamtis and once again the Singphos, from the country to the east of the Hukong valley'.[33] By tracing the linguistic genealogy of Khasi, he established that the Khasis belonged to the Mon Khmer Austro-Asiatic family of languages, and thus their origins are linked to migratory movements from Indochina. Discussions derived from similar ideas albeit with updated findings and variations were published by Khasi intellectuals in the following decades.

Set apart from colonial scientific and historical ideas, various origin myths of *U Hynniewtrep* are rehearsed and remembered by inhabitants of the Khasi hills in the present day. One of these is celebrated by the practicians of the Seng Khasi or indigenous faith. It highlights the importance given to *Lum Sohpetbneng*, or the hilltop that connected the earth to the skies, which serves as a site for annual rituals and the rehearsal of oral traditions.[34] According to this origin myth which slightly varies based on who tells the story, the *Hynniewtrep* were among the sixteen clans or families who used a tall tree or ladder (this varies in different renditions) connecting *Lum Sohpetbneng* with the skies to come down in order to cultivate in the hills and return to the land of God or *U Blei*.[35] On one occasion, when only seven of the families had descended, someone cut down the ladder out of greed. Thus, the seven clans or *U Hynniewtrep* became the inhabitants of the hills. This story resonates deeply with the rupture that accompanied the establishment of sedentary agriculture in the plains of Sylhet. Colonial territorialization of the Bengal plains resulted in several groups being cut-off and labelled as 'hill tribals', thereby reconstituting their social, economic, and political relationships with inhabitants of the plains. The idea of separation within the sixteen clans—the seven clans that became inhabitants of the hills and the nine that remained in

[33] Gurdon, *Khasis*, 11.
[34] The literal translation of the name of the hill is 'heaven's naval'.
[35] K. U. Rafy, *Folk-Tales of the Khasis* (London: Macmillan, 1920), 8–9, mentions that the myth concerns a tall tree connecting heaven and the hill top; however, the Khasi words to describe this are *jingkieng ksiar*, literally meaning 'golden ladder' or 'vine'.

the skies—provides an insightful element of this story. It points towards a belief that the Khasis were originally part of a larger group, but connections between the two were later severed.

Another origin tale inscribes matrilineal kinship onto the landscape. In this tale, *Meiramew*, the mother of three daughters named *Ka Ding* (fire), *Ka Um* (water), and *Ka Sngi* (sun), came to earth to meet her daughters, and then fell ill and died.[36] The three daughters endeavoured to conduct final rites for their mother's body. As per matrilineal custom, the youngest daughter, *Ka Sgni*, was the first to conduct the rites; while her fierce rays scorched the earth dry, *Meiramew's* body nevertheless remained unscathed. *Ka Um* was the next to perform last rites, whereupon she produced incessant rains and flooding. But once the water subsided, they found *Meiramew's* body still preserved. Lastly, the eldest daughter *Ka Ding* set everything alight, which finally destroyed *Meiramew's* earthly remains. The endless plains that had characterized the earth were believed to have been transformed with the *Ka Ding's* flames into mountains, valleys, and gorges. In this landscape, trees, shrubs, and flowers grew again; water cascaded over hills; and lakes were formed. This tale also speaks to a sense of rupture: the death of *Meiramew* and the constitution of a new landscape.

Oral traditions that perpetuate Khasi conceptions of landscape mention a ceremony held annually at the beginning of the agricultural season of rice, when *Lukhmi* the spirit or goddess of grain is welcomed into the hills. This three-day annual ceremony of *keh loh Lukhmi*, or fetching *Lukhmi*, practised in the northern Khasi hills close to the Assam border, gives us privileged access to local ideas about history by looking at repetitive practices or performances that explain the development of sedentary agriculture in the hills. The important aspects of this three-day ritual include the act of fetching the spirit of paddy, which signifies the recent origins of paddy cultivations in the hills; the walk up to *Nongbah*, literally meaning 'capital' but considered to be the first site of settlement of the Khasis; and the performance of egg divination to ascertain from what direction *Lukhmi* will come each year. Desmond Kharmawphlang has noted that '[while] it is generally believed that the *Ka Lukhmi* originally came from the plains ... the very act of performing divination to ascertain

---

[36] *Meiramew* can also be understood as everything that constitutes the landscape.

whence *Ka Lukhmi* will come—from the Khasi hills or from the low lands reveals how the *Ka Lukhmi*-woman turned benefactor—has gained acceptance in the cultural milieu of the Khasi hills adjoining Assam.[37] The hill, or *Nongbah*, is an essential component of this ceremony. It has historical, political, and social significance. The very act of repetition and performance in fetching *Lukhimi* from a site called *U Mawsieng*, which translates as boat-stone and which is her carrier, reflects several dimensions of conceiving, recollecting, and articulating the past. For instance, the rituals and oral traditions surrounding the annual fetching of *Lukhimi* reinforce communal memory of paddy cultivation as a practice that was indigenous to the hills. Further, practices of divination, along with other ritual performances that confirm both *Lukhimi's* arrival and goodwill, also reflect processes of accommodation and adaptation to changing socioeconomic patterns such as rice cultivation and sedentary agriculture.[38] Together the ritualistic rehearsing of communal memory, historical transformations, and settlement is a story of belonging in the hills.

Belonging did not imply only being situated in the physical confines of the hills. Place-making which resisted being co-opted into a colonial geography manifested itself in alternative forms and planes of existence. There were multiple ways of 'being' in the place of *Hynniewtrep*: either as *rngai* (also called *syrngi*), meaning shadow of ancestors, as *rngiew* or spirits of shamans who could physically traverse two conceptual worlds or realities, and others.[39] These immaterial forms were considered to be important social agents through which the power of nature was harnessed, and they represented the power and legitimacy of the hills in terms that were inconsistent with colonial legal definitions. The Syiem's

---

[37] Desmond Kharmawphlang, 'The Ka Lukhmi: A Khasi Rice Myth', in 'Where the Sun Rises When Shadows Fall: The North-East', special issue, *India International Centre Quarterly* 32, no. 2/3 (2005): 132.

[38] For a reproduction of the oral traditions concerning *keh loh Lukhmi*, see Desmond Kharmawphlang, *Khasi Folk Songs and Tales* (New Delhi: Sahitya Akademi, 2006), 2–27. For a description of the three-day ceremonies, see Kharmawphlang, 'The Ka', 122–136.

[39] I have used translations that are consistent with those used by Desmond Kharmawphlang in his work. However, in my interviews I often found variations; for example, 'shadow of ancestors' are often translated by Kharmawphlang as 'spirit of ancestors'. The *rngiew* is often translated as 'guardian' or a 'constant presence in the lives of people'. See Desmond Kharmawphlang, 'In Search of Tigermen: The Were-Tiger Tradition of the Khasis', in *The Human Landscape*, eds. Geeti Sen and Ashis Banerjee (Delhi: Orient Longman, 2001), 160–176; Esther Syiem argues that even oral traditions have their own *rngiew* or aura that permeates all living beings: see Syiem, 'Negotiating the Loss', 80–89. See also R. S. Lyngdoh, *Ka Histori ka Thoh ka Tar: Bynta I and II* (Shillong: 1979 and 1983).

power, within this framework, did not represent the epitome of local indigenous authority. Taken together, in fact, the non-human elements represented a significantly greater power due to their incommensurability
with colonial legal, spatial, and temporal frameworks.

Legends about the interaction between humans and non-human elements are very common in folk traditions of these hills. Many folktales
provide a sense of direct engagement between the constituent elements of landscape or *meiramew*. There are also conceptual or alternative spaces identified as *ramia*, and located within *meiramew*, which
can only be inhabited by *rngai* and *ka rngiew*.[40] *Ka rngiew*, according to
Kharmawphlang, is 'an essence, a power which shapes and determines
most of man's actions, thoughts and motivations. It gives shape to his
dreams and visions, and charts the course of his life and is regarded as
imperishable and immutable'. This concept is distinguishable from the *ka
met* (body) and *ka mynsiem (soul)*.[41] The concept of *ka rngiew* can thus
be understood as a feminine (denoted by prefix *Ka*) energy that accom-
panies the person in their lifetime and does not perish after death. It pro-
duces specific actions and thoughts, and bestows the power to transcend
the real inhabited space. *Ka rngiew* then is attributed with the power to
exist both in the physical landscape and in spaces that transcend it.

This point emerges clearly from the performative tradition of Khla
Phuli or Tigermen. Selected individuals—usually male elders designated
as shamans—are vested with a power whereby their *rngiew* embodies
the form of a tiger and enters the space of *ramia*. The person inhabiting
this alternative space may or may not be asleep. The shaman is believed
to have had the power to transform physically into a tiger in the past,
whereas nowadays, only the shaman's *rngiew* transforms into *Khla Phuli*
(tiger) or *San Saram* (four clawed one). An extract from an interview he
conducted in a village from the northern Khasi hills with one of the elders
there demonstrates the Khasi understanding of this practice.

KHARMAWPHLANG: What is the reason for turning into tigers?
MAJI: For the reason of clinging and holding.

[40] Desmond Kharmawphlang has translated this word as 'hallucination', 'illusion', or a 'dream';
he does nevertheless caution that these words cannot capture the meaning of *ramia*, especially in
the context of tigermen.
[41] Kharmawphlang, 'In Search of Tigermen', 161.

KHARMAWPHLANG: Clinging of what?

MAJI: the religion.[42]

In the above extract from Kharmawphlang's interview with Shaman Maji, I find the emphasis on 'clinging' significant. The transformation from person to tiger, and then inhabiting an alternative space is likely the product of an anxiety to protect and preserve what is considered to be under threat. Kharmawphlang refers to instances when the tigermen or the *rngiew* had an obligatory role to protect their territories (variously interpreted as villages or alternative spaces) in the event of some encroachment by 'outsiders': i.e. people and/or other tigermen who did not belong to the particular *Hima* (polity, village, or religious unit). If the shaman had the metaphysical power to guard the *Hima*, then this was a significant supplement to the Syiem's power, the titular head of the *Hima*. It is not surprising, however, that the shaman's role has been significantly marginal(ized) compared to that of the Syiem. In many *Hima* today there are no living shamans.

Caroline Humphrey has pointed out, in relation to Mongolia, that the landscape could be framed either as shamanistic or as chiefly because these were the types of figure who had pervasive power and authority over their people.[43] While much of what Humphrey describes resonates with practices in the Khasi hills, there are nevertheless some major differences. Both chiefs and shamans were vested with religious power and social agency, and the Syiems often sought the shamans' counsel on various socio-political issues. Both positions were acquired through matrilineage and were typically held by male actors. The most significant difference between shaman and chief was that shamans worked alone in their roles as protector and defender of *ramia*, whereas Syiems primarily relied upon the support of family and village elders, or of the *darbar*, in order to maintain the exercise of his agency. The shamans were in a sense peripheral, just as the *ramia* was peripheral to the physical landscape. The shamans also served as the nexus for a complex of relationships linking community, ancestors, and geography. The space of the *ramia* also allowed for

---

[42] Ibid., 163.

[43] For an elaborate analysis of landscapes conceived of as shamanistic or chiefly, see Humphrey, 'Chiefly and Shamanist Landscapes', 135–162.

unrestricted movement and wandering. In the interview extract reproduced above, the clinging to religion mentioned by the interviewee was
less about the performance of specific rituals, and more about a broader
desire for and exercise of continuity with the past. Shamans were neither agents of religion nor were they responsible for performing religious
functions, a role that was usually given to Lyngdohs. To cling to religion,
as one shaman noted, was also to protect and preserve a space that was as
just as much socially and politically relevant as it was sacred. This was a
metaphorically idealized space that was prone to incursions and attacks,
and thus inflected the contestations of the physical landscape.

The roles performed by the tigers varied, according to Kharmawphlang.
He writes of three different shamans:

> U Dsing Marin's idea of guarding was to protect humans from tigers. U
> Joid Marki's was to protect the area from incursions of alien were-tigers
> who could come to create disturbances in the village. And according
> to Shanti Barim, the iapnagar tiger deity used to thwart the attempts of
> alien tigers from entering his domain. Whether the village here is the
> human or tiger village is unclear, but there are portions of the inter-
> views where there are clear references to the imprisonment of alien
> were-tigers.[44]

The shaman's power to transform was transferred from maternal uncle
to nephew in accordance with matrilineage. Once the shaman enters the
state whereby his body remains visible and inhabits the physical world,
but his *rngiew* inhabits the *ramia*, then he is guided by the *ryngkew*.
Ryngkew, as mentioned above, are guardians of particular places. The
ryngkew would lead the *rngiew* into the *ramia* where the *rngiew* would
transform.[45] The need to appease the *ryngkew* is paramount, both in
the alternative spaces of the *ramia* and in the physical sacred forests. In
the cryptic and metaphorical narrations of such experiences, it is often
reiterated that a failure to follow in the footsteps of the *ryngkew* (literally in the *ramia*, and figuratively otherwise) leads to *ka klim ka khla*

---

[44] Kharmawphlang, 'In Search of Tigermen', 169.
[45] I have avoided the translation of *ryngkew* as deity, since there is no known process of deifica-
tion involved.

which translates as committing adultery signifying severe transgressions of norms.

Ramia is a place of contestation, rather than religious or spiritual. The encroachment by alien tigers or people is commonly understood to be the reason for the shaman's journey. To be invested with the power and authority to access these places beyond physical space, shamans were required to live by strict disciplinary codes.[46] Not only did their power come from the knowledge required to access the *ramia*, but it was also a product of their authority to protect and defend both the knowledge and these places. The absence of colonial accounts about these places might have resulted from the refusal on the part of the hill inhabitants to divulge or share information with the colonizers. Nevertheless, the *ramia* was not a place isolated from the colonized or geographical landscape of Khasi polities, but rather it represented dreamlike interpretations of ecological, political, and social realities.

The *ramia* is a manifestation of a place where the shaman can accordingly inhabit the physical spaces that mark his *Hima*, village, and home. There is no attempt to deny the existence of colonial or postcolonial geography in the articulation of the *ramia*. Nor is the *ramia* declared to be a space that predates colonialism. The *ramia* is nested within a colonial and national geography, but it is not subsumed by that same geography. The *ramia* defies the spatial and temporal boundaries of colonial and national states. In this way, the *ramia* is not just an alternative space, or a time that is lost. It is in excess of geographical space and linear time, what Skaria has described as 'extra colonial'.

Orality and its relationship to memory have been deployed by scholars in their critique of 'history' as a synonym for western civilization and modernity. In the vast literature on the relationship between memory and history, two strands of argument must be examined before closing this chapter. First, oral traditions and oral histories challenge dominant written narratives, and often serve as critical sites of memory that enable alternative historical imaginations.[47] This points us towards questions of

---

[46] Tambor Lyngdoh (whose uncle was a shaman and his father a traditional healer) explains that present-day shamans are either very old (or dead), and that there are hardly any from his generation owing to a strict and a disciplined lifestyle required for the position; Tambor Lyngdoh, interview by Reeju Ray, June 2012.

[47] See Ajay Skaria, *Hybrid Histories*; Saurabh Dube, ed., *Historical Anthropology* (New Delhi: Oxford University Press, 2007); Prakash, *Bonded Histories*.

method and methodology when using oral sources to produce written histories. Second, and related to this, memory itself is susceptible to appropriation in the pursuit of history that serves various ideological and political agendas.[48]

Skaria suggests rethinking historical imaginations by tapping into the radical possibilities in the 'other' of history.[49] Approaching orality as a site of memory challenges modernist, universal representations of what history ought to be. Memory can exceed the limits of written records that are held up as the most valid sources of history as modernity. The state of 'being in excess' of the colonial modern can be read into spaces such as the sentient ecology of the frontier hills represented in the *ramia*, *mawbynnah*, *law kyntang*, and in the rehearsing and repetition of oral traditions.

Thus far, we have explored the various places that embody living memory. Such places are framed within and through ideas of custom and kinship. If, as argued earlier, custom is not the opposite of law—i.e. custom does not amount to law's 'other'—then the places like the sites of oral traditions and folklore, of living megaliths and sacred forests, and *ramia* are also spaces of law. Here it is necessary to return to the primary question that has run throughout this book: how does law reconfigure spaces?

Kinship and Place

Spatial reconstitution, legal exceptionalism, and ethnocentrism were undercurrents defining and shaping gender norms in the nineteenth century. Instead of pursuing an additive analysis that shows that *women too* were part of historical processes, I want to attempt to locate *where* gendered identities were shaped and formed (see Figure 7.3). Through this enquiry I will also trace the transformative role of law in processes of place-making. The written accounts on indigenous religion and custom were sites that provided validity to patriarchal institutions and voices in

[48] Pierre Nora, 'Between Memory and History: Les Lieux de Mémoire', *Representations* 26 (1989): 7–24.
[49] Skaria, *Hybrid Histories*.

Figure 7.3 Women farmers on a hill. By Tarun Bhartiya

the colonial and postcolonial period. Differently articulated nationalisms (state and regional), together with processes of globalization, have hardened the authoritative claims based on custom and religion. These claims reinforce patriarchal spatiality wherein arguments against women's rights range from defining women as ethnic border guards to challenges made to the matrilineal system. It is no surprise that patriarchal interests representing Hindutva ideology have aligned with ethnocentric interests. The heterogeneous interests that have appropriated *Niam* or Indigenous religion range from defenders of matriliny to those who severely challenge it.

Feminist analyses of the Khasi hills have often focused on matriliny as the site of struggle for women. To challenge the assertion that women have superior rights within the matrilineal system, feminists have contended that the institution of matriliny binds women to the household, which in turn precludes their participation in public and political life. The argument of confinement is not new. Whether confined to the land or the private sphere, women have been understood as having restricted mobility in the matrilineal societies of these hills. In many ways, this restriction is visible and such an analysis remains valid, albeit simplistic and limited. How then can we navigate questions concerning the historical silencing of women's voices? How did the spatio-legal transformation of the frontier gender place and bodies within it? What does place-making mean in a region fractured by economic divisions, and with social and physical boundaries? What are the pitfalls of using matrilineal social structure as an alternative map affirming ethnic connectedness? These questions inform the discussion below.

Despite variations across the hills and over time, a matrilineal kinship structure orders and underpins practices related to land in the Khasi, Jaintia, and Garo hills. A sense of 'being in place' refers to heterogeneous articulations of people's relationship to land, landscape, and environment. The discursive framework within which people articulate their sense of 'being in place' is that of kinship. Matrilineal kinship provides a site for the articulation of a feminist place for a majority of inhabitants living in the hills.

Kinship orders the relationship between land, religion, and people everywhere, but it has become the focus of anthropological studies on tribal societies in particular. Several such studies have focused on the role of women in the biological and cultural reproduction of ethnicity. Others have studied their relation to space, the organization and division of work, patterns of physical movement, right over children, the nature and character of marriage, matters relating to property, or authority and decision-making.[50] Frederik Engels in his *Origins of Family Private Property and*

---

[50] For instance, Leela Dube argues that kinship is the framework that guides the distribution and management of resources, the formation of groups, membership in groups and their functions: see Leela Dube, 'Who Gains from Matriliny? Men, Women and Change on a Lakshadweep Island', *Sociological Bulletin* 42, no. 1–2 (1993): 15–36. David Schneider states that matrilineal decent groups are defined as units with decision-making functions. This type of activity and corporate organization directly entails an 'interest' on the part of each member, which he argues

State attributed evolutionary privilege to patrilineal societies by showing that it is a natural successor of matrilineal societies.[51] This position has influenced several prominent anthropologists.[52] G. Arunima, in her study of matriliny in Kerala, points out that anthropologists have tried to extrapolate abstract rules regarding marriage, inheritance, and residence practices without concern for historical processes.[53] Matriliny is a historically evolving institution that is shaped by social, political, and economic processes. Attempts to legislate changes within a supposedly rigid matrilineal social structure in the Khasi hills in recent decades have further demonstrated a complex interplay of ideological, economic, and political forces.

An examination of social organization through kinship gives access to the spatiality of gender relations.[54] The undercurrents of a kinship-based form of social organization are visible in the discourse about place-making and its multiple shapes—ranging from the patriarchal and exclusionary to critical feminist, with a range of positions in between. Land is the locus of kinship, and both remain heavily contested in the present day. The social production of spaces like the frontier, the hills, land, and home simultaneously bear the markings of embodied experiences of places. Space is not greater than place, nor are socially structured relationships in space

---

implies that each member has 'rights': see David Schneider, 'Introduction', in *Matrilineal Kinship*, eds. David Schneider and Kathleen Gough (Berkeley and Los Angeles: University of California Press, 1961), 10.

[51] Friedrich Engels, *The Origin of the Family, Private Property and the State* (New York: International Publishers, 1942).

[52] Despite variations in how different matrilineal societies are transformed, Gough shows that they share the feature of becoming integrated into a unitary market system. The privatization of land, resources, and human labour stimulates the disintegration of matrilineal societies. Others have focused on the resilience of matrilineal societies, or on differential interests between the sexes that orientates such societies towards Christianity. Men look at matrilineal obligations as a drain on their limited resources; thus, in order to protect their commercial interests, men prefer to align with Christian religious groups. Women, in contrast, largely because of their weak marital bond, see the advantage in retaining their alliance with their uterine kin rather than in the ties established through the church. See Schneider and Gough, eds., *Matrilineal Kinship*, 445–556; see also Tiplut Nongbri, 'Khasi Women and Matriliny: Transformations in Gender Relations', *Gender Technology, and Development* 4, no. 3 (2000): 359–395; Govind Kelkar, Dev Nathan, and Pierre Walter, eds., *Gender Relations in Forest Societies in Asia: Patriarchy at Odds* (New Delhi: SAGE Publications, 2003).

[53] G. Arunima, *There Comes Papa: Colonialism and the Transformation of Matriliny in Kerela, Malabar, c. 1850–1940* (New Delhi: Orient Longman, 2003), 3–4.

[54] Doreen Massey has argued that spatial relations amount to social relations that have been 'stretched out': see Massey, *Space, Place, Gender*. See also Doreen Massey, 'Don't Let's Counterpose Place and Space', *Development* 45, no. 1 (2002): 24–25.

more historically significant than the actions and experiences that give meaning to place. Matrilineal kinship structured through *Kpoh* (womb) and *Iing* (home/household) embody the gendering of space and the multiple articulations of self and fractured identities of place.

The home and the body have long been theorized as sites of place-making. Harcourt and Escobar theorize place in the contemporary historical moment of globalization. They identify home and body as places where women are engaged in political struggles in their encounters with global processes.[55] Centring place-making within the frontier space gives way to a feminist materialist approach to social and historical relations in the hills. This section focuses on the discursive construction of matriliny and thereby excludes 'others' who inhabit the hills but follow patrilineal and caste-based norms.

With the above lacuna in mind, the diversity and multiplicity of hierarchies that mark the socio-economic groups living in the hills means that women in the hills do not occupy the same place. Their articulations of history, identity, and belonging cannot be understood in singular terms. The heterogeneity of place itself can offer historical depth in analysing the frontier space that frame and dominate knowledge on the Khasi hills. A discussion of matrilineal societal organization situates gendered subjects in these hills and reveals crucial iterations of place-making.

The structural organization of Khasi society is based on the dual institutions of *Kpoh*, which refers to a domestic unit tracing descent from one great grandmother, and *Iing*, or home or family. Chie Nakane, in her anthropological study of Garo and Khasi matrilineal systems, wrote that the function of the Khasi *Kpoh* is that of a religious or ritual unit, which unites its members in a shared sense of identity that traces descent through a common process of disintegration of the domestic unit.[56] Tiplut Nongbri concurs, and more succinctly describes the *Kpoh* simply as a descent group.[57] *Kpoh* literally means the *womb* and signifies the line

[55] Wendy Harcourt and Arturo Escobar, eds., *Women and the Politics of Place* (Bloomfield: Kumarian Press, 2005); see also Wendy Harcourt and Arturo Escobar, 'Women and the Politics of Place', *Development* 45, no. 1 (2002): 7–14.

[56] Chie Nakane, 'Garo and Khasi: A Comparative Study in Matrilineal Systems', in *Cahiers de L'Homme: Ethnologie, Géographie, Linguistique*, vol. 5 (Paris and The Hague: Mouton and Co., 1967).

[57] For a comparison between the Taravad in matrilineal Kerala and Kpoh, see Schneider, 'Introduction', in *Matrilineal Kinship*, 4.

of descent traced from an ancient grandmother. The *Kpoh* and *Iing* are both sites of legal contestation.[58]

Succession and inheritance mark the *Iing* as a spatio-legal unit. Keith Cantlie's 1934 monograph, *Notes on Khasi Law*, focused on disputes concerning inheritance and property rights, marriage and divorce, and religion and custom, all of which centred on the *Iing*.[59] Nongbri states that the *Kpoh* constituted one or more *Iing*s which were 'bound together by shared sentiments of genealogical connectedness, joint land ownership, and a shared cromlech where the bones of the death [*sic*] are deposited'.[60] The relationship with the past through genealogical tracing, communal interest in land, and rituals that mark the land are aspects of place-making.

Nongbri also emphasizes that within matriliny, the *Iing* constitutes the identity of its members' children, but not of their spouses, even if these latter are co-residents. Sons, and thereby husbands, belong to their mother's *Iing*. The ancestral property of the *Iing* in Khasi society passes through the youngest daughter of the family. Nongbri has argued that despite the right to inheritance, the role of the youngest daughter in fact ends up restricting her mobility, and binds her to the household. She states that families that comprised an *Iing* were economic units responsible for their agriculture, and the *Ka Khadduh* who inherited the ancestral house was responsible for the maintenance or support of any member of her *Iing* who was dispossessed or in need of shelter. Each member is also responsible for adhering to social practices, including inheritance customs and various rituals associated with birth, death, marriage, and divorce, all of which together ensured membership within a *Kpoh*. Guardianship of the *Iing* is a male prerogative held by the maternal uncle. Nongbri argues that

---

[58] The *Iing*, literally meaning 'house', is the lowest order of clan and lineage segmentation. A *Kpoh* sometimes included two or more *Iing*s. Children belong to the mother's *Iing*. However, the spouses of *Iing* members, even when co-resident, are actually excluded from the *Iing*. For instance, a husband does not belong to his wife's *Iing*, even though residence is matrilocal. The more frequent type of household comprises wife, husband, their children, and the wife's unmarried sisters and brothers, including those who may be widowed or divorced. Less frequent is a larger household that contains three or more generations of people tracing their descent from a single woman; such circumstances amount to the ideal type known as *Kpoh*.

[59] Keith Cantlie, *Notes on Khasi Law* (1934, Reprint, Shillong: Ri Khasi Press, 1974). Cantlie not only offered 'solutions to legal problems', but also offered opinions about matrilineal system itself. For instance, he stated that the youngest daughter was not an heiress but a custodian of ancestral property.

[60] Nongbri, 'Khasi Women and Matriliny', 367.

the religious function of the *Iing* ensured matrilineal solidarity on the one hand, and a 'permanent position' (of authority) for sons in their natal *Iing*.[61] In this way, the spatiality of the *Kpoh* and *Iing* structure gender relations from the household to the clan.

Three stones that traditionally surrounded the hearth in the *Iing* represent *Ka Iawbei*, or the first grandmother/'primeval ancestress'; *U Thawlang*, the first father of the clan; and *U Suidnia*, the first maternal uncle.[62] Nongbri points out that the emblem of the hearth has been distorted in recent representations that have replaced the stone representing Iawbei with an image of the Syiem. This, she argues, is part of the onslaught against the matrilineal system by patriarchal interest groups that depict matriliny as regressive, and promote the transition to a patrilineal system among the Khasis.[63]

Nongbri draws particular attention to organizations such as *Synkong Rympei Thymmai* or Association of New Hearths, Hynniewtrep Endeavour Society, the Khasi Students Union, Central Riwar Youth Federation, as well as individuals and government representatives at the Khasi Hills Autonomous District Council.[64] Their voices found legal validity in the Lineage Bill of 1997, passed as the Khasi Custom of Lineage Act 2005, and which has received several amendments in recent years. Under the guise of codifying the matrilineal system, the Council introduced a set of proposed reforms that reaffirm the dominant position of men in Khasi society. The Lineage Act imposed severe restrictions on women by controlling their sexual choices and their right of descent. Directed at all members of Khasi society, the legislation has the power to revoke ethnic/tribal rights if anyone fails to 'observe the Khasi matrilineal system of lineage or Khasi laws of inheritance and succession, consanguinity and kinship, or has adopted personal law of a society not compatible with Khasi personal laws and customs'.[65] The law places the specific onus of preserving Khasi ethnic identity on women. Children born of Khasi mothers and non-Khasi fathers are those who are most vulnerable

[61] Ibid., 368.
[62] Tiplut Nongbri, 'Family, Gender and Identity: A Comparative Study of Trans-Himalayan Matrilineal Structures', *Contributions to Indian Sociology* 44, no. 1–2 (2010): 161.
[63] Nongbri, 'Family, Gender and Identity', 172.
[64] Nongbri, 'Khasi Women and Matriliny', 381.
[65] Ibid.

to the loss of their privileges according to the Lineage Act. Concerns of demographic obliteration of 'pakka' or pure Khasis due to the increase of mixed blood progeny have been put forward as a significant concern by those who support the law.

Women have challenged such patriarchal assertions with diverse and public movements to secure their rights. The 1997 bill, according to Nongbri, flouted the most significant matrilineal principle of the right of descent. The demands by sections of Khasi civil society that children of mixed marriages forfeit Khasi ethnic status and inheritance rights have highlighted the exploitation of Khasi women by non-Khasi men to obtain Khasi women's property rights. The Bill posited Khasi women as repositories of ethnic identity and imposed upon them the role of ethnic border guards. Additionally, appropriate behaviour ensured the continued rights to that identity. The current legislation, as amended in 2018, places the reproductive family at the centre of defining and preserving cultural and historical identity.

This law has provoked protests led by different women's organizations representing varying levels of disagreement. Yet Nongbri has pointed out that women did not protest the Bill in as large a capacity as expected. This, she suggests, is because of the invocation of moral, social, and ethnic responsibility to *embody* Khasi identity. According to Nongbri, because women were caught between expectations to perform the role of a Khasi woman responsible for the proper exercise of matriliny and to ensure their loyalty to their ethnic identity, many of them chose not to voice their opinions on this debate.[66]

While ongoing debates in the public sphere focus on women's biological and cultural reproductive roles, class divisions and colonial/postcolonial property and land relations have been flattened in much of the discussion on kinship. Place is a contested terrain where women defend the right to their matrilineal *Iing* (household) and *Kpoh* (womb). What makes place a contested terrain is differential access to land and property, and lack of autonomy over one's body. Place is also transgressive. Kinship has been used as a critical analytic against dominant representational politics as well as the oppressive nexus between law and custom. Women

[66] Ibid.

have spoken out and organized against institutional and everyday violence in fighting for their rights over land and livelihood.

A reading of place-making allows for an understanding of spatiality as multi-temporal, experienced, negotiated, and conflictual. This is a move away from the abstract nature often attached to understanding legal spatiality.[67] Inhabitants of the hills embodied the frontier as legal space through active engagement, both material and imaginative, whether as participants in colonial legal processes or in actively resisting colonial law and geography. We have seen in previous chapters how inhabitants participated in the production of the legal space of the frontier. To examine this point further, the present chapter has located contemporary practices of place-making and conflictual negotiations that form spaces of law. Overall, the chapters have shed light on the spatial processes that characterized governance strategies of the colonial state and produced territorial and situated subjectivities. Law and spatiality imbue the locally experienced place with a universal character. The deeply local time of law does not deprive the global connections and flows that inform place-making. Place in this conceptualization is neither an authentic locality nor does it emphasize difference as plurality. Place is a historically shaped locus of struggle, informed by the violence of law and spatiality of violence.

[67] Irus Baverman, Nicholas Blomley, David Delaney, and Alexander Kedar, eds., *The Expanding Spaces of Law: A Timely Legal Geography* (Stanford: Stanford University Press, 2014).

Conclusion

This book has argued that colonial law was central to the spatial transformation of the region known as the north-east frontier of the British Empire in India. The book begins with an examination of the relationship between law and space. The frontier was not a geographical site at the periphery of colonial territory. In fact, the frontier is a particular type of political-legal space that was integral to the imperial project. The book rejects commonly assumed binaries between law and custom, British and non-British territories, and colonial and indigenous knowledge.

The book is a story of rupture, radical transformations, and social transmutations caused by colonial law. Each chapter looks carefully into the processes, instruments, and mechanisms of colonial legal ordering that created a frontier spatiality. The book begins with the travels of law beyond imperial jurisdictional spaces such as the Bengal Presidency. Through the signing of contracts and agreements communities inhabiting the regions north and east of Bengal including plains and hills were brought within the frame and work of colonial law and commerce. Inhabitants of lands under such contractual agreements were classified as tribal, concomitant to landscape and its resources. The colonial categories of 'hill tribal' and 'hill polities' were misleading in terms of describing both inhabitants and the topographical extent of polities that reached far into the Sylhet plains.

The 'hill tribal' was a peculiar subject of law, not recognized as a British subject but bound within colonial law, and circumscribed by colonial infrastructure. While in the initial decades of the nineteenth-century contracts gave greater negotiating power to the rulers and Chiefs of the 'hill polities', over the course of the nineteenth century the template of contracts changed significantly reducing the political role of local rulers.

Placing the Frontier in British North-East India. Reeju Ray, Oxford University Press. © Reeju Ray 2023.
DOI: 10.1093/oso/9780192887085.003.0008

Inaction on the part of the colonial administration to define a specific legal policy combined with overlapping jurisdictions between colonial and local authorities facilitated violence within the ambit of law. The book shows how colonial boundary-making on the north-east frontier between British and non-British territories produced the legal and political category 'tribal'. Colonial law generated and deployed this and other categories such as 'frontier' to formulate a linear temporalization of space. In other words, law became both a measure and embodiment of time that differentiated colonial spaces along gradations from primitive to modern. The book also shows that the colonial spatial-legal project was key to the circulation of capital and trade and ordered the relationship between the colonial government and European private traders.

The second half of the book shows how the frontier hills were shaped by law. Both identity and geography were configured hegemonically through the lens of tribal ethnicity and kinship relations. Both space and place were fashioned through multiple often conflictual negotiations including custom and kinship, orality and literacy, class and gender. The book shows how colonial law was both informed by, and gave legitimacy to colonial knowledge produced on the frontier hills. The role of different disciplines is examined starting with geography and cartography, geology, anthropology, and linguistics. Languages—both English and standardized Khasi—appear as important conduits of law and spatiality.

Autonomy, legal pluralism, and indirect rule have been commonly used concepts in colonial history in the northeast frontier. Such understandings evade the deeply pervasive and violent transformations brought on by colonial law. Recent historical research has been demystifying the commonly assumed ideas of putative primitivism, isolation, exceptions, and difference. This book locates itself in this new historiography of frontiers and borderlands. Traversing the judicial archive from late eighteenth century onwards, a critical reading of colonial correspondence, and a contrapuntal reading of scientific and non-scientific narratives from the nineteenth century, the book demonstrates the interface of law, custom, and non-normative ordering of people through systems of colonial and Indigenous knowledge. The book shows the mechanisms through which colonial law transformed the region into a frontier, thereby creating distinct ideas, relationships, and conditions. The book intervenes in the new historiography with its focus on the spatiality of law.

A related concept of place offers towards a deeper understanding of historical and lived experience. The history of the frontier as place demonstrates that imbricated and weaved into a long durée of the Himalayan foothills are visible articulations of histories and geographies that have been in a dialectical relationship with various religious, imperial, and dominant systems of knowledge. The latter include the systems of knowledge and practices of monastic geographicity, Brahmanism and Islam, Christian missionary teachings, and a gamut of Western scientific and empirical records of the frontier space. With the spread of literacy due to Christian missionary education and the subsequent emergence of a Khasi public sphere written articulations of identities based on kinship, land, location, legal, and civilizational status became available. Place-making understood as heterogenous articulations of lived experience, rootedness, and identity is visible in several sites including the public sphere, landscape, myth, and memory.

The hills recast as frontier space was the locus of political and social struggle that produced new politico-economic realities, new forms of knowledge, new cosmological possibilities, new avenues and platforms for deliberation and contestation. The inhabitants' experience of these swift and sustained changes over the course of late eighteenth and into the twentieth century are examined in this book with considerations to the *where* of history. The book finds that despite the transformative force of law interruptions to hegemonic spaces are contained in varied forms of social resistance and relationships between people and landscape. The frontier hills offered counter-spaces, or places wherein inhabitants variously narrated their history and belonging. Thus, place emerges as a relational, dynamic, and embodied site where people variously narrated their histories.

The multiple renegotiations (spatial, political, religion, ideological) are part of the living memory of the inhabitants of the hills and form an integral part of contemporary lives. For instance, in the present-day discourses on indigeneity and custom in the hills are embedded in conceptions of the past shaped by colonial and national discourses on tribal identity, customary law, and frontier governance. Oral sources such as folktales and legends have engaged with written histories for over two centuries inflect the coexistence of linear and non-linear conceptions of the past. With this in mind, the book ends with a historical account of the conditions of possibility for multiple articulations of the past. It identifies feminist materialist narratives embedded in landscape and orality that challenge and deny essentialist and hegemonic constructions of identity. Political articulations of a feminist materialist place can be found in resistance to the legality of custom, struggles for rights of livelihood and against ecological destruction. The embodied experience of localized place and global space is visible in these struggles.[1]

---

[1] Massey disagrees with treating space as a universal abstract category and place as meaningful, subjective, and experiential location. She argues that spaces and places are relationally and historically formed. Historically forged places allow an understanding of belonging free from essentialist and exclusivist characteristics. See Doreen Massey, 'Geographies of Responsibility', *Geografiska Annaler. Series B, Human Geography* 86, no. 1 (2004): 5–18. See also Doreen Massey, *Space, Place, Gender* (Cambridge: Polity Press, 1994).

Index

For the benefit of digital users, indexed terms that span two pages (e.g., 52–53) may, on occasion, appear on only one of those pages.